THE DIE-HARD FAN'S *Guide to* SOONER FOOTBALL

THE DIE-HARD FAN'S *Guide to* SOONER FOOTBALL

JIM FLETCHER

An Eagle Publishing Company • Washington, DC

Library of Congress Cataloging-in-Publication Data
Fletcher, Jim, 1962–
The die-hard fan's guide to Sooner football / Jim Fletcher.
p. cm.
Includes index.
ISBN 978-1-59698-530-8
1. Oklahoma Sooners (Football team)—History. 2. University of Oklahoma—Football—History. I. Title.
GV958.O4F57 2008
796.332'630976637—dc22
2008025839

Published in the United States by
Regnery Publishing, Inc.
One Massachusetts Avenue, NW
Washington, DC 20001
www.regnery.com

Manufactured in the United States of America

10 9 8 7 6 5 4 3 2 1

Books are available in quantity for promotional or premium use. Write to Director of Special Sales, Regnery Publishing, Inc., One Massachusetts Avenue NW, Washington, DC 20001, for information on discounts and terms or call (202) 216-0600.

To James F. Fletcher, Sr., Thelma Fletcher,
and James F. Fletcher, Jr.
I look forward to seeing you all again
some glad morning, when every day
will bring a national championship.

CONTENTS

Foreword

Through a series of events that I have come to appreciate more and more as the years have passed, I came to play college football at Oklahoma for Bud Wilkinson. I had taken visits to some places, including Notre Dame. To go to Notre Dame, to be recruited by them and see that place, was a great experience.

But there was just something about OU that appealed to me. The other places were fine, but I could see around Norman just how much people cared about football. I had the same feeling in Norman that I had had in Breckenridge.

Today, I can't really describe what it means to have played for a national champion at Oklahoma. I am truly blessed to be a part of this great tradition. I've been to twelve Orange Bowl games, played in two of them, and won both. My kids grew up on Oklahoma football. Getting to know the players who have made OU great over the years has been one of the highlights of my life.

I go to the games today and see everyone from my good friend Barry Switzer to fans from all over the country. There's no thrill like Oklahoma football, and it's been that way for over fifty years. And it will be that way fifty years from now.

This book is a fond look at the great times, and it's written by a fan, for fans. That's something Jim and I share with you—we are Die-Hard Fans!

—Jakie Sandefer, '58

Introduction

They still run in our memories. The galloping ghosts of Bennie Owen, the aging men of the glorious Streak, Switzer's Wishbone ponies. Billy Vessels is still alive, sprinting away from Notre Dame defenders in 1952. Billy Sims isn't middle-aged, he's sliding and high-stepping through Nebraska's black-shirt defense on a cold day in Lincoln. Bobby Warmack is youthful, with a crew-cut and fresh face. Joe Washington is still "smoke through a keyhole," as Darrell Royal put it.

I'm just a fan; that's all I am. A terror as a backup nose-guard in the eighth grade, I never ran through a tunnel, signed autographs, or waited for my name to be called on draft day. But I know what the heat is like at Owen Field on a Saturday in early September. I've known it from the beginning of my life—literally.

The setting: OU vs. Syracuse, the season-opener of the 1962 season. The real bedlam game, between Kennedy and Khrushchev, was still a month away. Bud Wilkinson's last bowl team had had all it could handle from the Orangemen, and with less than five minutes to play, the home team was down, 3–0. No offense at all that day. Oklahoma's dominance in college football was heading into a transitional period, but one spark remained.

Joe Don Looney, a man who fit his name better than anyone since Fatty Arbuckle, fumed on the sidelines. Looney had a thoroughbred's body and the heart of a hippy. Wilkinson, fed up with the phenom's bizarre, antisocial behavior, had benched him. Looney paced and paced, waiting for an opportunity.

My father was pacing, too. Twenty-nine, with a good government job, impeccable manners, and a dislike of anything Soviet, my old man was a true-blue conservative and hot-blooded Oklahoma football fan. He would become a father in three short months. In fact, he'd been kind enough to take Mom to this game, four days after her birthday. I suspect his intent was to indoctrinate me in the womb.

It worked.

When Looney could stand it no longer, he ran up to Wilkinson and said something insane, a cry from a demon that wanted to get on that field and help his team win. Bud thought about it, looked at the scoreboard, and sent Looney into the history books.

The play came into the huddle: Right 72 Y Pitch. The fans were sitting on their hands, with no reason to stand or even think about cheering. It was embarrassing watching a Sooner team get blanked.

That's when I did my thing.

"... the child leaped in her womb ... ." (Luke 1:41)

Suddenly, Mom grew nauseous. The heat, the smoke from Dad's Pall Malls, and my restlessness in her belly... it was too much for her. She turned to my dad and said, "Jim, I need to go to the bathroom. Will you help me?"

He looked at her, looked at the sorry mess on the field, snapped his cigarette onto the cement, and took her by the arm. In my mind's eye, I see him as Jack Webb, curtly escorting some dame with a string of hot checks down to the lockup.

In the bowels of hallowed Owen Field, Mom struggled to the bathroom. Dad leaned against a wall and wiped his face.

JOE DON LOONEY takes it sixty yards for a game-winning touchdown against Syracuse in 1962. My dad got to see him run off the field.

Suddenly, the roar of the crowd made the sweat on his back run cold. Forgetting he was married, an expectant father, and everything else one usually considers important in life, Dad raced up the steps to see Looney tossing the ball to a ref while trotting out of the endzone and off the field. He had taken a pitch and raced sixty yards for the winning touchdown.

As Mom's luck would have it, this happened in the days before ESPN or instant replay. Shoot, I don't even think they had a television set at home.

She staggered up the railing in time to see Dad's furious face. It was the same crimson color as the OU jerseys. "MY GOD," he yelled, "COULD YOU NOT HAVE WAITED FIVE MINUTES?"

It's a funny story now, I think, forty-five years on. I don't approve of what Dad did. The conditions were not fun for Mom that day. He should have been more understanding. He should have taken her home long before, tucked her into a cool bed, and listened to the game on the radio.

I don't approve at all of my father's behavior that day.

But I understand it.

For the love of everything holy, I understand it. I've torn paper up into little pieces during games, pounded the floor with my fists, stomped on hats, scared dogs and children, and said some really bad words in the first half of the 2002 OU-Texas shootout. (That last one, in fact, was Nate Hybl's fault for throwing multiple interceptions.) For decades now, I've bled red during the tight games and seen a great White Light during the big wins, basking in its warmth for at least seven more days.

I understand my father's obsession. Because I have it.

When Thomas Lott was stopped on fourth-and-one by Texas's Johnny Johnson in 1977, I lay face-down on the floor for two hours, drained, defeated, and demoralized.

The agony is worth it, though, for the times when we reach the mountaintops. The national championships; the cold wins against Nebraska in those Lincoln Novembers; seeing All-Americans in the flesh; recruiting season; spring football; the hot anticipation of summer; two-a-days in August;

opening day; October's Red River Shootout with Texas; and of course, being driven home by my son, Curtis, after the epic 2000 national championship Orange Bowl win over Florida State, because I was a twitching, babbling, weeping goof with Albert Einstein hair.

This is the life of a die-hard Sooner fan.

For the most part, we're laid-back Okies except for Saturday afternoons in the fall. Then, we transform into something else. As Patton said about war, "God help me, I do love it so."

Oklahoma football has been built on huge wins. As the King, Barry Switzer, used to say, "Hang half-a-hundred on 'em."

That's what we love—the fifty-point wins. Praying that we will live to see the End of the Age, when a modern college football team, preferably the Sooners, will put up a hundred on a single afternoon.

That's how Oklahoma has played football for sixty years. It's how Oklahoma wins. It's what the fans devour.

This is a fan's look at the proud story of University of Oklahoma football. It's not a blow-by-blow, game-by-game account from John A. Harts' 1895 squad to today's "Stoops' Troops," but rather an impressionistic, joy-filled walk through the years. We'll recall everything from the genius of Switzer and Wilkinson to the dedication of super fan Cecil Samara. Tailgaters, and tear-away jerseys in the Wishbone's heyday, and the tough kids of the 1990s who held the fort down until Bob Stoops arrived—they'll all find their way onto these pages.

This is a book by a fan, for fans. We'll share our memories, both the good times and the bad.

But mostly the good.

Like the ancients did, we'll focus on our tremendous victories. We'll let the juice of an orange run down our chins one more time.

We'll have interviews with legendary names: Mildren, Selmon, Washington, and Heupel, to name just a few.

Some of us Sooner fans are from broken homes, while others have seemingly coasted through life. There are those of us who can buy anything we want, and others who live paycheck-to-paycheck. Some are intellectuals, and some didn't make it through high school.

What we share, though, is that bond that can never be broken. The images that flicker in our minds and hearts. The images that began as black-and-white, grainy ghosts, and which have, over the years, become the full-color Crimson and Cream.

They still run in our memories.

Chapter One

BIRTH OF THE BEAST

OKLAHOMA FOOTBALL, 1895-1946

It had rained the week before.

The first football game at the University of Oklahoma took place on a cold December day in 1895. The team that played it bore little resemblance to the powerhouse that the program would eventually become.

It is well-documented that John A. Harts organized OU's first football team in the Risinger and Jones barber shop (now remembered as "Bud Risinger's barber shop") on Main Street in Norman. The details associated with the team's first game, however, are not so widely known.

The school had been founded as Normal Territorial University in 1890. It was established on an appeal from the territorial governor, George Steele, to the territorial legislature to create a higher education system. In 1907, when Oklahoma entered the Union, the school was renamed The University of Oklahoma.

The school was founded a year after the great Land Run, when settlers in what is now northern Oklahoma lined up to stake claims of land given for homesteading by the United States government. Pioneers had to "solemnly

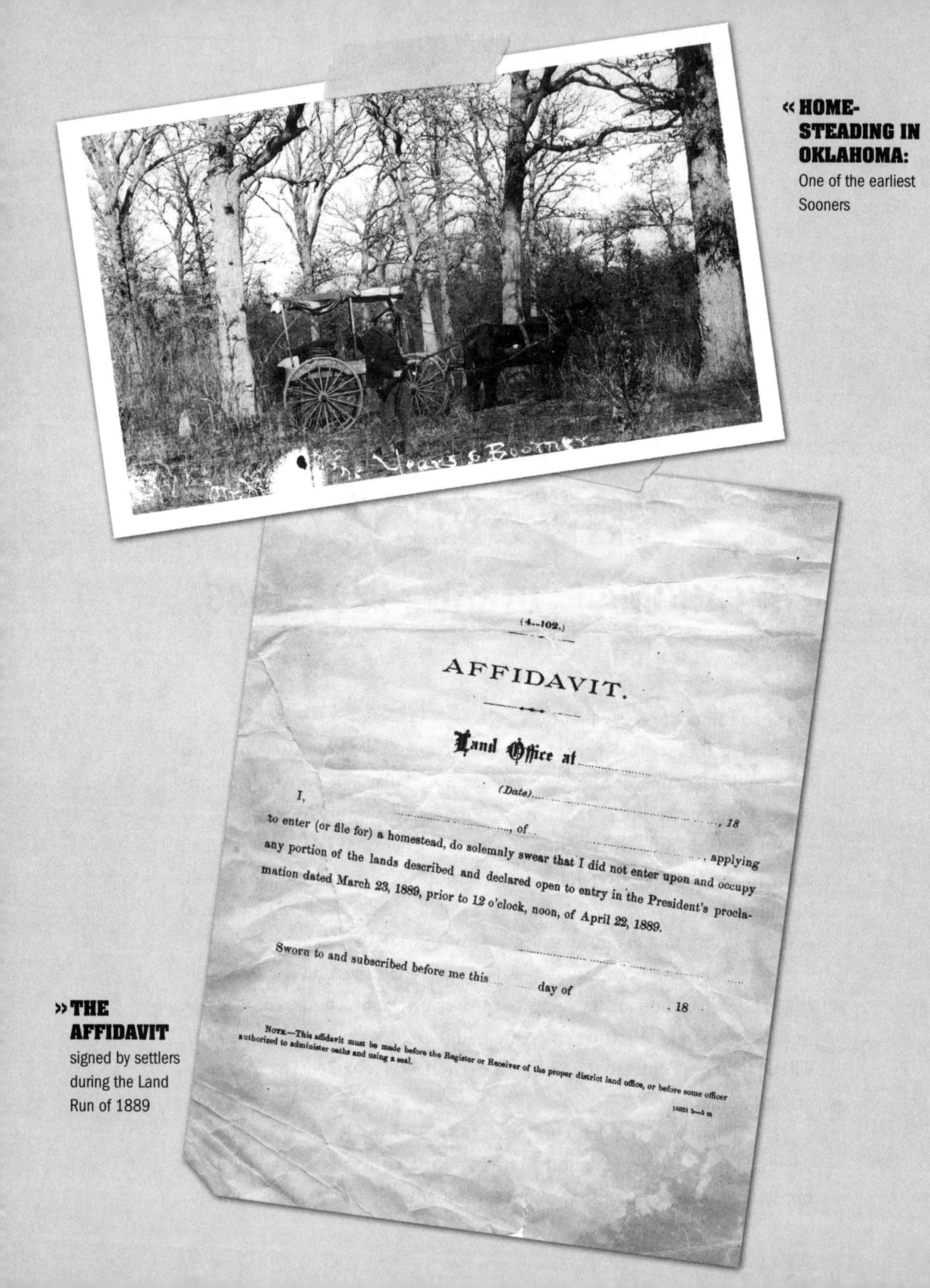

(4--102.)

AFFIDAVIT.

Land Office at ....

(*Date*)..., *18*

I, ..., of ...., applying to enter (or file for) a homestead, do solemnly swear that I did not enter upon and occupy any portion of the lands described and declared open to entry in the President's proclamation dated March 23, 1889, prior to 12 o'clock, noon, of April 22, 1889.

....

Sworn to and subscribed before me this .... day of ...., 18 ...

....

NOTE.—This affidavit must be made before the Register or Receiver of the proper district land office, or before some officer authorized to administer oaths and using a seal.

16051 b—5 m

« **HOME-STEADING IN OKLAHOMA:** One of the earliest Sooners

» **THE AFFIDAVIT** signed by settlers during the Land Run of 1889

swear that I did not enter upon and occupy any portion of the lands described and declared open to entry in the President's proclamation dated March 23, 1889, prior to 12 o'clock, noon, of March 22, 1889." This pledge notwithstanding, some pioneers tried to get a head start on the action, thus giving rise to OU's nickname—"The Sooners." This is also the source of the derisive nicknames ("Land Thieves," "Dirt Burglars," etc.) given to OU fans by rival fans at Texas (itself populated by people who had taken their state from Mexico a few decades before—albeit in a fair fight).

The citizens of Norman donated four hundred acres for the university, and the first school president, David Ross Boyd (for whom the football field would be named—later renamed "Owen Field"), insisted on extensive landscaping.

In the late nineteenth century, out on the Oklahoma prairie, people were noticing that the relatively new sport of American football was coming west. Naturally, pioneer pride demanded that a football team be formed in Norman.

Early in the fall of 1895, the *Norman Transcript* announced the formation of a "Football Club:"

> The Oklahoma University students not to be outdone by the members of any other University, have organized a football team and are practicing as if their lives depended on making a good score. Norman has to keep pace with every progressive move.

This modest notice was a far cry from the multi-page coverage that heralds nearly every element of OU's football program today. It indicates just how far Oklahoma football has come from its humble beginnings over a century ago.

The *Transcript*'s announcement was sandwiched between an ad for "Cypress Tea" and this scintillating item:

> Geo. Smith has been looking after W. H. Carr of Lexington, who is supposed to have skipped away from his bondsmen leaving them in the lurch to the tune of $15,000. Carr is reported to have gone on the Rock Island railroad to Kansas City, Missouri, after leaving

> Noble on the 4th of this month and so far no further trace of him has been found.

"A FOOTBALL GAME"

The team was known as the Oklahoma Elevens, "elevens" being a common nickname at the time for any football club, referring to the number of players on both the offensive and defensive squads.

As the team prepared for its game against Oklahoma City High School, the chilly fall weather gave way to colder winter temperatures. Out on the prairie, the rain ensured that mud would be a key factor in the game. A front page announcement in the the *Norman Transcript* on Friday, December 13, reveals the embryonic moments of the Sooners:

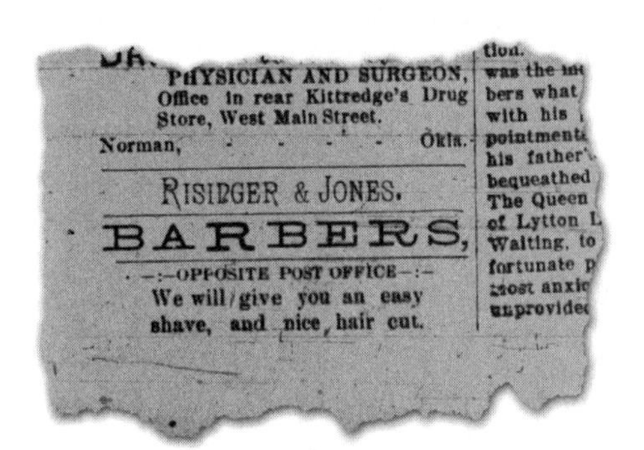

PHYSICIAN AND SURGEON,
Office in rear Kittredge's Drug Store, West Main Street.
Norman, Okla.

RISINGER & JONES.
BARBERS,
—:—OPPOSITE POST OFFICE—:—
We will give you an easy shave, and nice hair cut.

AN AD for Risinger and Jones barber shop in the *Norman Transcript*, 1895

> **A Football Game**
>
> The University boys and the Oklahoma City club are to play a football game on the University campus here Saturday afternoon. It will be a strong game as both clubs have some members that are experienced and skillful. The Oklahoma City club is coming down with the determination of carrying back the pennant of victory, while the University boys think they can give odds and beat them. Go out and witness the game.

In a 1942 article, Harold Keith, OU's masterful sports information director for so many years, provided a brief description of the Sooners' less-than-stellar first game:

> The first University team ignominiously failed to score a point. Its only game was with the bigger, rougher and vastly more experienced Oklahoma City Town Team. The contest was played in Norman right

out on the prairie north of the present Fine Arts Building. Wearing home-made uniforms, the University boys were soundly licked, 0 to 34. Harts twisted a knee and had to retire, and before it was over, the befuddled Norman boys were borrowing the Oklahoma City subs so they'd have a full lineup. A large crowd watched the fun with mixed emotions and wondered what devilment the giddy Norman college boys would think up next."

Fortunately for us, in the records at the Oklahoma Historical Society in Oklahoma City, the genesis of Sooner football is found in both the *Transcript* and the Oklahoma City paper, the *Daily Oklahoman*. Although today's version of the *Transcript* provides good coverage of the Sooners, we can agree that the "reporting" of this first game was, well, skimpy:

Oklahoma City, 34; Norman, 0.

It was the same old story at Norman yesterday, the University team going down before the high school boys by a score of 34 to 0. Time of game, seventy minutes. Referees; D.W. Harts and Dr. Van Nuys.

The Norman Transcr

A LIVE REPUBLICAN NEWSPAPER—DEVOTED TO THE BEST INTERESTS OF NORMAN AND SOUTHERN OKLAHOMA

NORMAN, OKLAHOMA TERRITORY, FRIDAY, DECEMBER 13, 1895.

A PLUCKY STUDENT.

TERRITORIAL ROUND-UPS.

Some Facts of Interest Gleaned From All Parts of Oklahoma

The McLoud News has suspended publication.

Waukomis is holding Evangelist meetings this week.

Ed. B. Stephens has again taken charge of the Lexington Leader.

The Santa Fe railroad company pays over $7,000 taxes in Kay county.

The Rock Island has discontinued running Sunday trains on its Territory branch.

A Football Game.

The University boys and the Oklahoma City club are to play a football game on the University campus here Saturday afternoon next. It will be a strong game as both clubs have some members that are experienced and skillful. The Oklahoma City club is coming down with the determination of carrying back the pennant of victory while the University boys think they can give odds and beat them. Go out and witness the game.

The Next President.

The city of St. Louis, Missouri, will have the honor of being the place ... nomination of the next president of ... United States ...

STATEHOOD CONV

THE NORMAN TRANSCRIPT as it appeared on December 13, 1895. The announcement of OU's first football game is at the top of the third column.

> The Oklahoma boys were accompanied by some thirty or forty football cranks, and the crimson and black, accentuated by the high school football yell, was very much in evidence. The boys were treated very nicely, and returned loud in their praises of the Norman people.

The *Daily Oklahoman*, provided some "meatier" coverage on its front page, although the account was wedged between news stories about the "Indian Territory Townsite Bill" and the unfortunate case of a Mrs. Wolf, who, it was determined, was accidentally shot through the hip by her husband as he "was carelessly handling" a revolver. The couple's farm, in the Chickasaw Nation, was visited by a Dr. Hudson.

In any event, with all the fanfare we can muster, the Die-Hard Fan gives you:

> **The Football Game**
>
> In the football game last Saturday between the team of the Oklahoma City High School and that of the University here, the Oklahoma City boys came out victorious, the score being 34 to 0. The game lasted seventy minutes and was hotly contested[!], the Norman boys putting up a strong game even though they failed to score. Two of the University team's best players were unable to play and that fact coupled with the one that the boys had practiced together but little, placed them at a serious disadvantage to their opponents who are a strong team and one experienced in playing. There was a good attendance at the grounds and a large number of Oklahoma City people witnessed the game. The Norman people treated their guests courteously and all the players are to be commended for their gentlemanly conduct. The University boys propose to practice up and be prepared to conquer when next they meet.

OU bounced back from its drubbing the following year, when, within a two-week period in October and November 1896, the "University boys" defeated another high school team, Norman High School, 12–0 and 16–4. Tellingly,

"No Coach" is listed for this squad, which notched the first two wins in school history. In fact, these being the only games the team played that season, the 1896 lineup became the program's first unbeaten team.

The epic rematch against Oklahoma City High School took place almost two years to the day after the initial blowout. In Norman, a crowd of four hundred watched the Sooners win 16–0, avenging the inaugural whitewash. This team was coached by Vernon Parrington, who was OU's first "real" coach.

Parrington's squads had discipline, posting seven shutouts in twelve games over a four-season period. Keith described some of Parrington's first players:

> Some of the better-known players of the Parrington regime were Fred Roberts, a 190-pound farm boy from Mayfield, Kansas, who Norman old-timers declare was the greatest back ever developed at Norman; two fine tackles in rugged Joe Merkle, another hard-twisted farm lad, and Ed Barrow, a mixed-blood Indian from the Chickasha country; Jap Clapham, a plucky end who still lives at Norman; Tom Tribbey, a 230-pound young Goliath from the Pottawatomie country who had never ridden on a railroad train prior to the Texas game of 1900, C.C. Roberts, Clyde Bogle and others.

The first OU-Texas clash came in 1900. The Longhorns got lucky, eeking out a 28–2 victory. Parrington's squad apparently took it out on a hapless Fort Reno team two weeks later, crushing them 79–0.

Mark McMahon's 1903 team tied Texas, 6–6, at Austin, before dropping a follow-up game, 11–5, in Norman. OU would get its revenge soon enough, but it would come under the direction of a new coach.

After a blowout loss to the Longhorns in 1904, Bennie Owen arrived in Norman to take the reigns of the program. OU never looked back. Owen, who had played on Kansas's unbeaten team of 1899, led the Sooners for twenty-two seasons and became the program's first legendary coach. Today, his name is given honorary first mention in the popular mantra of OU's great

"The Texas-Oklahoma game transcends tradition. It is American history overlaid on an athletic contest, a game that's been played for a century, an outlet for marrow-deep passions and ancient grudges. But it is still 60 minutes of football, and in keeping with a more recent tradition at the Red River Shootout, the Sooners beat the snot out of the Longhorns."

—*Sports Illustrated*'s Austin Murphy, after OU beat Texas, 65–13, in 2003.

coaches—"Bennie, Bud, Barry, and Bob." He is remembered with reverence by Sooner fans as they watch their team play at "Owen Field."

In September 1905, the *Daily Oklahoman*—replete with its own sports page—previewed the upcoming season:

Football Season Is Now at Hand

Now that the baseball season has closed, football can have its inning. The local football season will in itself far surpass anything in a similar line heretofore. The local high school will be quite a factor in the interscholastic championship race, and for intercollegiate honors we have the University of Oklahoma from our section of the territory. The Swede-Oklahoma game here Thanksgiving day will be the crowning event of the season's games, locally.

THE FIRST TEXAS WIN

Owen's first team went 7–2, shutting out six of nine opponents. Both losses came at the hands of Kansas teams: the Jayhawks and Washburn.

One opponent that season stood out from all the others: Texas.

On October 7, the *Daily Oklahoman* announced an upcoming match against Texas:

Oklahoma and Texas Elevens to Play Here
University teams will roll the pigskin at Colcord Park November Third

Assistant Secretary A.W. McKeand, of the Chamber of Commerce, yesterday completed the negotiations for the big football game in

Oklahoma this season, which will be played at Colcord park, Friday, November 3, between the Oklahoma University and University of Texas elevens. This was an open date for both elevens and there is every promise that the game that day will be a bitterly contested one.

The University of Texas eleven is considered one of the fastest in the south. A year or so ago, the Texans defeated the Oklahoma players at Austin and since no game was played between both teams last season, the Oklahoma university is desirous of turning the tables this year and present indications point that they may be able to do so.

The university team this year is an exceptionally good one and under the training of Coach Bennie Owen, are rounding out in good form.

The Thanksgiving Day game will also be played in Oklahoma City, although the eleven which will be pitted against the University is not known. The Swedes of Lindsborg called off the game, which was scheduled here for that day, some weeks ago. The game between the Oklahoma and Haskell Indians elevens will be played October 16.

The day before the game, the *Oklahoman* reported on the public anticipation of the match:

Norman Coming En Masse.
Special to the Oklahoman.

NORMAN, OKLA., NOV. 2—The excitement in anticipation of the game with Texas tomorrow is growing and it is thought that by the time the special leaves here tomorrow at 1'oclock that there will be not less than five hundred people ready to go up and support the university football team.

The team went through its last practice tonight. Last night Coach Owen worked them till it was too dark to see the ball, for almost two hours they bucked the scrubs up and down the field, and then after the scrubs were sent in the varsity was put through another half-hour of signal practice after which they were told to hurry in. Tonight's work consisted entirely of signal practice, and the boys were well worked out, Bennie speaking to each one individually if the play did not go off smoothly. There will be quite a change in the line-up of the team from that of the Haskell game, part of this is due to a better man in the position and part of it is on account of injuries, the worst loss of this kind is Action [sic], the half back, who will not start in tomorrow's game, on account of a bum knee.

This is a heavy loss and it is thought that if the game should for any reason go against us that Acton may go in the last part of the game. Reeds, who takes his place, is a stronger player and is probably the best man outside of Acton on the squad, but he does not seem to have the power to jerk away from tacklers that Acton had. The other change is at center, where Runbeck is replaced by Severin, the Swede, being moved to tackle and letting Long out. Huges [sic], who played half last year and who this year seemed to have Captain McCreary's place as half-back cinched until he was out of the game for two weeks on account of a bum shoulder, has been put back in and McCreary will play end in Severin's place. Severin at center is very light, but is sure at passing the ball, having played that position for three years in the high school. His weight is only 156.

Game day, Friday, November 3, brought out this exclusive report:

Both Elevens Ready For Game
Large crowd will witness annual
Texas-Oklahoma Game Here Today

The Oklahoma and Texas elevens are ready for the big game to be played this afternoon at Colcord Park. The Oklahoman team will arrive on this morning's Santa Fe train and at noon a special train will arrive with almost the entire student body of the university to witness the game. Coach Hutchison took the Texas men to the park yesterday afternoon where they indulged in a sharp signal practice for an hour. The visiting team appears to be in fairly good shape for the game, altough [sic] showing the effects of the present trip and the games at Vanderbilt university and at Fayetteville, Ark., where they defeated the Arkansas University by a score of 4 to 0.

Excursion rates have been granted over nearly all the routes entering Oklahoma City for today's game and there is every promise that a large crowd will be in attendance. The game will be called at 3:30.

The fact that the Haskell Indians defeated the Texas team a few weeks ago by a score of 18 to 0 and that the Haskell team was defeated by the Oklahoma men by a score of 18 to 12 a few days later adds additional strength to the interest and efforts which will be put forth today by both teams to win today's contest. The line-up will be as follows:

Oklahoma		**Texas**
Runbeck	Center	Hamilton
Mathews	R. G.	Parish
Wolf	L.G.	Mainland
Monett	R.T.	Fisk
Long	L.T.	Ramsdell
Severin	R.E.	Duncan
Pickard	L.E.	Jones
Cross	Q.B.	Francis
McCreary	R.H.B.	Henderson
Acton	L.H.B.	Robinson
Truesdale	F.B.	Caldwell

As it happened, it was a good thing the Sooners had their skinny center, because he made the key play of the game, one somewhat reminiscent of Roy Williams' famous "Superman" play of 2001. With both teams finding it tough to move the ball, Severin broke through and tackled Robinson, the halfback, for a safety. Final score, 2–0.

Here's how the *Oklahoman* described the game:

Owen's Men Won

Robert Severins, center, saved the day for Oklahoma University. With the ball in Texas possession, off the latter's five yard line, Captain Robinson was given the ball for a line-buck through left tackle. As the ball was put in paly [sic], Severins broke through the line, tackled Robinson and with a number of the Oklahoma men back of him pushed the Texas captain across the goal line, for a safety netting two points. This was the the only score made by the either team. Both teams played hard and it was not until a minute before the whistle blew in the final half that the safety was made. Both teams were about evenly matched as regards offensive and defensive playing and neither team appeared to have the advantage in this respect, despite the fact that the Lone Star state eleven outweighed the team from Norman. Features of the game were brilliant end runs by Acton, Hughes, Mathews and McCreary, a fifty yard dash by Hughes, through tackle, splendid line plunging and bucking by Robinson, Hendrickson, Francis, McMahan, Hastings, and Crane. Captain Robinson brought cheers from the Texas "rooters" by his repeated end runs for long gains. The first half opened with Runbeck kicking off to Francis on the ten yard line. The ball was carried fifty five yards before they were forced to kick. A twenty-yard run by Hendrickson and a fifteen yard run by Robinson being the features. Oklahoma took the ball but was unable to make much headway. Fumbles by both teams were numerous and the teams were penalized for ten and fifteen yards often because of off-side plays. The ball was kept in Oklahoma's territory during the major part of the half, which ended with the ball in Oklahoma's possession near the center of the field.

> The Oklahoma team carried the ball fifty yards soon after the second half commenced, losing it on Texas' thirty yard line. Texas was forced to kick but later regained the ball and carried it from the center of the field to the five yard line.
>
> With the ball within half a yard of the goal line a line buck was attempted the ball being fumbled and the territory got it again on their five yard line. On the second down, Hughes broke through the line and ran a distance of fifty yards before being downed. Acton, Runbeck, Hughes and Mathews carried the ball to Texas' five yard line, where the team was held for downs. Robinson in attempting to advance the ball through the left tackle was carried by Acton behind the goal line for a safety and the game ended with the score, Oklahoma 2, Texas 0.

Not a bad write-up for 1905! The writer was no Rick Reilly or Barry Tramel, and aside from the fact that the lead paragraph conflicts with the last (did Severins or Acton actually pull Robinson down? We'll never know for sure!), this is a remarkably detailed account of the first Sooner win over rival Texas.

REEDS BECOMES OU'S FIRST ALL-AMERICAN

Coming off a disappointing 5–4 season in 1912, Owen's team looked to improve. Among the team's best players was Claude Reeds.

Reeds, born in Norman on November 12, 1890, was a special athlete. A fullback, he was considered an integral part of the Sooners' plans for 1913.

The team bounced back with a vengeance, defeating its first three opponenets—Kingfisher College, Central Oklahoma, and Northwestern Oklahoma State—by an incredible combined score of 258–0. Owen's use of the forward pass, which usually allowed the Sooners to score quickly, was gaining a national reputation for Oklahoma football.

A controversial eligibility ruling kept Reeds out of Oklahoma's narrow, 20–17 loss to Missouri in Columbia. Conference rules allowed players to play three seasons. Although Reeds had only played two, he, along with Elmer Capshaw, were kept out of the game anyway. Tiger coach Chester Brewer kept his team in the university's gymnasium until Oklahoma's Bennie Owen agreed to sit Reeds and Capshaw.

Owen needed his star for the next game, a key match in Norman against the Kansas "Jayhawkers."

Kansas, coming off two consecutive losses to Oklahoma, entered the Halloween afternoon game leading the Missouri Valley Conference. Owen's team, which the coach characterized as "Oklahoma's greatest," defeated Kansas, 21–7.

Only the narrow loss to Missouri and a similar outcome against Texas kept the Sooners from going unbeaten in 1913. Against Northwestern Normal that year, Oklahoma had thirteen runs of forty yards or more in the course of a lopsided 101–0 win—a foreshadow of dominating Sooners teams far into the future!

THE BEGINNING OF THE LEGENDARY 1915 SEASON

Several young players from 1913 had become seasoned players two years later. In the meantime, a world war had erupted, and football was a nice distraction.

"Benjamin Gilbert" Owen looked forward to the season, and with good reason. By late August, the coach had assembled a team that was the envy of the region. Indeed, a reporter remarked that the Sooners had "superhuman speed and grit"—another hallmark of later Sooner teams.

Owen had the nucleus of a good squad returning, although Billy Clark and quarterback "Rip" Johnson had used up their eligibility. It was also rumored that Willis and Oliver Hott, younger brothers of former Sooner great Sabert Hott, might have to remain on the family farm at Wakita. But by mid-September, the Hott boys decided to return to school.

MEMBERS OF an "elevens" squad in the Oklahoma territory around the turn of the century

Owen's forward passing game merely had to reload, since "Hap" Johnson at quarterback and Forest "Spot" Geyer at fullback could throw well enough. Additionally, the team took on track star John Jacobs. The move was indicative of the Sooners' innovative approach of getting the ball to skill players, in lieu of the "battering ram" approach to offense favored by most teams at the time.

Owen implemented other innovations as well, such as putting the team through strenuous summer workouts. He also devised a tackling dummy that resembled a live player. Thanks to the growing popularity of the teams he was putting on Boyd Field, thirty-five players tried out for the 1915 team, more than double the number of the previous season.

Player competition was the norm in those days, a mantra often repeated by Stoops and embraced by Wilkinson, too. For the 1915 opener, Owen announced that only Geyer, a team captain, and Johnson had secured starting spots. Everyone else would have to fight for it, with Owen intending on using tune-up games to solidify the starters. An observer noted:

> Not only in the backfield, where there are four sets of halves, will the competition be keen, but there are spots in the line that are being looked over every day by the keen eye of the coach, and there will be many substitutions in the line as well as in the speed division at the rear.

One might mistake this Oklahoma team for one from decades later, as fans eagerly anticipated not only the returning stars, but new players who might become stars.

The *Daily Oklahoman* noted that sophomore Vic Cline was giving the fans something to talk about (its description of Cline would fit 1955 sophomore Clendon Thomas as well):

> He is one of the speediest men of the team, built solidly and yet is rangy and runs hard and straight. He has been picking holes in the opposing line remarkably well so far, and is known as a hard man to

stop. Fans are watching his daily workouts with a great deal of interest, and his future looks promising. He will be given his first baptism of varsity play in Saturday's game.

The paper also noted that Charles Swatek was similar to Cline, but was a more dangerous open field runner with plenty of moves.

It went on to describe Owen as being a hands-on kind of guy:

> In preparation for Saturday's game Owen has had his coat off and has mixed more than usually right in amongst the plays, giving out lightning-quick personal rebukes and encouragement. He singles out the faults of every player, one at a time, and gives them the correct information even while the quarterback is calling the signal for the succeeding play.

As the season got underway, Geyer showed that he understood something early on that all Sooner greats who came after him have grasped: the team *has* to beat the Longhorns.

"If there is one thing above another that we're starting out to do," said Geyer in September, "it is to beat Texas. We should have done it last year [a 32–7 loss] and it looks like we will have a good chance this year, and we're certainly going to do our best."

The Sooners' first scheduled game of the season was a much-anticipated matchup against Central Normal (Edmond). The opponents looked forward to unleashing star fullback George Perdue. A five-foot-eleven, 185-pound native of Edmond, Perdue was said to possess "speed to burn" and "that rare article, headwork, to go with it." He was also a great kicker, and Oklahomans were intrigued by the anticipated battle between Perdue and Geyer.

Unfortunately the game, which was scheduled for Fair Park in Oklahoma City, was cancelled on account of inclement weather. Despite rain, humidity, and tropical temperatures, both Owen and Central coach Charles Wantland had worked their squads tirelessly. Owen, planning to play regardless of the weather, had worked his team out on Friday afternoon in the rain and mud. But I. S. Mahan of the Oklahoma State Fair and Exposition visited the park Friday evening and then instructed both teams not to come. Sadly for the fans, motorcycle races scheduled for after the game were struck from the program as well.

Owen and Wantland tried hard to reschedule the game—Wantland even declared that Central "was prepared to be carried off the field before O.U. should be returned a winner." However, to play OU, Central would've had to reschedule a game against Oklahoma Methodist in Guthrie, and this could not be done because the Ringling Brothers circus was in town on the only day the game could be made up.

After the Central game was cancelled, Owen turned his attention to tune-up matches (called "secondary school practice games"—the equivalent of Stoops' "East Popcorn State" moniker of the twenty-first century) against Kingfisher College and Northwestern Normal.

The two sacrificial lambs bled out, 169–0, to the red-and-white-striped Sooners. Kingfisher never got past the 20, the modern red zone, and its defense "crumpled" from the start. Six players alone alternated at halfback.

Geyer scored the first touchdown of the season five minutes into the game, soon after Johnson returned a punt to the Kingfisher 40. On the first play from scrimmage, a "Congregationalist" picked off a Sooner pass, but fumbled on his 25. Cline did most of the work on the ground before Geyer bulled his way in from the 1. Geyer scored again from short yardage a minute later, followed by a touchdown pass to Oliver Hott, another Geyer score, and yet another by Cline. In what would become typical Oklahoma fashion, the score at the end of the first quarter was 34–0.

Owen substituted a new team for the second half, with Elmer Capshaw and Raybourne Foster doing most of the damage on the ground through both long and short runs.

Meanwhile, Owen managed to get what he wanted: plenty of experience for everybody.

Oklahoma was off to a booming start for 1915.

Next up was a hastily scheduled tune-up game against Southwestern Oklahoma State at Weatherford on October 5. Only twenty Sooner players made the trip with Owen and assistant coach Edgar Meacham. Southwestern still didn't stand a chance.

Rolling to a 38–0 halftime lead, the Sooners won 55–0. Southwestern had only one chance to score, on a long pass. Several Sooners recovered in time, though, to drop the receiver.

Northwestern Oklahoma State was the underdog at the next game on October 9; nevertheless, the Sooners were afraid their opponents would be able to run up a high score.

They needn't have worried.

With Geyer scoring four times, the "crimson-sweatered" Sooners demolished Northwestern, 102–0. The visitors made only two first downs and snapped the ball just once in Oklahoma territory. (The game was eerily reminiscent of OU's dominaton of Nebraska at Norman in 1973, in which defense coordinator Larry Lacewell remarked, "I'll take this defense and go fight Russia.")

A reporter noted that either Northwestern was "weak and ignorant," or else Owen had another tremendous line. In a sign of the times, he also related that the Sooner faithful were offended by an opposing player, McConnell, who used "deliberate loud profanity" during the game.

OU, thanks to Geyer's running and Johnson's passing, led 41–0 at halftime. Curiously, up 67–0 at the end of three, Owen put his starters back in.

Geyer intercepted a pass and brought it back thirty yards for a touchdown. Johnson then fielded a Rangers punt at midfield and followed a wall to the endzone. It was reported that "Sooner fans wildly cheered the heady quarter after his dash."

Nine different players scored touchdowns, while Geyer kicked every extra point.

DID YOU KNOW?

Legendary professional wrestling commentator (currently on WWE Raw) Jim Ross is a huge OU fan. "JR" is a fixture around the OU scene when he can get away from his multifaceted career of announcing, running restaurants, and writing cookbooks.

With the tune-ups out of the way, the Sooners turned their attention to the season's opening match against Missouri. Although Owen and the players were tight-lipped about forecasting the outcome, long-time Sooner observers predicted that Oklahoma's passing game would lead to something like the previous year's 14–0 victory,

Although Missouri claimed that up to six starters were injured and would not play, Owen cautioned his team not to believe "those Missouri bear stories." Owen, however, did his own investigating and discovered that the Tigers were on the up-and-up about their injuries. Only center Curly Bell was hobbled for the Sooners, but Owen felt he'd play anyway.

Sure enough, Oklahoma out-gunned Missouri in Columbia, relying on the pass. Geyer both threw and caught passes all day as the Sooners won convincingly, 24–0. Missouri outgained Oklahoma on the ground, 166 yards to 134. But it was the pass that doomed the Tigers, with OU connecting for 260 yards. Missouri only gained thirty yards in the air and was forced to punt a staggering fourteen times!

Incredibly, Owen used only thirteen players (to Missouri's twenty-three) while baffling the Tigers with his catch-and-run passing game.

Upon the team's return from Columbia, the Oklahoma student body spilled into the streets, yelling and cheering. They marched to the university's administration building and demanded a holiday to commemorate the victory.

A WAR IN DALLAS

After the win against Missouri, a headline in the paper on Sunday, October 17 said it all: "Next On Sooner Schedule is to Brand That Texas Longhorn." The Red River Rivalry was on.

A survey revealed that upwards of 2,000 Sooner fans would make the trek to Dallas for the Oklahoma-Texas matchup at the state fair. Students secured a special railroad car and raised enough money for twenty band members to make the trip as well.

Beginning with the summer workouts, the slogan "Beat Texas" echoed from Oklahoma's bleachers. The intensity of the rivalry rose to fever-pitch by the time the game rolled around, as a "burning desire for retaliation" arose among the Sooner faithful.

On the Friday before the Texas game, the *Oklahoman* reported, "While the crimson-sweatered football men crashed back and forth on Boyd field, Pepmaster 'Ne-Hi' High led five hundred fans in the bleachers in the final rehearsal of songs and yells, and the band did their last practice march round the quarter-mile track."

Although the Texas line outweighed the Sooners' by an average of eleven pounds (174 to 164), and the Texas backs outweighed their counterparts by nearly double that, Owen was privately confident. Texas fans, however, predicted a double-digit Longhorns win.

A crowd of 5,000 was expected—the largest ever to see a football game in Texas—but 12,000 showed up to see the Sooners pull off a thrilling victory in the last three minutes.

> **"We place our entire emphasis on speed."**
>
> —BUD WILKINSON

Quarterback Montford "Hap" Johnson scored both Oklahoma touchdowns. Twice earlier in the game, Geyer missed field goals. Texas scored late to take a 13–7 lead, but a touchdown pass from Geyer to quarterback Johnson pulled the Sooners even. Geyer trudged to the spot for the placement, measured the distance to the uprights, and gauged the wind. He then backed up in the face of thousands of screaming Longhorn fans.

> Geyer's kick, from a difficult angle, was sure, and Oklahoma took the lead.
>
> Willis Hott's defensive play was a key factor; at one point he stopped Texas backs six straight times.
>
> With the 14–13 win, Oklahoma advanced to 5–0 and looked forward to playing Kansas, Owen's alma mater. The Oklahoma team was

> first on the field, presenting an imposing appearance as, wrapped in their brilliant crimson blankets, they crossed the north end of the gridiron to the space reserved from just outside the east sidelines. Five minutes later, from the far northeastern corner came the blue-sweatered Jayhawkers, a big squad strikingly promising.

The game turned out to be a classic. Fifty Jayhawk students made the trip from Lawrence, and they were treated to an offensive extravaganza. Six thousand Sooner fans, the largest crowd to watch a football game in Oklahoma at that time, saw their team use its superior quickness to counter Kansas' size advantage.

The game had some surprises, as Kansas gave Oklahoma a little of their own medicine, throwing the ball effectively. The Sooners, on the other hand, gashed Kansas' defensive line and produced a number of great running plays.

Early on, Oklahoma was able to move easily between the 20s, but stalled in scoring position. Kansas scored first, two minutes into the second quarter, from Oklahoma's 15. The Jayhawk quarterback threw to his receiver, Reber, but the Sooners' Johnson made a break on the ball and appeared to have intercepted it. Reber managed to grab possession, though, and fell across the goal line.

Kansas threatened again when Geyer was intercepted. Driving, they were stopped from opening up a two-touchdown lead when McCain (who was playing despite his back injury, and would later break his wrist) recovered a fumble.

Oklahoma tied the game at the end of the first half. Geyer had begun hitting Howard McCasland, and the little end took one fifty-five yards to the Kansas 5. McCain swept left end on fourth down for the touchdown.

At halftime, the "show" consisted of Kansas students flocking onto the field to do a snake-dance; a news account reported that "their demonstration surpass[ed] any ever seen before on Boyd field." Not to be outdone, the Sooner faithful assembled in front of the visitors' grandstand and staged a mock funeral for a dead Jayhawk.

Geyer scored on the opening drive of the second half. A few minutes later, Johnson took a Kansas punt at his 35 and dodged and twisted for a touchdown. Geyer missed the extra point, but later made a 37-yard field goal, something of a novelty in those days. In the end, Oklahoma outscored Kansas, 23–14.

Newspapers reported that with their sixth victory of the year, the Sooners were cruising to an unbeaten record with four games remaining. Oklahoma, they said, was expected to "make a clean sweep of the remaining games."

As Oklahoma moved into what was supposed to be the easy part of its schedule, more people began to talk about a potential postseason matchup with mighty Nebraska, which had been unbeaten since 1911.

Cornhusker Head Coach Jumbo Steihm mentioned the possibility, since his team had to turn down an invitation to play—we're not making this up—Kansas City Veterinary College. Coach-speak didn't really exist in those days, so Steihm simply admitted that Nebraska had nothing to gain from such a contest. "Such a game could not add to our prestige," he said dismissively.

However, the appeal of a Sooner-Husker matchup was clearly intriguing. Both teams wanted to be known as the lone power of the Southwest. Nebraska fans remembered the game with the Sooners at Lincoln three years before, when a Claude Reeds pass to Raymond Courtright was stopped just short of the endzone in a 13–9 Husker win.

KENDALL, KENDALL, RAH-RAH!

First, though, the Sooners had to take on Henry Kendall College (Tulsa). With an unbeaten season for the taking, and a possible marquee game with Nebraska at the end, Oklahoma could be forgiven for overlooking Kendall.

They did, and it almost broke their hearts. The *Oklahoman* reported that OU players were "surprised by the versatile and powerful attack of the Presbyterians," in what was surely the one and only time in history that particular sentiment has been put to paper.

SNAPSHOTS from the 14–13 win over the Texas Longhorns in Dallas, 1915

Kendall scored first only three minutes into the game, having won the toss and electing to receive with a wind at their backs.

On the last play of a ten-play drive, a Kendall halfback faked out both Johnson and Geyer to score standing up from twenty yards out. A crucial missed extra point would later prove decisive.

With a minute left in the first half, Geyer hit Johnson with a 20-yard touchdown pass and Geyer kicked the extra point to give OU a 7–6 lead. To open the third quarter, Kendall used a fifty-yard pass to score from in close.

Rousing themselves in the third quarter, the Sooners relied on the running of halfback Fred Capshaw, who scored a crucial touchdown at the end of the third.

Late in the game, Kendall had the ball in Oklahoma territory. But with the sun setting fast, Kendall missed on a fourth-down attempt at the Sooner 10.

Oklahoma barely won, edging out Kendall 14–13.

PIG SPIES

With a game looming against Arkansas at Norman, the Sooners went back to practice. The big news that week was the accusation from Arkansas circles that the Sooners had sent spies to Fayetteville to observe the Razorbacks' new plays. A newspaper article noted that "two suspicious looking characters were seen in town Wednesday" skulking around the practice field. Oddly enough, the article went on to provide a fairly detailed account of Arkansas' practice and the coaches' interaction with their players.

Unsurprisingly, the article declined to speculate how any such spies could have made it back to Norman in time for the Sooners to use the supposedly illicitly gained information.

In the game, Capshaw ran for 110 yards to lead the Sooners to a 23–0 win. It was a good thing that the running game was successful, since the team's vaunted passing attack went 2 of 15 for just forty-five yards. The victory was sealed late in the game when, with Oklahoma up 16–0, Homer Montgomery picked up a blocked kick and ran eighty yards for a touchdown.

"MEX"

Roughly during the years of World War I, OU's first mascot, a dog from Mexico nicknamed "Mex," was brought to Hollis, eventually making his way to Norman. He sported a red sweater and chased stray dogs away from the field. He passed away peacefully in 1928 and, according to legend, is buried somewhere under Owen Field, presumably near Jimmy Hoffa.

DOWN AND DIRTY WITH THE WILDCATS

A few weeks before the Kansas State game, the *Daily Oklahoman* sparked a lot of heated discussion across the plains when it broke the story that Nebraska's coach would consider a post-season game against the Sooners.

As time went by and no action was taken by Nebraska, the *Oklahoman* asked the six members of the Missouri Valley conference about the prospect of such a matchup. When Nebraska got wind of this the school issued a defensive statement, which was reproduced in a *Daily Oklahoman* article:

> The possibility of a post-season engagement between the Cornhuskers and the Oklahoma Sooners now is remote. Even if Nebraska's pulverizing victory over Kansas failed to settle all doubts as to supremacy of the Huskers to the Missouri valley section, it is fairly well settled that conference approval to a post-season contest could not be secured.

With a potential OU-Nebraska game torpedoed by premature publicity, Nebraska began angling for a game in Pasadena, California against, possibly, the University of Washington.

The *Oklahoman* article, carrying the headline "Someone in Cornhusker Land is Monkeying, Trifling with Sooner Football Aspirations," went on to mock the Huskers and accuse Nebraska representatives of various forms of dirty dealing. In those wild and woolly days of newspapers, it was common for reporters to editorialize to an incredible degree in what were ostensibly straight news stories. The comments sometimes even took on a racial character; for example, in the article quoted above, the *Oklahoman* writer twice declared that "there's a 'nigger in the woodpile.'" That expression, coupled with similar ugly sentiments sprinkled throughout the article, illustrate just how pervasive racism was in those days.

But back to football.

As Oklahoma got ready for its ninth game of the year—against the Kansas State "Farmers"—the talk of the country was the Sooners' passing game.

However, that didn't turn out to be a big factor in the game. In a detailed account of the Sooners' 21–7 victory, the lead paragraph in the following day's paper used the humorous vernacular of the day; note the use of the word "dope," which was a common expression back then:

> **Aerial Style Fails Oklahoma Heavers**
>
> Playing true to dope but abandoning their aerial style of football for line plunges and trick plays, the University of Oklahoma eleven Friday defeated the Kansas Aggies by the score of 21 to 7 in a game which was a whirlwind from start to finish and was marked by the absence of successful forward passing on the part of both teams. The game was a wonderful demonstration of the most modern type of ground playing known to the football world of today.

In fact, no one completed a pass until the fourth quarter, when K-State connected on a 30-yarder! Evidently, the strong northwest wind swirling in Manhattan, Kansas that day shut down Geyer and Johnson's passing.

K-State struck first, recovering a fumble that was returned fifty-three yards for a touchdown.

After stopping the hosts on another drive at the Sooner 11, the visitors began an 89-yard march for a touchdown. They ran behind Foster, McCasland, and Montgomery, with the latter scoring from in close. In the second quarter, Johnson scored on fourth-and-goal to put the Sooners up by seven.

Kansas State moved the ball on the ground twice in the first half, but Oklahoma stiffened on defense and took a 14–7 lead at halftime.

In the third, Oklahoma relied again on its rotating backs, with Hott scoring on a five-yard run for the final touchdown.

In the fourth, K-State's great back, Randalls, got loose for a 55-yard touchdown run, but it was called back on a holding penalty. The hosts didn't give up, driving late in the game to the Sooners' 15, before Geyer intercepted to seal the win.

With the Kansas State game behind them, Oklahoma sparked a great deal of interest in the Bedlam game against the Oklahoma "Aggies," which was played in Oklahoma City on Thanksgiving Day.

It was noted after Monday's practice that Oklahoma students watching from the bleachers "talked about the great amount of wildness, craziness and desperation that has enveloped the Stillwater aggregation in the past day or so by the discovery of what a victory over the Sooners would mean."

"If there is one thing above another that we're starting out to do, it is to beat Texas."

—Forest "Spot" Geyer

The Sooners were in generally good physical shape for the game, although Montgomery had broken his nose in the game at Manhattan, and the "midget man" Jesse Fields had a bad ankle. With the few injuries, Oklahoma had to use people in other spots. It was pointed out that "Capshaw and Swatek were used a great deal, and are doped to shine in the coming contest."

Doped!

Owen took no chances. In the final practice on Wednesday at Boyd Field, the coach spent an hour going over each player's individual assignment, as it was felt that the Aggies would try to duplicate K-State's effective pass defense.

A whopping 7,000 people watched the game, all the more remarkable considering the holiday. The crowd stood and cheered when the players ran onto the field, later repeating their appreciation at the game's conclusion.

Although Geyer would become Oklahoma's star player that year, it was "Trim" Capshaw who scored twice against the Aggies. Geyer scored once, and kicked a field goal and three extra points.

Early on, Aggie fans were overjoyed when their team took a 7–0 lead—it was the first time in eighteen games that the Aggies had a lead over the Sooners! However, "That touchdown seemed to be the thing needed to make demons out of the men from Norman." Oklahoma proceeded to score seventeen more points before halftime, the last touchdown coming on a drive that featured a pair of 20-yard runs by Johnson.

The 26–7 win sealed the Sooners' greatest season to date, as they finished 10–0 and forever wondered what might have been had someone not "monkeyed" with their aspirations.

The unbeaten 1915 team mirrored its coach, just as later Sooner squads would reflect coaches like Bud Wilkinson: disciplined, conditioned, and emphasizing speed.

Players like Montford "Hap" Johnson proved not only their versatility, but their skills in particular areas. Fans would long remember kick returners like Joe Washington and Antonio Perkins, but Johnson's returns go down as some of the greatest in Sooner history.

Clifford Meyer, through sheer determination and perseverance, became the kind of player that Barry Switzer would extol many decades later. He was one of those good, solid players that a coach needs in abundance to complement the truly great players—the All-Americans—in order to assemble a successful team. Meyer played himself into a job at center and, amazingly, spelled Johnson at quarterback against the Oklahoma Aggies.

Homer Montgomery, one of those amazing Muskogee players from that little eastern Oklahoma town's football pipeline, was also a forerunner of great players to come. Ends like Ben Hart, Tinker Owens, and Malcolm Kelly would later earn honors and become receiving legends, but Montgomery was

GAMEDAY HAUNTS

The Mont, located at the corner of Boyd and Classen in Norman, is a favorite of fans on game day. Originally opening as the Monterrey in the 1920s, the restaurant has been serving great food as The Mont since 1976.

one of the Sooners' first great ends. His ability to catch the ball in traffic and make twisting, difficult catches was key in Owen's undefeated 1915 team.

Willis Hott established himself as a great defensive lineman. A Texas fan in Dallas that year remarked, "That man didn't play mere All-Southwestern football—he played several minutes of All-American stuff!"

Tackle George Anderson was the only player in 1915 to play every snap in every game. The Ardmore native passed up his senior year of football to concentrate on medical school.

With so many great football teams remembered at Oklahoma, it's time we tipped our hats to the undefeated Sooners of 1915—a memorable team, indeed.

Chapter Two

RISE OF A DYNASTY

FROM SOUPY AND SNORTER TO THE BUD WILKINSON SHOW

In any era, football fans want to see greatness and dominance from their teams. And if Providence smiles on them, perhaps they'll get a dynasty. Think of the Green Bay Packers of the 1960s, Pittsburgh in the '70s, and San Francisco in the '80s. In the college ranks, Southern Cal had a good run in the 2000s. Miami has had some extraordinary seasons. Many of these teams' performances were breathtaking.

And OU surpassed them all. With a string of dominating teams, an unmatched forty-seven-game win streak, and even a quarterback who never lost a game, OU went to work in the mid-twentieth century assembling a powerhouse football program destined to leave its mark on the sport itself.

As the 1920 season approached, Owen found that, for the first time, he had enough players to put two men at each position on the field, thus creating the first real "depth" Oklahoma had ever had. Twelve lettermen returned to serve as the team's nucleus.

Sooner fans grew anxious as the season approached because the squad's playing equipment was delayed in shipping for a month. However, they

Photo courtesy of Oklahoma Historical Society

A "RAUCOUS" GROUP of fans watch the Sooners defeat Missouri in 1924

anticipated a great season from players like Roy "Soupy" Smoot, Lawrence "Jap" Haskell (later an Oklahoma assistant coach), and Dewey "Snorter" Luster (later a Sooners' head coach), all of whom provided not only terrific play, but the requisite colorful nicknames so coveted in those days.

Harry Hill was expected to challenge for playing time at halfback, and his twelve-hour work days on his father's Chickasha ranch prepared him well for OU's punishing training regime. Hill's physical conditioning was not unusual for Sooners back then; many were literally straight off the farm by the time practice rolled around, and no doubt practice was almost a vacation compared to their previous jobs.

As the Sooners readied for the 1920 opener against Central, there was a hang-up in the practice schedule: "Engineering students were working on [the tackling dummy] this week but had been having trouble in inserting a lever that would stand up under the weight of the husky Sooner linemen."

Quickly recovering from their preseason technical problems, the Sooners went on to manhandle nearly all their opponents. The team opened with a 16–7 win over Central, then rolled to three more victories before blowing out the Oklahoma Aggies, 36–0. They tied Kansas State, then finished the season with a 44–7 win over Drake at Norman.

Playing just three games in Norman, the Sooners' pre-Thanksgiving contest at Kansas State, which ended in a tie, was the only thing that prevented Oklahoma from posting a perfect record. Finishing the season at 6–0–1, the team was the third undefeated team in Owen's career at Oklahoma, coming after the thrilling 1915 season and his 1918 SWC champions, who went 6–0.

Owen went on to coach for six more years at Oklahoma. His final team, in 1926, lost close games to both Kansas state schools and, sadly, tied the Oklahoma Aggies in his final game in Stillwater.

In the coach's twenty-two seasons in Norman, his teams went 122–54–16. He was Oklahoma's first iconic coach.

FIRST ORANGE BOWL

The Sooners had four coaches during the 1930s. They had fair success, going 49–33–12.

The team dropped several close games to Texas during the decade, but beat the Longhorns in 1933 under Lewie Hardage, tied them in 1937 under Tom Stidham, and then won in 1938 and 1939, again under Stidham.

Stidham's 1938 team became the most noteworthy of the Depression-era squads.

After a one-point win in the season opener against Rice at Houston, the Sooners went on a tear. A crowd of 28,000 turned out to watch Oklahoma defeat Texas. Incredibly, the 1938 Big Six champions pitched eight shutouts and only gave up a total of twelve points during the regular season. A season-closing December win over Washington State at Norman set the stage for Oklahoma's first post-season game.

Photo courtesy of Oklahoma

A REPORTER interviews OU assistant coach Lawrence "Jap" Haskell, 1930s

Although Orange Bowl appearances would later become almost routine for the Sooners, the first was a source of tremendous excitement for Oklahoma fans. A headline in the *Daily Oklahoman* described the enthusiasm of the Sooner faithful, albeit somewhat oddly: "Oklahomans in Florida Turn Orange Bowl Trip Into Gay Winter Vacation."

Fans enjoyed themselves to the hilt in Miami, where the scenery provided a stark change from the prairies of Oklahoma. The *Daily Oklahoman* reported on an amusing incident that occurred two days before the game, when a radio announcer mistook some Sooner players for Tennessee boys:

> **Whoa, There, Husing—These Are O.U. Boys!**
>
> Ted Husing, that glib microphone man who will broadcast the University of Oklahoma's Orange Bowl game with Tennessee at Miami Monday afternoon, has let himself in for a bit of feudin' with the Sooners.
>
> Admittedly an "Oklahoma" fan and an official of Miami's bowl, the radio football authority made a slip of the tongue while he was doing his stuff from the site of the Orange Bowl game Saturday afternoon. Husing, doing a preview commentary on Monday's game, had just interviewed Tom Stidham, Sooner coach, and Waddy Young and Hugh McCullough, Oklahoma stars. He then took his roving microphone out on the practice field where the Tennessee team was running through its final drills.
>
> "What a handsome bunch of boys these Vols are," Ted said with sugar dripping from every word. "There goes Gene Corrotto, dark and handsome. Girls, Robert Taylor, Clark Gable and Tyrone Power are pikers along side him. And there's Jim Thomas, a guard, a very handsome lad, and Earl Crowder, another back also a might pretty boy." Of course, Corrotto, Thomas and Crowder are Sooners, but the man of the mike never caught up with himself for a correction.
>
> However, in part, Husing did redeem himself, as he extemporized on the Sooner possibilities for a victory in Monday's game. He

> interviewed Stidham "... whom I have known for years, since he was assistant at Northwestern under Dick Hanley, and today is perhaps the outstanding coach in the nation." Stidham, sounding like a professional radio announcer, did not commit himself, but did have a lot of nice things to say about the Sooner team, Miami's scenery, and the general manner in which the team has been treated. It remained for Waddy Young, Oklahoma's All-American end, and Hugh McCullough, ace back whom Husing compared with Marchie Schwartz, Red Grange and Red Cagle as one of the nation's most versatile back-field men, to predict a victory for the Sooners Monday. Both players were "sure that Oklahoma would win." Following the Husing broadcast a local program, originating from the bedside of Howard "Red" McCarty, injured Sooner backfield ace who is in St. Anthony's hospital, gave the Pauls Valley redhead opportunity to express himself.
>
> "I feel confident that Oklahoma will win by a couple of touchdowns," Red said. "If the boys are going at top speed the score should be 19–0. If the Sooners receive the opening kickoff you can look for a touchdown in the first five minutes of play."

Things didn't quite turn out like that for the Sooners, who got a rude welcome to bowl competition.

On Monday, January 2, 1939, Tennessee decided to show the country it had had enough talk about Oklahoma and its eight shutouts. In a game marred by the ejection of four players, Tennessee vowed to "give the Sooners a licking they'll long remember."

The Sooners had their work cut out for them—the humid, 85-degree weather disoriented the players as much as the Vols' renowned blocking skills.

In the first half, McCollugh sent a punt toward Tennessee's great George Cafego, who returned it to the Sooners' 27. Four plays later, Bob Foxx scored easily. Cafego had gained eight key yards to the 13 during the drive.

The point-after was dramatically blocked, but a Tennessee player alertly picked up the ball and ran into the endzone.

With a minute left in the first half, Tennessee hit a field goal to take a 10–0 lead. The half had been ugly for the Sooners, who were stymied by penalties and mistakes in the kicking game. Kick returner Otis Rogers was dropped several times deep in his own territory. By contrast, Tennessee successfully returned McCollough's punts to get into Oklahoma territory and keep the game on that end of the field.

In the fourth, Tennessee got the ball on its own 27 to start its final scoring drive. Two penalties looked like they would doom the Vols, who reached the Sooner 14 before a 5-yard penalty set them back. A 19-yard touchdown run on the next play deflated Oklahoma for the moment.

As they've done so many times over the years, though, Oklahoma mounted a late rally. McCollough began hitting passes and but for a motion penalty would have been deep in scoring position. Tennessee then picked off the Sooners.

Oklahoma later drove to the Vol 8 but couldn't convert. This allowed Tennessee to run out the clock.

Oklahoma managed only five first downs and 110 total yards. The Sooners also had six turnovers—five of them fumbles—and punted thirteen times.

The 17–0 final impressed the Sooner players as well as their fans. One OU fan summed up the game nicely: "Those squirrel-shooting hillbillies from Tennessee have got a heck of a lot better football team than I expected them to have."

Indeed.

The Sooners would have better luck in future Orange Bowls. . . .

THE WAR YEARS AND BEYOND

After Stidham and quarterback Jack Jacobs—an All-American and one of the great punters in Oklahoma history—led the Sooners to a decent 6–3 record in 1940, Dewey Luster came back to coach his alma mater.

"Snorter" would go 27–18–3 while navigating the Sooner program through the turbulent war years, when most teams scrambled to field a competitive squad as players were shipped off to fight overseas.

In 1941, Oklahoma had a promising team, led again by Jacobs and incoming freshmen like runningback Joe Golding. Other factors, however, would interfere with Sooner aspirations again, as the country turned its attention east to Japan and west to Germany.

A week after the Sooners dropped a one-point game to Nebraska at Lincoln, the Japanese attacked Pearl Harbor. Football took a backseat to more pressing wartime issues for the next several years. OU again went 6–3 in

"DEWEY'S LUSTER"

DEWEY LUSTER

Born at Tahlequah, Indian Territory, in 1899, Dewey Luster had always been interested in sports, but his slight frame looked like it would prevent him from competing on the gridiron. As a high school freshman, Luster was "a little shaver," weighing only eighty-five pounds! However, former Sooner player Art Reeds, coaching at Chickasha, decided that his team needed a little Luster, and he gave the quarterback reigns to Dewey. By 1916 Luster was also spending time in training camp for field artillery officers.

Luster was also a law student, earning his degree in 1922. At five-foot-eight and 151 pounds, he was an early proponent of weight-lifting. He worked out year-round at his Chickasha home in a custom-designed weight room.

Luster saved some of his best play for games against the Oklahoma Aggies. His later coaching career would also see some memorable games against Oklahoma's Bedlam rivals. As a player and a coach, he broke Aggie hearts more than once.

In an exciting match at Oklahoma City in 1919, Luster overcame the icy field conditions to block a punt and score on a 23-yard end-around.

1941, dropped to 3–5–2 in 1942, rebounded nicely with a 7–2 season in 1943, then rounded out the Luster era with a combined 11–8–1 record for 1944 and 1945.

As the war came to a close and America looked to the future, it was Tatum Time at Oklahoma.

A charismatic head coach, Jim Tatum was a sharp dresser who began a whirlwind tour of the state when he arrived in Norman in 1946 to take charge of the Sooners. Staying just one year at OU, Tatum operated more like a demanding CEO than a football coach à la Tom Stidham, delegating day-to-day management of the team to his talented young assistants, led by Charles "Bud" Wilkinson.

A fascinating account of Oklahoma's first game against a great Army team—along with intriguing details about Tatum—was written by Jeff Linkowski for the website Soonerstats.com:*

> In '46, a North Carolina alumnus named Jim Tatum, who had spent a few years as an assistant at Iowa Preflight under former Missouri coach Don Faurot, interviewed for the head position in Norman. Along with him for the visit was his assistant coaching counterpart and buddy, Bud Wilkinson, and together they impressed the administration. Tatum got the job with a three-year contract that totaled $27,000, comprised of yearly salaries of $8,000, $9,000 and then $10,000, but Wilkinson also had to come with him, and he would get a $6,800 salary.
>
> Coinciding with the end of World War II, college football had an influx of players returning, most of them older and in their mid 20s, and eligibility requirements were so loose that they could move from school to school without any problems. Tatum devised a massive recruiting effort that included tryouts and spring and summer practices, and with the number of conventional high school players

*Reprinted with permission, Soonerstats.com

coming in, players numbered in the hundreds of which Tatum could pare his squad. As a result the Sooners were able to get a lot of great talent, but it didn't come cheap, for reputedly, Tatum had spent the athletic department's entire surplus of more than $100,000 before the first game.

Oklahoma's imposing array of talent notwithstanding, there was a fairly substantial feeling throughout the Big Six that Missouri was the team to beat, for Faurot had done a similar mass recruiting. But Tatum, who thought his team would do well to win half their games, was installing the same "Split-T" offense with the Sooners that he had learned under Faurot. Given the heavy financial investment, all those involved in Norman would quickly find out if it were all worth it as Oklahoma's opener was against the finest collegiate football team in the land, the United States Military Academy.

An absolute powerhouse, the Cadets entered '46 as two-time defending national champions, and since there was no reason to believe that the "Touchdown Twins" were going to slow down, Army was favored to win its third straight national title. If any other team wanted it, they had to go through West Point.

The first AP poll wouldn't be released for a few weeks, out on October 8th, but everyone in the college football universe knew what team would be at the top. The Cadets kicked off their '46 campaign against Villanova at home, powering to an easy 35-0 victory to run their winning streak to 19 straight games. But it was costly, as [fullback Felix "Doc"] Blanchard had suffered a serious knee injury that would sideline him for at least a minimum of a month, if not longer. The challenge for Army had just become greater, and next up for [Army coach Earl "Red"] Blaik and his Cadets was their first-ever meeting with Oklahoma.

In front of over 25,000 in Michie Stadium at West Point along the Hudson River, a gathering that included United States President Harry S. Truman, Blanchard was in uniform and walked out to the center of the field for the coin toss, but that was about the extent of his duties. Once the game got underway, with the visitors being anywhere from three to four touchdown underdogs, it was Davis who would assume the brunt of the burden.

Once the whistle blew to begin play, it was the determined big and scrappy Sooners that inflicted most of the punishing early on in a fierce and bruising game. They did it by using a defensive alignment that had seven down linemen and two linebackers so close behind that it almost amounted to a nine-man front. Army could not get out of its tracks against the array, and while the alignment seemed an invitation to pass, Cadets [Arnold] Tucker and [Glenn] Davis were constantly overpowered as they tried to launch aerials.

After a scoreless opening period in which the Oklahoma offense experienced the normal learning curve associated with having a new offense in less than a month of practice time, it was their defense that turned in a big play. With regular punter Blanchard sitting on the sidelines, Army had to call in a green plebe, Joe Green, to kick from behind their own goal line. He fumbled the snap from center, and before he could get the punt away, the Sooners' Stanley West blocked it, and teammate Norman McNabb fell on the loose ball in the end zone for a touchdown. A successful extra point by junior Dave Wallace gave the visitors the lead, and a once-seemingly invincible team trailed 7–0.

When Army took over for their next possession, they had only made two first downs and had been slammed down on almost every attempt to rush or pass the ball by the tough Oklahoma defense. But then it was Tucker, maybe just a little under-appreciated before, who proved just how valuable a cog he was to their "T" when they took over at their 39. Along the way, he fired a 46-yard pass right down the middle of the field and into the arms of Davis, who had been mauled and battered to a standstill for the first 28 minutes of play, moving the Cadets close as the half drew near to a close. Tucker then fired a four-yard scoring toss to Hank Foldberg, and the extra point from Jack Mackmull tied the game, 7–7, with just 47 seconds left in the

DID YOU KNOW?

CBS newsman Walter Cronkite spent 1937 broadcasting OU football games with an Oklahoma City radio station.

half. Army hadn't lost in three years, but at halftime the Sooners had the game dead-locked at 7–7.

After intermission, and early in the third period, giant cadet Barney Poole, a demon on defense, blocked an Oklahoma punt on the Sooner 15. Then it was Tucker again who fired a nine-yard pass to Davis. It set up Fuson's one-yard touchdown burst, and Army had their first lead of the game. The successful extra point made it 14–7.

Late in the third, and after Army's berserk line had hammered the Sooners into a state of grogginess for Poole and Foldberg, Oklahoma and their Split-T offense put together a substantial and rip-tearing march of 74 yards. Once again though, it was Tucker who came up big. First, he broke through two blockers to throw freshman halfback Darrell Royal back to the six-yard line on a sweep after a first down had been registered at the Army 3. On the next play, tucker leaped into the air and snared Royal's pass to squelch the threat. It was Tucker's pair of spectacular defensive plays that halted the Sooner advancement at the Army three-yard line, denying a possible game-tying touchdown.

The Cadets had no sooner taken possession of the ball than a fumble gave it right back to Oklahoma at the 18. Sooners' halfback Joe Golding, a powerful runner who had lettered with the team back in '41 before the war, carried the ball to the 8½-yard line as the third stanza ended with the visitors threatening.

On the first scrimmage after the teams switched sides, Oklahoma sophomore quarterback Jack Mitchell lobbed the pigskin back to Royal, but sizing up the play was an alert Tucker, who came in like a flash and gobbled the ball out of the air, and before any Sooners could realize what had happened, he was off. Oklahoma's players reacted late, and Tucker had opened up a lead of about ten yards in the other direction. With the stands on both sides a bedlam of screaming and cheering fans, including Truman who was seated in the superintendent's loge and trying to remain impartial, Tucker sped the required 86 yards across the goal line for a touchdown. The extra point made it a 21–7 fourth quarter Cadets' lead, and the Sooners appeared drained.

Oklahoma did manage to come back to make one last try of it. Golding threw two passes to reach the Army 44, but the final ten minutes of the game found the Cadets recovering fumbles and intercepting passes, and two new backs, John Shelley and Bill West, did some of the best running of the afternoon. As such, Army was completely in command and then in eventual possession of one of the most dearly earned victories of the last few years, a 21–7 triumph representing their closest game in three seasons.

To appreciate the fight the Cadets had on their hands, the Sooners had gained 129 yards rushing while holding Army to the unbelievable total of just 83. The Oklahoma defense, led by senior lineman Plato Andros and junior John Rapacz, had held Davis to a mere 19 yards on 12 carries in the contest, his all-time low, and zero points. The visitors also had two more first downs than their hosts, 9-7, and they averaged 50% more distance on their kicks.

The Sooners had battled valiantly. Given their first game with a new offense, the usual growing pains were to be expected, and it was their turnovers that were principally responsible for their undoing in the form of four lost fumbles and three thrown interceptions. But Tatum had to be proud, regardless of how tough the defeat appeared, for if Army represented the measuring stick, Oklahoma certainly had stacked up.

Oklahoma, led by key players like Golding and others returning from the war, also benefitted from an infusion of talent from players like Darrell Royal, of tiny Hollis, Oklahoma. Royal started as a freshman in the backfield with established stars such as Golding, quarterback Jack Mitchell, and halfback George Brewer.

Linemen Jim Tyree, Homer Paine, Buddy Burris, John Rapacz, Dee Andros, and Wade Walker gave Oklahoma a ton of top-level talent to lead the way for the Sooners' glittery backfield.

After the opening-day loss to Army in the 1946 season, Oklahoma dropped close games at Texas and Kansas. But the team looked forward to a match against North Carolina State in the Gator Bowl in Jacksonville, Florida, which would give them a chance to avenge their loss to Tennessee in the 1939 Orange Bowl.

When NC State tied it early at 7, Joe Golding took the kickoff to his own 35 and appeared stopped by the 'Pack. Golding, however, flipped the ball to a trailing Charles Sarratt, who went sixty-five more for the touchdown. Oklahoma never looked back, piling up twenty-seven points by halftime and winning 34–13.

After his inaugural 8–3 campaign, the future looked bright for Jim Tatum and his Oklahoma Sooners.

The 1947 season was shaping up to be an exciting one, and would prove to be just that, for reasons not yet known.

BUD WILKINSON'S CHARM, ELEGANCE, AND HIS DECIMATION OF OPPONENTS

It is likely that the Sooners would have been very good had Jim Tatum stayed longer than one season. It is even conceivable that they would have become a heavy gorilla on opponent's backs.

But it is unlikely the program would have become King Kong without Bud Wilkinson at the helm. He brought sound ideas, discipline, motivation, and gifted assistants like Gomer Jones, Pop Ivy, and Bill Jennings. He brought innovation and a sanguine method of motivation that drove young men to attempt what no one had ever done before. He also brought a football mind that was at once brutal and elegant.

He was always a gentleman, yet his teams just pulverized opponents. Quarterback Jimmy Harris, who went unbeaten in college, had this to say

Photo courtesy of Oklahoma Historical Society

OU COACHING great Bud Wilkinson

twenty years after his playing days were done: "I guess the thing is I really would have liked to have played more. We got ahead, especially my senior year, and never did get to play enough. I enjoyed playing. Of course, you don't enjoy running the score up on anybody and Bud never did try; he really didn't."

Harris also noted that Wilkinson had long-range plans and a systematic way of achieving his goals: "He made a statement the spring of my freshman year, when I was starting because Gene Calame and Pat O'Neal were hurt. Bud said our group would get Notre Dame when we were seniors and we would be ready for them. I know he really didn't point for just that game. But we came out with all kinds of stuff—split backs and a completely different offense than we'd ever shown. We could have run the score a lot higher than we did [40–0]."

When interviewing a large number of former OU players, the one thing that comes through more than anything else is their competitiveness. Some are nice, others gruff; many are self-effacing, while others are openly confident. But it doesn't matter. They are all competitive for their entire lives. This can be traced, in large part, to Wilkinson's influence.

Clendon Thomas was once asked what his most memorable game was. He replied, "Every year when we played Oklahoma State. I think, because they wouldn't give me a scholarship. If you'll look back, I think you'll find that I had exceptional days in those games." Against the Aggies in 1955, Thomas scored OU's second touchdown on a sixty-five-yard punt return; his convoy included Wayne Greenlee, Bill Krisher, Don Stiller, Tom Emerson, and Bob Timberlake. He also ran for forty-six yards on nine carries.

Oddly enough, the teams Thomas played on each scored fifty-three points on the Aggies, giving up only six; the first two games were shutouts. In Thomas's junior year—the great 1956 team—he scored twice, taking the national scoring crown from Tommy McDonald. Thomas scored once from a yard out then, ironically, took an 8-yard TD pass from McDonald for OU's third score.

In 1957, Thomas ran for 162 yards and two touchdowns against the Aggies, while hitting one of two passes for twenty-four yards. Yes, Oklahoma's players were—and are—competitive.

Wilkinson counted presidents as friends, was cordial with fellow coaches, and even ran for the U.S. Senate upon resigning from OU at the end of the 1963 season. Everyone who knew him acknowledges his charm and sophistication.

Yet he clearly enjoyed dominating opponents—this in an era when many teams scored far fewer points than the teams of today. Neighboring Arkansas fielded several fine teams that routinely posted scores along those lines. Texas schools usually battled each other by matching wits among defensive coaches.

DID YOU KNOW?

In the 1930 Marion Davies film *The Florodora Girl*, in a game between two college football teams, the band plays the tune of "Boomer Sooner."

Oklahoma was hanging half-a-hundred on teams when Barry Switzer was in high school. Gifted athletes like Max Boydston, Buddy Leake, Eddie Crowder, Tommy McDonald, Prentice Gautt, and many others scored almost at will against opposing teams.

Wilkinson's teams were made up of guys who were not always highly recruited, but who had the "team" concept down pat. Thomas, who would become an All-American halfback, wasn't exactly deluged by recruiting letters out of Oklahoma City's Southeast High School. His team only won two games his senior year. He claims that he only received two solid scholarship offers—from Tulsa and Central State. However, like many of Wilkinson's players, he went on to excel not only in college, but in the pros.

Wilkinson also fostered loyalty from everyone with whom he worked. Gomer Jones, his long-time assistant, stayed with the head coach until he replaced Wilkinson in 1964. Gomer's two teams at OU were not up to the Sooners' standards, but it wasn't because of him. Jones had been an integral part of OU's unmatched success, and he managed to keep the program

GOMER: BUD'S "WING MAN"

GOMER JONES

A 1960 piece on Gomer Jones, Wilkinson's long-time assistant coach, summed up succinctly how OU felt about the former center from Ohio State:

GOMER JONES, looking angelic as a Buckeye lineman, 1935

Thinking of Bud Wilkinson without Gomer Jones is akin to thinking about a hot dog without the weiner, cabbage without corned beef or a Big Eight Conference championship-crowning ceremony without Oklahoma.

Through 13 autumns, Jones has served as Wilkinson's right-hand man during strategy mapping meetings and practice sessions. And on 137 pressurized Saturdays, Gomer has roamed the sidelines of the football world at Bud's side. A man of few words but possessor of a keen mind and dry wit, Jones complements Wilkinson perfectly. When they disagree on some point of strategy, the eventual compromise usually turns out to be just what the doctor ordered.

There has been an amazing parallel in the careers of Jones and Wilkinson. While Wilkinson was playing guard and blocking back for Minnesota from 1934 through '36, Jones was the center on Francis Schmidt's Ohio State outfits. Both made All-America but their teams did not meet. Both served in the Navy, Jones enlisting in 1943 and playing 2½ seasons with St. Mary's Pre-Flight. Like Bud, Gomer got coaching experience at several places. After a year of pro ball with the Cleveland Rams, Jones was freshman coach at Ohio State from 1938 to 1940. Gomer's 1941 Martin Ferry's Ohio, High School club was all-victorious and he was named Ohio Coach of the Year. After leaving the Navy, Jones served as aid to Bernie Masterson at Nebraska in 1946, then joined Wilkinson at Oklahoma.

Several colleges and universities have offered head coaching jobs to Jones, but he has spurned them to remain with Wilkinson and OU. To queries about why he declined such posts, Jones quips: "I've already got an ulcer, why do I need to be a head coach?" Jones is probably the best-paid assistant coach in college football but most observers say he isn't getting half as much as he's worth. Certainly, Wilkinson is only half-joking when he remarks: "If Gomer ever left, I'd have to quit."

together until his successors came in and transitioned the program to new heights.

To this day, Wilkinson's former players tear up at the mere mention of his name. Devotion like that doesn't come along every day.

> **"Come on . . . 47 wins, and 26 shut outs? That is mind-boggling, and will NEVER be seen again."**
>
> —Comment on OUInsider.com

His 10–0 national champions of 1956 are considered by some to be the greatest of all time. It's hard to argue the point—the team scored 466 points and allowed only 51.

Wilkinson's 1953 team, which started the famous forty-seven-game winning streak, had a memorable Orange Bowl game against Maryland, the national champions. It proved the Sooners' resourcefulness and tenacity, after having dominated so many opponents. These traits perfectly describe Wilkinson himself, as a team is usually a reflection of its coach.

Tied late, and without injured quarterbacks Gene Calame and Pat O'Neal, Wilkinson turned to little-used senior Jack van Pool of Oklahoma City. At halftime, van Pool asked his coach, "What shall I call this half?" Wilkinson answered, "It's your ball game; you call it." The story goes that when van Pool entered the huddle for the first time, he extended his shaking hands. He said, "If you guys stick with me, I promise I won't fumble." They did, and he didn't.

Late, van Pool pitched out to halfback Larry Grigg, who ran, then bulled his way into the endzone. With that, alongside the extra point, the Sooners took the game, 7–0.

"Although Jack van Pool hadn't even made some of our trips, he was an example of our squad's great attitude," J.D. Roberts remembered. "Van Pool didn't make a single error. He played super."

Van Pool and hundreds of other Sooners were super, and they were winners, both on the field and off. They were truly a reflection of their iconic head coach.

Chapter Three

GLORY DAYS

THE WISHBONE OFFENSE AT OKLAHOMA

There may be more important things in life than the Wishbone—okay, there *are* more important things—but any Sooner fan old enough to have seen it remembers how it made us feel to see this beautiful offense run to perfection. Those were good days.

The Wishbone formation uses four men in the backfield rather than three. Lining up directly behind the quarterback is the fullback, used primarily for blocking. On either side of the fullback, slightly behind him, are the right and left halfbacks. They are primarily ball carriers, but they block as well.

This formation gives a team several more options for running the football. Consequently, it also eliminates a wide receiver, thus lessening options in the passing game.

As several coaches pointed out to the Die-Hard Fan, the Wishbone helped to bring championships to Texas, Oklahoma, and Alabama. Those three teams dominated college football in the '60s, '70s, and '80s with an offense that was difficult to prepare for and nearly impossible to stop.

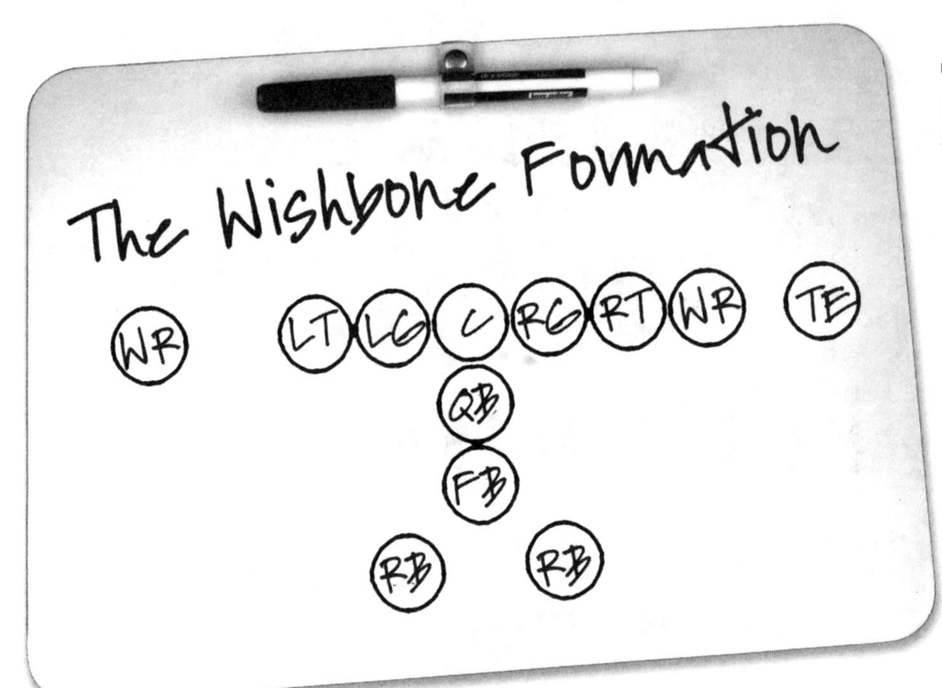

THE WISHBONE, used to devastate Sooner opponents.

The Texas program played a key role in the development of the Wishbone. Because Texas is such a big state, a lot of Texans get the feeling that everything started there—as if the Garden of Eden were originally located at Darrell K. Royal Stadium in Austin, and the Tower of Babel dispersion occurred near Houston, where various Texan dialects sprang up.

You get the idea.

Despite these conceits, we Oklahoma fans must acknowledge that the first real, live version of the Wishbone offense in college football did, in fact, arise at the University of Texas. The offense was unveiled on the heels of a couple down seasons following the national championship of 1963. Oklahoma, of course, debuted it in 1970 against (of all teams) Texas, and then went on a two-decade-long tear.

A year later, Alabama's Bear Bryant adopted the Wishbone and proved, with quarterbacks like Jeff Rutledge and Richard Todd (both of whom went on to significant pro careers), that the Wishbone wasn't just a running offense, but could include lethal passing, too.

THE SOONER QUARTERBACKS

Seven men really made their mark as Wishbone quarterbacks at Oklahoma: Jack Mildren, Dave Robertson, Steve Davis, Thomas Lott, J.C. Watts, Danny Bradley, and Jamelle Holieway. While other quarterbacks skillfully executed the Wishbone at OU, it was these seven who carved their names in Sooner football lore.

THE WISHBONE WIZARD

Jack Mildren is the standard-bearer. As the first OU Wishbone quarterback, Mildren established standards for running the Wishbone that are still in vogue today, even though the offense is mostly confined to the service academies now.

Mildren went to OU in hopes of becoming the next Bobby Warmack, the Sooners' marvelous passer. He was the object of a ferocious recruiting war, having played on winning teams since the fifth grade and become a widely known high school star in Abilene, Texas. He produced stunning numbers for any era, but especially in the '60s. In his senior season of 1967, Mildren completed 147 passes for 2,076 yards and twenty touchdowns. In a precursor to his OU career fame, he also ran for 787 yards and twenty-four touchdowns. In *Saturday's America*, author Dan Jenkins writes that Mildren "had all the attributes that made recruiters dance and holler—size, speed, arm, brains, moves, family, church, statistics, leadership and handshake."

His brothers had wanted Mildren to play for TCU or Texas, and Mildren had seriously considered SMU. When it came down to it, however, the family decided his college should be within a "reasonable driving distance" from home. That kept Oklahoma on the list. Later, Chuck Fairbanks came calling on a recruiting visit, telling Mildren that they could win a national championship together at OU.

JACK MILDREN pitches out to Greg Pruitt against Kansas in 1971

Photo courtesy of the *Daily Oklahoman*

Finally, it came down to Oklahoma and Arkansas, which had the great Frank Broyles. Mildren eventually opted for Oklahoma and phoned Broyles the morning he made his decision.

When Barry Switzer was named head coach at OU in February of 1973, *Daily Oklahoman* writer Bob Hurt profiled the new Sooner boss and related an anecdote from Mildren's recruitment:

> It was a warm spring night in 1968 in Abilene, Texas. This car stops in the middle of the street and two figures hop out and start going through strange gyrations under a street light.
>
> The older fellow goes into a semi-crouch, hands extended in front of him, and starts yelling numbers like a bingo caller. Then, he

turns abruptly and extends his hands farther in a sweeping motion. The younger guy watches intently, nodding his head in understanding. Most of the traffic detours around them. Some cars stop to see what is going on.

"But there wasn't much traffic," said Jack Mildren. "Abilene is not the wildest town after dark."

The scene remains vivid in Jack's mind. It returned to his mind when I asked Jack what kind of a recruiter Oklahoma's new football coach, Barry Switzer, would be.

Jack, now employed by a Tampa, Fla., oil company and the Baltimore Colts, seemed an ideal person to ask. A prep phenom, he was highly recruited. He attracted more coaches than a convention. The recruiting battle was won by Oklahoma and Switzer.

"He didn't pressure me," recalled Jack. "Mostly, we just talked football—like that night we were driving around and we stopped the car and he showed me quarterback techniques under that street lamp."

That's how the story unfolded.

"He didn't hound me or anything," Jack continued. "And he didn't run down the other schools—like Arkansas doesn't have this or Texas doesn't have that. We just talked about Oklahoma and football. I guess the big thing was I just liked him."

At OU, Mildren did what Fairbanks said he'd do: he started as a sophomore.

It fell to Mildren (along with Greg Pruitt) to save the coaching staff in 1970. OU had been running the Veer with mixed results. Looking for a more powerful offense,

DID YOU KNOW?

Actor James Garner is a Sooners fan. Born in Norman on April 7, 1928, Garner left the city as a teenager to join the Merchant Marines. He received an Honory Doctor of Human Letters degree at OU in 1995. After receiving two Purple Hearts for service in Korea, Garner returned to OU in hopes of making the football team, but injuries kept him off the squad. He then headed west to become one of the most famous actors of his generation, starring in *The Great Escape* and *Support Your Local Sheriff*, and playing iconic television roles as Bret Maverick and private investigator Jim Rockford. In 1980, during the final season of *The Rockford Files*, a freshman cornerback by the name of Jim Rockford enrolled at OU and became a key defensive player He was drafted by the Tampa Bay Buccaneers in 1985.

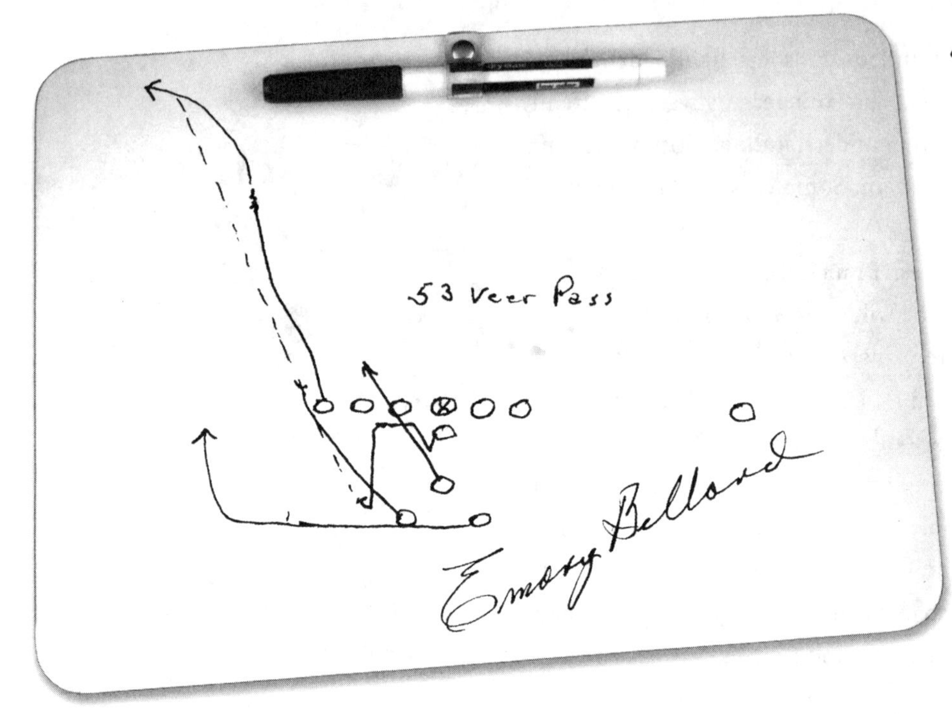

"RIGHT 53 VEER PASS," as diagramed by Emory Bellard, who invented the Wishbone offense. This play was proof that the Wishbone could be a passing offense.

OU's coaches couldn't help but notice how Texas had won championships with the Wishbone.

So OU tinkered with it, finally unveiling the new formation in 1970 against Texas, the defending national champions. The Longhorns blinked, then went to work and left the Sooners in the dust, 41–9. But Mildren ran the ball tough. It was a start.

Oklahoma went on to finish 7–4–1 that year. They tied Alabama in the Bluebonnet Bowl, with Greg Pruitt earning the game's MVP award and showing why he would become a superstar the next two years.

By 1971, Mildren was getting ready to show the world how the Wishbone could really be run. Seemingly born to play quarterback in an option offense, Mildren took OU on a run that will probably never be equaled. Almost four decades later, OU fans still recall that the '71 Sooners ran for an average of 472.4 yards per game. That's sick. Their total offensive average of 566.5 yards per game is only slightly less remarkable.

SITTING DOWN WITH THE GREAT

EMORY BELLARD

In a profession dominated by giant egos, it's refreshing to see that many of the iconic coaches of the past give credit where credit is due. As it pertains to the triple option, no less than Barry Switzer, Darrell Royal, Frank Broyles, and Merv Johnson point out that the Wishbone was conceived in the mind of one Emory Bellard. In fact, Switzer and Royal have honored Bellard with the designation "Father of the Wishbone."

In an interview with the Die-Hard Fan, Bellard explained how the Wishbone came to Oklahoma:

> We gave it [the Wishbone] to Alabama, we gave it to Oklahoma. I mean, their execution knowledge and so forth of the offense came from us; we gave it to Oklahoma. I just saw Barry [Switzer] the other day. He was offensive coordinator at Oklahoma and Chuck Fairbanks was the head coach and Darrell came into my office one day and we'd already just wore Oklahoma out a couple years and he said, "Chuck is in trouble, he's gonna lose his job and they want to put in the Wishbone. Barry is gonna be calling you, help him all you can." I shook my head, I said, "Darrell, you got to be joking." He said, "No, I wanna help him." I said, "Well, I can admire your wanting to help somebody but gosh darn, not them."
>
> That's true, too, because they got to where they had so much speed it was hard for us to catch them. He [Royal] called me about four or five months ago. He calls every now and then and I call him every now and then. But anyhow, he called and said, "You know, I was just sitting here thinking, I might not be as benevolent if I had it to do over again." I said, "I hope not, Darrell. I don't think we could go through that again."

> **"Steve Davis is an ideal Wishbone quarterback. Durable, intelligent, highly competitive, he has never failed to sparkle in showdown contests."**

The offense was so good that OU rolled over opponent after opponent. Slowly, the excitement began to build for the titanic clash scheduled for Thanksgiving Day. Nebraska was a defending national champion and had a great coach in Bob Devaney, along with superb players like Jerry Tagge, Johnny Rogers, and Rich Glover.

National magazines spotlighted the upcoming game. It was labeled "The Game of the Century" and became one of the few big matchups that lived up to its billing.

By the time the top two teams in the country met in Norman, few could contain their excitement. In the end, Nebraska eeked out a last-minute, 35–31 victory. Mildren, forced to pass because of a Nebraska defensive alignment that focused on stopping Pruitt wide, burned the Cornhuskers for two touchdown passes to former high school teammate Jon Harrison. He also ran for over 100 yards. Mildren nearly willed OU a win, but it wasn't to be.

Capping his career with a blowout win over Auburn in the Sugar Bowl, Mildren spent some time in the NFL before going on to a successful business career. Having served as lieutenant governor of Oklahoma, he remains a beloved figure in Sooner lore.

THE CHAMPION OF 1972

Dave Robertson is one of those players who achieved great success almost in anonymity. Many Sooner fans would scratch their heads if asked to name the guy who directed the Sooner Wishbone *between* Jack Mildren and Steve Davis. It didn't help that he only started one season.

But what a season.

As Oklahoma headed into 1972 after walloping Auburn in the Sugar Bowl, Sooner fans were unsure just how good OU could be with a new quarterback who, well, simply wasn't Jack Mildren.

But Dave Robertson had been around the program and had paid his dues. The six-foot-two, 199-pound California quarterback was known more for his passing ability than for running. For the season, he totaled only 278 yards on the ground, but threw for over 1,000. His passing ability was key in beating a tough Nebraska team at Lincoln, as well as Penn State in the Sugar Bowl.

"WE CAN'T LOSE TO THESE PEOPLE"

All fans are partial, of course. Certain players stick in people's minds for certain reasons. At Oklahoma, it's silly to argue that one player was better than another. The truth is, there have been so many great ones. A Sooner fan really can't say that Jack Mildren was "better" than J.C. Watts, or Adrian Peterson was better than Joe Washington or Tommy McDonald or, heck, Claude Reeds.

They were simply Sooners, and they were all great. As the Bible says, they were beautiful in their time.

Still, a die-hard fan will remember some a little more fondly than others. Steve Davis was that kind of player.

Coming out of Sallisaw and finding himself seventh on the depth chart in 1972, Davis could easily have given up. If he had, Oklahoma fans would

STEVE DAVIS leading OU to a 35–10 victory over Nebraska in 1975

"LITTLE" JOE

One would be hard-pressed to name a player more exciting than Joe Washington. It seems inconceivable that more than a quarter-century has passed since Joe juked and flashed his way to football immortality at OU.

The Die-Hard Fan well remembers Washington's punt return against OSU in 1974. (Check it out on YouTube!) The crowd sat down in despair when he got hemmed-in on the sideline by half the Cowboy team. Suddenly, we got back on our feet and let out a roar as Joe streaked into the endzone.

Washington, after a long NFL career, now works at OU. We caught up with him soon after he assumed his new duties as director of the Varsity "O" Association.

Asked what his actual height, weight, and 40-speed were while he played at OU, Washington replies, "Five-nine and three quarters, 168, 4.5." That should settle some debates between long-time OU fans who have often wondered just how big and fast Joe was back in the day. His 3,995 career yards rushing overshadow his versatility; he was a dangerous punt returner, passer (he shocked Texas with a 40-yard bomb to Tinker Owens in 1973), and punter. Washington's 86-yard quick kick killed Texas's comeback hopes late in the '75 game in Dallas. He could also catch; two great grabs in his senior year helped beat OSU and Nebraska.

In the NFL, Washington ran for 4,839 yards and caught passes for another 3,413.

He remains the most elusive runner in OU history.

"Rest assured, there wasn't any way I wasn't going to get the first down."

—Joe Washington

Washington came by his versatility naturally, playing for his father in Port Arthur, Texas.

"I played tailback, mostly, and we ran from various formations," he remembers. "I played fullback, halfback, wide receiver, and quarterback." Bill Michaels came calling from OU first, followed by Wendell Mosley. Mosley had joined the OU staff in January 1972, after a high school coaching career in Houston. He had a real affinity for the players, and he knew Texas well.

"As a kid, I thought about all the great schools—Notre Dame, Texas, Navy, Stanford," Washington says. "As I got into high school, Texas, more than anyone, appealed to me. In the end, it came down to Texas, OU, and Houston."

The Sooners won out—and thank goodness for that!

"The stars just lined up right," Washington says today. "Getting to play in the same backfield with Greg Pruitt my freshman year was great."

After running for 630 yards as a freshman, Washington ran for 1,173 and 1,321 yards in his sophomore and junior years, respectively. He finished with 871 as a senior, behind a rebuilt line.

His 71-yard TD run to save the Missouri game in 1975—and the season—is one of the most electrifying runs in Sooner history. On the play, Oklahoma had a fourth-and-one from its own 29, with five minutes left. More importantly, OU was down, 27–20, as Mizzou's Steve Pisarkiewicz had passed the Sooners silly for the entire second half. He was helped by tailback Tony Galbreath, who kept the ground game going. Switzer decided to go for the first down, reasoning that OU might not get the ball back. Offensive coordinator Galen Hall called "Eleven Hammer," an option pitch to the best player.

Washington had been concerned about the footing all day, but the high-stakes play brought out that ol' Oklahoma competitiveness.

"Rest assured, there wasn't any way I wasn't going to get the first down," the soft-spoken Washington says. "I got the pitch from Steve, made two cuts, and then I thought, 'Wow, this could go all the way.'"

It did, and OU ran the same play on the two-point conversion. As recounted in the 1976 book, *The Winning Edge*, "Great pressure was placed on the freshman tight end, Hicks. He had to read a Missouri stunt, and then release down the scrimmage line in much the same manner he had done on the previous play. He did it exactly right. Davis faked to Littrell and pitched to Washington, who was hit at the two, fought, squirmed, and leaped into the endzone."

Washington's hips bounced on the goal line and the referee threw up his hands. The Sooners rejoiced, then held off a late Missouri field goal attempt, as Switzer knelt on the field.

The game set the stage for an OU runaway win over Nebraska the following week. Later, in the Orange Bowl at Miami, Washington and his Sooners dispatched Michigan, 14–6, to win their second consecutive national title.

For two years, Washington and Ohio State's Archie Griffin dueled for the Heisman. Griffin won both, yet Washington wouldn't trade his experiences for a personal trophy; he understands that champions are forever.

"To be honest with you, until you just mentioned it, I never thought about feeling 'cheated' that I played in the Wishbone," Washington says. "It was fun, it was an exciting offense. And people never realized how much we blocked; I really enjoyed that part of it, the blocking. It made me a tougher player, a better player."

That unselfish nature sets him apart from some of today's top players.

As far as rivals went, Washington remembers some classics.

"Nebraska had the most meaning to it in the sense that if you could beat Nebraska, you could win the Big Eight championship. We were always respectful of Nebraska, and they were respectful of us."

Being a Texas native, the Longhorns stood out, too. "Texas was another matter. That was for bragging rights."

And there was one more: "Oklahoma State, you were supposed to beat them, but they were a lot tougher than people realized."

The "Punt Return" still gives Washington a chuckle, all these years later. "It's funny how people do remember. It's impressive to me that people remember. It's flattering."

Thanks for the memories, Joe.

Photo courtesy of Bill Horn

JOE WASHINGTON (24), with Billy Sims (20), at the 1992 Varsity Alumni game

have been robbed of iconic moments on the field. Davis had good physical attributes, but at the end of his career, he had something more important: a drawer full of championship rings.

No quarterback except Jimmy Harris had a similar run. Davis won two national championships and three Big Eight championships. He never lost to Nebraska, Texas, or Oklahoma State, and he went unbeaten in bowl games, having piloted the 14–6 Orange Bowl win over Michigan to cap his career.

As a green sophomore in 1973, Davis was the missing puzzle piece for Oklahoma. Young players like Joe Washington and Tinker Owens helped form a powerful offense. The defense was stellar, fielding the likes of Rod Shoate, Lucious Selmon, and Randy Hughes. Davis had time to grow into the position.

GAMEDAY HAUNTS

Legends Hotel at I-35 and Lindsey is an OU-themed hotel for fans. The rooms, restaurant, and lobby are decorated with Sooner memorabilia and photos.

Davis's competitiveness is legendary. Leaning against a locker room wall in the fall of 1975, the week of the Oklahoma State "Bedlam" game, Davis declared, "We can't lose to these people!" He didn't, posting a 27–7 win.

Although he had a reputation as more a runner than a passer (as is natural with option quarterbacks), Davis was an effective thrower. He burned Texas for 185 yards and two touchdowns in a 52–12 dismantling in '73; half his completions (eleven) in 1974 went for touchdowns; and his forty-yard post pattern to Tinker Owens in the 1976 Orange Bowl, when a great block by Elvis Peacock gave the quarterback enough time to throw, set up Billy Brooks' thirty-nine-yard end-around, which gave OU a lead it wouldn't relinquish.

Davis went on to become a successful real estate developer. But he will always be remembered for his performance at OU, where his statistics were good, his leadership and competitiveness better, and his championship legacy was sterling. No quarterback has ever won more games at Oklahoma.

A LOTT OF BANDANAS

It wouldn't be too much of a stretch to liken Thomas Lott's running of the option to the beauty of Vladimir Horowitz's Chopin, or, even better, Allen Collins' guitar solo on "Free Bird."

Lott did his thing better than anyone else ever has. He was a born runner who controlled a running offense. His smooth-as-buttah work on the corner, after which he'd weave his way through the secondary and accelerate away from gasping safeties... well, it was a beautiful thing.

The San Antonio native was another of those Texas thoroughbreds who came across the Red River to bedevil opponents.

Lott was really a halfback that Oklahoma turned into a quarterback. At five-foot-eleven, 205 pounds, with 4.5 speed, Lott was a load as a running quarterback. He could also throw, helping stave off Stanford in his senior year. He finished his football career by tossing a 50-yard TD to Victor Hicks in a 62–7 demolition of Oklahoma State.

Lott came to OU in the celebrated class of 1975, playing for the JV his first year. Early in 1976, after Dean Blevins, the heir-apparent, had won the starting job at quarterback, Lott was left to bide his time.

OU's offense loped along until it came time for Texas, when Blevins was felled by an illness. Suddenly, the Sooners had to go into the RRS with a totally green backup.

It wasn't pretty. Texas had one of its usual stout defenses, but OU's was pretty good, too. The game remains a textbook lesson in offensive ineptitude. OU ran for just ninety-five yards, with Lott completing two passes to Victor Hicks for another thirty-eight. Down 6–0 late, in Darrell Royal's last go against Oklahoma, Lott got another chance.

Earl Campbell fumbled and left OU thirty-odd yards from a touchdown. Lott didn't waste the opportunity. Grinding it out, Horace Ivory finally scored. A bad snap spoiled the extra-point try, leaving the teams tied. Still, Lott was now battle-tested.

The next week at Kansas, he came into his own. The Jayhawks, of course, had upset OU in spectacular fashion the year before in Norman. They had done it without completing one pass. Kansas had a salty Wishbone backfield with plenty of speed, athleticism, and power. It was comprised of quarterback Nolan Cromwell, fullback Norris Banks, and halfbacks Laverne Smith and Billy Campfield, several of whom went on to play in the NFL. By the time the teams rematched in the Bicentennial Year, it was Cromwell who commanded national attention.

OU was getting beaten again in '76 when Cromwell went down with an injury. At halftime, a light came on for Lott. In the second half, he scored on weaving runs of thirteen and thirty-three yards, giving OU a 28–10 victory.

OU righted its ship, finishing the year at 9–2–1 and becoming conference co-champions. Lott also directed a 41-7 rout of Wyoming in the Fiesta Bowl.

The 1977 and 1978 Wishbone teams he directed remain among the smoothest in school history. Lott was simply an incredible operator. Games such as the 38–7 blowout of Nebraska in '77 and the '78 win over Texas cemented his reputation as a natural.

Lott's trademark in those days was a collection of bandanas used to keep his afro from becoming creased in his helmet. During game week, Lott would set out his bandanas, finally whittling the collection down to two the night before a game. He would then select which one to wear, and the tail of each knotted bandana waived to opponents while he ran down the sidelines.

Lott finished his playing career in the NFL with the St. Louis Cardinals. Today he coaches in Texas.

"THE SOONERS HAVE ANOTHER PREACHER"

The *Tulsa World*'s incomparable Bill Connors wrote a 1979 profile in *Big 8* magazine of new Sooner signal-caller J.C. Watts. The article captured the various pressures Watts faced as he took over the Wishbone offense:

> The last thing a despondent freshman wants to hear is that it will be two years before he has an opportunity to play, because it is planned to redshirt him as a sophomore. That is tantamount to giving him a one-way ticket home.
>
> But such a message in 1976 influenced J.C. Watts to remain at Oklahoma.
>
> The quarterback who is the key figure in the Sooners' 1979 rebuilding plans packed his bags and went home to Eufala two or three times during a trying freshman year. Football was not fun; it was challenging and brought him no enjoyment, Watts told his father.
>
> His father, a Baptist minister, reminded Watts "that if it was easy, everyone would be doing it." Barry Switzer expressed similar sentiments in an attempt to soften Watts' disillusionment.
>
> Nevertheless, Watts was "ready to go home and not come back" when offensive coordinator Galen Hall used a more blunt approach to change his mind.
>
> "Coach Hall said they planned to redshirt me the next year and I would not play again until my third year," Watts said. "I was impressed by Coach Hall's honesty. It took a lot of guts to tell a kid

who was ready to quit he was going to be redshirted. Nobody wants to be redshirted, especially a freshman who is already low.

"But he said they wanted to do it this way, so I would have a chance to start for two years. I know that schools do this with players all the time. But I don't think many are honest enough to tell the players. I thought I would like to play under a coach who was that honest with me."

Watts stayed, paid his redshirt dues and understudied Thomas Lott last year. Now, after "it seems like I've been here forever," Julius Caesar Watts' time has come to be Oklahoma's sixth Wishbone quarterback. His predecessors left a legacy that tempers as surely as it fascinates.

THOMAS LOTT, left, gives J.C. Watts advice on the sideline in 1978. Watts's passing ability bailed OU out of several games in the two years he started, including the 1981 Orange Bowl.

... [Watts] takes over an offense that has a new line and a new fullback. Also, this offense may not have complementing weapons. Oklahoma's defense looks tender and its kicking is suspect. The truth is that Watts and the offense need to be very good very soon if the Sooners are to maintain their elite status of the '70s. Clearly, Watts is on the spot.

He is under no illusions. He brings to his mission a combination of maturity and personality. Married and the father of two children, Watts is an honor roll student majoring in public relations. He says the Bible enabled him to get through the darkest days of his freshman year, and he is the favorite baby-sitter of Switzer's children.

Watts also realizes none of the above qualities will shelter him from abuse if he fails to engineer enough touchdowns and victories.

"I know we are expected to win, and if we do, I will probably get more credit than I deserve," Watts said. "And if we don't win... I know that any time a team is not as successful as fans expect, they want the scalps of the quarterback and the coach."

... Watts admitted he sensed the pressure to excel. But he said he does not feel any pressure to be another Lott or Davis or Mildren.

"I am not trying to be those guys," Watts said. "I will not try to play up to their level. I don't concern myself with anybody's expectations except my own. I know I can play. And I am confident things will work out for the best, because I know Jesus Christ loves me.

"People will compare me with those other guys. That's inevitable. I just hope they compare my first year with their first year, not their last."

The five-foot-eleven Watts, who weighed 202 pounds as a high school senior, weighed 200 in spring practice and hopes to play at 192 this season. He is not quite as fast as his predecessors, or as slick on the option as Lott. But his speed (4.65 or 4.7 seconds in the 40-yard dash) is adequate. Watts' passing skills, despite a 34 percent completion rate last year, may exceed those of any OU quarterback since

MERV TALKS THE

WISHBONE

Like many of Barry Switzer's assistants, long-time offensive line coach Merv Johnson knows a fair amount about the Wishbone. He had seen some of it at Arkansas and even Notre Dame. Building effective offensive lines in an era of transition, Johnson crafted the road-graders that paved the way for OU's great runners.

In the late 1970s, SMU and Nebraska were the first option-I teams to begin placing huge offensive linemen at guard. It took OU a few years to catch up to this trend, and it took some great Texas defenses to make it happen.

The Longhorns, led by big, physical defensive tackles in their 4–3—guys like Kenneth Sims and Bill Acker—shut down several of OU's Wishbone teams. Johnson saw that his athletic, undersized guards needed to beef up.

"Because Texas played the 4–3, the guards we had weren't physically able to block them. Nebraska was also running the 4–3, so we decided to put our bigger, stronger guys at guard," Johnson remembers.

He is fond of his former players, both for their abilities and for the kind of people they were. "It was a fun time for a line coach," he says.

Oklahoma began stockpiling bigger athletes during Johnson's early days at OU.

"Louis Oubre and Paul Tabor were terrific athletes, and Don Key was a heckuva player. Bill Bechtold at center was a terrific athlete; he had played quarterback and safety in high school."

Johnson also recalls two players who were the first bulldozers he had at guard at OU: "Steve [Dr. Death] Williams and Paul Parker were the physical presence we needed at guard." Williams and Parker were able to physically manhandle opponents while retaining enough athleticism to compete at a high level.

The Sooners had simple criteria for selecting potential offensive linemen.

"Most of our offensive linemen came to college to play defense, and they were great athletes," Johnson says. The thinking was that if a player's knees couldn't take the pounding on the defensive line, or he had to wait behind too many great players, a move to the offensive line might be just what the doctor ordered.

The new, physical presence on the offensive lines did not go unnoticed. Orville Henry, the long-time sports editor for the *Arkansas Gazette*, was shocked at the athleticism of OU's huge offensive linemen after the 1987 Orange Bowl. He remarked in a column that it was startling to see offensive tackle Greg Johnson—all 320 pounds of him—escorting Spencer Tillman to the endzone on a 77-yard TD run.

Johnson also laments the scholarship limitations that came into effect. "We had guys like Sammy Jack Claphan and Lyndle Byford—late bloomers—that probably wouldn't get a scholarship today."

Johnson's experience gave him a unique perspective on how the Wishbone operated.

"In that style of offense, the quarterback essentially blocks a lineman by getting him out of the way [during the reads]. The Wishbone could work again if you could find a guy who could throw well enough. You sure could, and you could probably devastate people with it."

Johnson laughs when contrasting the styles of offense OU ran under Switzer with those under Bob Stoops.

"In those days [of the Wishbone], they wanted us to throw; today they want us to run the option!"

Robertson. Switzer and Hall plan to exploit this potential in a multiple Wishbone scheme that may make the 1979 Sooners look more like Alabama than the Oklahoma of recent years.

> **"The Wishbone could work again if you could find a guy who could throw well enough. You sure could, and you could probably devastate people with it."**
>
> —Merv Johnson

"I expect we will break the bone a lot more this year by sending people in motion, using a wingback and the I-formation," Watts said. "Using the other formations will make it easier to pass. Alabama has passed pretty well from the Wishbone, and we threw the ball a lot from the Wishbone in high school."

Of course, with Heisman Tropher winner Billy Sims to take handoffs and pitchouts, Watts knows Oklahoma's percentage of pass plays will remain relatively low. And how he executes those pitchouts and handoffs and carries himself will outweigh his passing in importance. Reservations about this phase of Watts' play arose last year when Lott was injured and Watts had an opportunity to start against Kansas.

Watts expected OU to win by at least three touchdowns. The Sooners escaped, 17–16. "I felt great and confident, but it looked like a disaster," Watts said. Even after sharper performances in mop-up roles against Kansas State and Oklahoma State, there were fears Watts lacked the speed to be effective in the Wishbone.

Apparently it was just a matter of refining his mechanics, a deficiency Watts thinks he corrected in spring practice, with the help of Lott. Just as Lott in 1976 mastered the Wishbone by studying film of Kansas quarterback Nolan Cromwell, Watts learned by studying film of Lott.

"No matter how much you practice or go to meetings or listen to the coach, it takes a while before it all sinks in," Watts said. "Coach Hall kept telling me last year that I was not getting enough depth on my first step. I bet he told me that a thousand times.

"But I did not comprehend what he meant until one day I got a reel of film on Thomas and tried to learn why he was able to execute so much better than I did. All at once I saw what Coach Hall had been telling me: I was not getting enough depth on my first step, and that threw the timing off on whatever we did on the option.

"Now, I've got it down. I don't expect to remind anyone of Thomas on the option. But I think I can get the job done. My time has come and I am ready."

Early on, it was thought that Watts lacked the necessary speed to effectively run the option. That proved to be a misplaced worry. What's more, in 1979 and 1980, Watts's passing ability added a dimension that OU had been lacking. He ended his career as perhaps the finest running-passing combination at the position that the Sooners would ever have.

> **"The wind conditions were horrible. Fortunately we don't have the season in the spring around here. That would be tough....We'd have to go back to the Wishbone, I think, if we were playing this time of year."**
>
> —Bob Stoops, after a Red-White game

Against Florida State in the 1980 Orange Bowl, Watts ran for 127 yards on fifteen carries. The following year, he beat the Seminoles by throwing for 128, most of it coming on a last-minute drive.

After Oklahoma, Watts played Canadian football for many years before returning to the U.S. and winning a seat in Congress in 1994.

OH, DANNY BOY

It is no exaggeration to say that Danny Bradley was OU's most valuable player, at least in 1984.

Like Watts, Bradley was a redshirt—a player selected to sit out a year in order to lengthen his eligibility to play in later years. Bradley didn't fit in well when OU scuttled the Wishbone to take advantage of Marcus Dupree's near-supernatural talents at tailback. In 1983, OU fell to Texas, 28–16, and Dupree skipped town. Suddenly lacking the personnel to run the I-formation, OU scrambled to save the season.

Fullback Stanley Wilson and others proved effective enough at tailback. After OU finished the season with a win over Hawaii in paradise, the Sooners began eagerly looking forward to 1984.

Switzer's staff had done a superb job bringing in fresh talent in '83—and proceeded to redshirt most of them. Another fabulous class in '84—Keith Jackson, Lydell Carr, and Rickey Dixon among them—boosted the team's abilities across the board. And, more than anything else, OU struck gold with the arrival of Danny Bradley.

OU's return to the Wishbone would not have been possible without the Arkansas native. A compact 185 pounds, Danny was an excellent option runner, and his passing skills suited the Wishbone perfectly. Because the 1984 version of the offense was not as explosive as some of its predecessors and heirs, Bradley's passing was critical.

DANNY BRADLEY rolls into the endzone against Stanford in 1984. OU won, 19-7.

Photo courtesy of Bill Horn

« **HOLIEWAY** grins during another half-a-hundred game.

Photo courtesy of Bill Horn

» **ERIC MITCHEL**, a highly recruited quarterback from Pine Bluff, Arkansas. Although a tremendous talent, Mitchel could never dislodge Jamelle Holieway.

After leading OU to a ho-hum 19–7 win over Stanford at home, Bradley steadily put his stamp on the team. Unfortunately for the Sooners, Bradley was injured in a game against Iowa State, forcing him to sit out the Kansas game.

Kyle Irvin gave the old college try at quarterback, followed by seventeen-year-old freshman Troy Aikman. It was ugly, with OU losing 28–11 to Kansas. The loss was especially bitter because 1984 was the first year in a long time in which no single team dominated college football. A win would have put OU in the driver's seat.

Bradley recovered in time to play Missouri a week later, leading his team to a 49–7 win. That week, as well as a week later against Colorado, he completed over 50 percent of his passes for 276 yards across the two games—a very impressive stat for a Wishbone quarterback.

But it was against Nebraska at Lincoln that Bradley really established himself as a star. The Cornhuskers were in another of those delusional moods when they felt it was time to embarrass their nemesis, Barry Switzer.

Bradley, though, had other ideas. He directed a smart game, scoring late on a 30-yard run, to drive a stake through Lincoln hearts, 17–7. That set up a key match against Oklahoma State. OSU was ranked third at the time, with OU second, and the Cowboys felt that an Orange Bowl berth was within their grasp.

With cornerback Brian Hall and safety Sonny Brown limping with injuries, and the Cowboys running the likes of Thurman Thomas, OU had excuses to lose. But they refused. Bradley performed wonderfully, the defense was sound, and a healthy Spencer Tillman at halfback ran for 100 yards.

In a column headlined "The Best Thin Team in OU History Won," *Tulsa World* editor Bill Conners commented that "the offense had quarterback Danny Bradley and Kansas as a reminder of his value." OU won the game 24–14.

In Danny Bradley's last game, the Sooners dropped a disappointing match to Washington in the Orange Bowl. Nevertheless, Bradley had established himself as a key player in a crucial period of transition for OU.

Some of the

MORE MEMORABLE

WISHBONE GAMES AT OU

Texas, 1971

The Sooners, in the space of one year, redefined how the Wishbone was run. Tough fullbacks and a tough quarterback were complemented by fleet halfbacks like Greg Pruitt, Roy Bell, and Joe Wylie. The offensive line, with Tom Brahaney at center, guards Darryl Emmert and Ken Jones, and tackles Robert Jensen and Dean Unruh, was stellar. Ends Albert Chandler, Eddie Franklin, and Jon Harrison completed the powerhouse offense.

Sooner fans had waited a long time and enjoyed every minute of the 48–27 track meet in which Pruitt ran for 190 yards. Texas under Darrell Royal never recovered in the RRS.

Kansas State, 1971

Mildren avenged the previous two defeats to the Wildcats, leading OU to a mind-boggling 75–28 victory despite having a 75-yard TD run called back.

Nebraska, 1972

Dave Robertson's passing helped OU knock off the Cornhuskers on Thanksgiving Day in Lincoln. Freshman split end Tinker Owens helped as well, and the pair had similar results in the Sugar Bowl against Penn State, winning 14–0 and proving that OU could throw the ball effectively.

Texas, 1973

OU threw for 225 yards—185 from sophomore quarterback Steve Davis—and the Sooners gave Barry Switzer his first win over Texas. It was a doozy, 52–13, as the Selmons throttled Longhorn fullback Roosevelt Leaks, while Washington and Co. dominated on offense.

USC, 1973

A tie, but an important tie. The Trojans were defending national champions, coached by John McKay, and playing at the Coliseum in Los Angeles. They were loaded with future NFL players, yet OU came in and arguably dominated. With a non-existent passing game, the Sooners still ran for over three hundred yards, ending the game in a 7–7 tie. The favorable outcome gave Oklahoma a huge boost in confidence and was a springboard to a dramatic run.

Nebraska, 1974

In one of those games fans relish for years afterward, Oklahoma ran for a staggering 482 yards on a very good Nebraska defense, while passing for...none. No completions, no yardage. Davis, Washington, and fullback Jim Littrell gashed the Cornhuskers into submission in the second half to drive OU to a 28–14 victory and its third consecutive Big Eight crown.

Kansas State, 1976

OU ran for 439 yards, with Thomas Lott gaining 195 on twenty-four carries, as the Sooners outscored Wendell Hendrickson (283 passing yards) and the Wildcats, 49–28. It would mark the first of two consecutive games in which OU would have zero passing yards. (They did the same against Missouri a week later, running for 436 yards in a 27–20 home win.)

Nebraska, 1976

Late in the game, the Sooners were in danger of not only losing, but of recording their third straight game with no passing yards. That was until Woodie Shepard hit Steve Rhodes with a 47-yard halfback pass, followed by Dean Blevins' flea-flicker to Rhodes and Elvis Peacock. The 20–17 victory sent Nebraska fans into another winter funk, while OU moved on to sunny Tempe.

Colorado and Nebraska, 1977

Lott, King, Sims, and Peacock completely overwhelmed these two teams on national television. The Sooners combined for fifty-six first downs and 931 total yards in beating Colorado 52–14 and pounding Nebraska 38–7.

Nebraska, 1979

Oklahoma used their feet and hands to break Nebraskan hearts again. Billy Sims, in his final home game at OU, ran for 247 yards on twenty-eight carries (an additional fifteen yards were called back on a bogus clip on Freddie Nixon), and J.C. Watts hooked up with tight end Forrest Valora on a 58-yard strike. Watts scored the Sooners' other TD on a short run as OU won, 17–14.

Colorado, 1980

This game is included here for the sheer blood-letting: eighty-two points, thirty-five first downs, and a mind-numbing 875 total yards, averaging eleven yards per play. It's the only game in the history of football in which a team threw the ball to hold the score down. (The Sooners completed five of seven for 117 yards.) OU won the wild match, 82–42.

Nebraska, 1985

It was the day that looked like Keith Jackson might be OU's leading ground gainer, receiver, and passer. He ruined the Cornhuskers, scoring a famous 88-yard end-around for a touchdown. In total, he ran for 136 yards on three carries and caught a 38-yard pass from Jamelle Holieway. On one reverse, Jackson looked like he wanted to pass, but pulled the ball back down and decided he could have more fun running it. The 27–7 win was one of total domination.

Missouri, 1986

Another obscene score, this time 77–0. The previous week, OU had run up 635 yards and sixty-four points on Kansas, with fullback Earl Johnson going for 205. Against Missouri, the Sooners had half-a-hundred by halftime and finished with 750 yards of total offense. Eric Mitchel narrowly missed taking off on a 99-yard run. After the game, Barry Switzer said of Missouri, "It'd be terrible to be in that kind of shape." OU fans stayed to the gory end, thoroughly enjoying the spectacle of walk-ons Eric Bross and Ron Counter running wild on the Tigers.

Arkansas, 1987 Orange Bowl

An ecstatic finish to the season, this was payback for the '78 Orange Bowl, which still appears to be the only win in Razorback history. In this splendid game, Spencer Tillman ran for 107 yards and two touchdowns by halftime, Lydell Carr had a 60-yard run, and Duncan Parham finished off the Hog barbecue with a 49-yard tight-end reverse. Oklahoma won 42–8, and Switzer said years later, "We could have hung half-a-hundred on 'em."

Nebraska, 1987

As if they hadn't learned their lesson before, Nebraska fans felt this was the year. The Sooners' Holieway and Lydell Carr had been knocked out by injuries against Oklahoma State, and the No. 1 ranked Cornhuskers, particularly defensive end Broderick Thomas, unleashed repeated taunts about nobody getting the keys to "their house." So OU reloaded with quarterback Charles Thompson and fullback Rotnei Anderson and went to town. The 17–7 final was much closer on the scoreboard than it really was, with Thompson, Anderson, and halfback Patrick Collins all gaining over 100 yards.

> **"Talk about Sooner magic; we didn't need any today. We dominated from start to finish. This was a dominating win. We faced the challenge; I like that."**
>
> —BARRY SWITZER, after his Sooners defeated Nebraska 17–7, on November 21, 1987

JAMMIN' JAMELLE

During the game in which Miami's Jerome Brown fell on Troy Aikman's leg at Owen Field in October 1985, the Sooner Nation was introduced to one of its most memorable players.

Jamelle Holieway, a true freshman quarterback from Los Angeles, flipped on his helmet and jogged to the huddle. Until that point, OU and Miami had engaged in an offensive shootout, with Vinny Testaverde snapping precision touchdown passes to Michael Irvin, and Troy Aikman tossing adeptly to Keith Jackson while doing a bit of nimble running himself. Spectators thought each team might hang half-a-hundred on the other.

But things looked grim when Aikman was carried off. OU would go on to lose that game, but they had found a quarterback. In the excellent recruiting class of 1985, Holieway came in with another super prospect, Eric Mitchel of Pine Bluff, Arkansas. Mitchel was six-foot-one, 200 pounds, and had run a personal-best 4.39 in the 40 in high school. He also had a big arm.

OU fans couldn't believe their luck, alternating between a preference for Holieway or Mitchel to start. Holieway, though, proved to be a natural-born Wishbone operator. Mitchel saw action, but ended his career in 1988 at halfback.

Holieway put his stamp on the team the week after the Miami game by tossing a 76-yard touchdown pass to Derrick Shepard in a 59–14 win over Iowa State. By the end of the year, in a game against SMU, Holieway was running the offense like Jack Mildren. In fact, against Missouri, he broke Mildren's single-game record for total offense, with 324 yards (156 on the ground, 168 in the air). He was a genuine phenom.

The grinning, personable Holieway seemed unfazed by the attention and pressure. He didn't seem to realize that a true freshman quarterback had never won a national championship at OU. He simply prepared for Penn

State and went to play them in Miami as if the game were a minor tussle with Kansas State.

OU's offensive line had sustained some injuries, and the Nittany Lions' defense was superb as always. These factors combined to slow down Holieway on the option. He was not able to break loose like he had in a fun blowout of Nebraska in Norman.

Still, he uncorked his throwing arm and hit Keith Jackson on a 71-yard touchdown pass in the first half. The play, called "72 Y Go," gave OU enough breathing room late in the running game to allow the Sooners to finish off Joe Paterno, 25–10. Incredibly, Holieway had led OU to its sixth national title.

Holieway ran for 861 yards and threw for another 517. He had a 41 percent completion rate—a fine average for the 'Bone.

In 1986 and 1987, he achieved what no Sooner quarterback has accomplished before or since—orchestrating forty-plus point games against Texas. His running of the offense was so smooth that Barry Switzer today calls him OU's best quarterback.

A late 1987 knee injury against Oklahoma State (ironically, on a play when no one had touched him) caused Holieway to lose a step of speed. Still, he returned for an effective season in his senior year.

Chapter Four

BENNIE, BUD, BARRY, BOB

HOW OU STRUCK GOLD

Four times in twenty-one tries, OU has struck coaching gold. One could argue for a few others, of course; Jim Tatum and Jim Mackenzie were stellar coaches, although hubris claimed the former and death struck the latter before they really had a chance to get started. And Chuck Fairbanks wasn't bad.

But there are four men who belong in the pantheon of great Sooner coaches. Bud Wilkinson and Barry Switzer are no-brainers, having won three national titles apiece. Bob Stoops, hired in late 1998 to reverse the slide OU had begun with the departure of Switzer a decade before, won it all in his second season; he surely ranks among OU's best. And old-time great Bennie Owen coached some fantastic teams that undoubtedly would have won championship games if they had been played back then.

While the coaching records of these four Sooner legends are widely celebrated, not as many people know how the great men ended up at Oklahoma in the first place. So let's take a look at how the cream of the OU coaching crop landed the jobs that would launch them into history.

BENNIE OWEN

It's too bad that Benjamin Gilbert "Bennie" Owen didn't win a national championship. It's too bad his great undefeated team of 1915 didn't have a chance at it. There had been talk of the Sooners playing Nebraska in the post-season, but mysterious forces scuttled the plan. Instead, the Cornhuskers went on to share the 1915 title with Cornell.

Owen, however, laid the foundation for everything that came after him. In his twenty-two seasons, the former Kansas Jayhawk built the OU program into a regional power and then some.

Owen didn't live in the era of multimedia, although local newspapers did a credible job reporting on the early Sooners. In their coverage, one can sense the increasing fascination and pride Oklahomans felt at the job Owen did.

An unintentionally humorous advertisement for the 1926 homecoming game offers a quaint glimpse of the nature of OU fandom in the 1920s:

> **Missouri vs Oklahoma**
>
> With a slick and shining well-groomed coat of fur, untorn by no defeats, a well-fattened Bengal Tiger shall soon stalk from the Missouri jungle. Constantly smacking his lips, the Missouri beast never has a satisfied hunger. Another gridiron prey is enjoyed. And, the beast's most relished feast is a homecoming occasion.
>
> With such a formidable foe, Oklahoma University Homecoming, November 6, will mean one of the hardest fought battles of the season. Preparations have been made to make the Tiger weep and wail. The red and white gridsters, The Sooners, who have pioneered a victory into camps that seemed invincible will tear the Tiger's pretty fur [*pretty fur?*]. When the Sooner and Tiger meet, it's a battle—a gridiron clash that is always remembered. It's a classic in which the breaks usually spell the outcome. So, soon it's homecoming at the University of Oklahoma. And homecoming in itself has a great meaning. To alumni, to the students, to the parents of stu-

> dents, to football enthusiasts all over Oklahoma, it means—"let's go to Norman."
>
> And, there are plenty of seats, if you order early. Plenty of entertainment. Missouri will, as usual, be accompanied with plenty of noise.
>
> Most of the 15,000 Reserved Seats in the New Stadium will be sold before the day of the game. It is therefore important that those desiring the best seats, get their applications in immediately. All seats $2.50. Mail applications with enclosed checks to Ben. G. Owen, Director of Athletics, Norman, Okla.

Fascinating! Imagine today being able to mail your ticket application to Bob Stoops! Incidentally, OU defeated Mizzou, 10–7, on that November day. It was Owen's last season, and a standing-room only crowd of 16,250 watched OU tame "the Missouri beast."

Interestingly, Owen showed a lot of characteristics common to his most famous successors.

Like Wilkinson, Owen stressed discipline and fitness. Like Switzer, Owen's offensive innovations—the forward pass, in particular—allowed the team to score early and often, transforming the Sooners into what one observer dubbed "the Terrors of the Midwest." And like Stoops, Owen was a hands-on coach, stressing perfection and readiness. He rode the players hard at practice and was a hands-on leader during games.

A reporter's description of Owen at a practice in the middle of his tenure gives us some great insight into the style of coaching he brought to Oklahoma:

> And from the unkind remarks the relentless Sooner coach hurled at his hard-working heroes during the three-hour grind Monday afternoon, an unknowing spectator would feel sure that Owen was working out a bunch of greenhands at the gridiron game. Up and down the field the coach was always right at the heels of the panting players, criticizing every defect in the execution of plays and

keeping silent when a maneuver was carried out flawlessly. The players never hear words of praise on the field from their coach and they don't appear to be much the worse off for their treatment.

BENNIE OWEN, OU's first great coach

Born in Chicago in 1874, Owen lived all over the Midwest as a youth. Although he was a doctor's apprentice at one point, he found his true calling while a student in Lawrence at the University of Kansas—football.

Legendary coach Fielding Yost mentored Owen, who starred at quarterback. Still in its early years, the sport of football needed innovators, and Owen learned quickly. His development of offensive formations began at KU as he absorbed Yost's systems while also studying others.

Owen was on his own for a season as head coach at Washburn College, but then rejoined Yost at the University of Michigan. He oversaw the Wolverines' "point-a-minute" squad. In 1901, Michigan scored a staggering 644 points—while allowing a paltry twelve to their opponents—in an 11–0 year. Owen then left to head the football program at Bethany College; ironically, Owen's teams dealt out losses to the Sooners in the two years before Owen was hired at Norman.

In 1905, in his very first season at OU, Owen led Oklahoma to its first win over Texas, which had already established itself as a powerhouse in the Southwest.

Owen coached the Sooners for two decades. In the roughly 1,100 games played in its history, Owen's teams scored over 5,000 of OU's approximately 28,000 points—this in an era just acclimating to innovations like the forward pass!

Owen achieved all this on a stingy annual salary of $3,500, during a time when financial difficulties sometimes forced his teams to travel to several schools in one trip and play multiple games per week. He persevered through some tough times and difficult personal experiences, most notably the loss of one of his arms during a hunting accident in 1907.

Little known to today's fans, Owen doubled as the Sooners' basketball coach, winning 70 percent of his games at that sport.

Thanks to the successful template established by Owen's early teams, and the juggernauts Wilkinson, Switzer, and Stoops later developed, Oklahoma ranks No. 1 nationally in all-time points scored.

Frederick E. Tarman of the *Daily Oklahoman* gave some keen insight into Owen in an article written a decade after Owen came to Norman:

> After the turning of nearly every cog in the Sooner wheel of undefeat this season, references to horseshoes and luck have emanated from the camps of enemies yet to be played regarding the 1915 football representatives of the University of Oklahoma, now all-victorious champions of the entire southwest. But the only application which can truthfully be made of such statements concerns events a long way removed from the work of the Sooners this season.
>
> The University of Oklahoma was lucky, some ten years and several additional weeks ago, in securing the services as coach of its football team a young man then directing the gridiron destinies of the 'Terrible Swedes' at Bethany college, Kansas. The university was lucky, it is admitted, to inducing this boyish coach to affix his signature to a contract before some other school recognized talent more or less hidden and secured the prize. Since that time the Sooners have earned every football honor acquired, with the earning power vested in the name of Benjamin Gilbert Owen, Sooner mentor, with a capital M.
>
> In October, 1905, not long after Owen took charge of athletics at the university, the Haskell Indians, then a powerful eleven which romped on Kansas and other strong western elevens with great regularity, journeyed to Norman and departed scalped by the score of 18–12.

DID YOU KNOW?

The cover story in the November 18, 1957 issue of *Sports Illustrated* was entitled "Why Oklahoma Is Unbeatable." A few days later, Notre Dame snapped the Sooners' NCAA-record 47-game winning streak, 7-0.

System Ten Years Effective

That was the first game I ever witnessed in which a Sooner team participated, but it had all the earmarks of the Owen coaching system which has predominated in the more than fifty games I have seen since that day, so quickly had the new coach transformed the gridiron tactics of the Oklahoma school.

That team had speed, dash, grit and a fighting spirit—a spirit which caused it to come from behind and score three touchdowns in the second half of the game, after the first half ended 13 to 0 in favor of the Indians. It was the first of many similar victories won since that day, and the last of which was recorded only last Thursday in the state championship affair with the Oklahoma Aggies.

In a few weeks time Owen had developed real football stars, including the now far-famed Harry Hughes, Owen Acton, Bill Cross and others never to be forgotten by Oklahoma football fans. Hughes and Acton at halfback positions get away in much the same manner as Capshaw and Swatek of present day fame.

It was simply Bennie Owen's brand of football, a brand which since that time has scored three victories in six games over the University of Missouri, four victories and a draw in the last five games with the University of Kansas, and a number of decisive victories over the University of Texas, all schools with two or three times as much material from which to select their elevens.

For Owen, as many football writers have pointed out, is coach at an institution where all the students are known to each other by nickname, where "Spot," "Trim," "Hap," and a host of other familiar titles cling to various gridiron stars and where the wizard mentor himself is referred to as Benjamin Gilbert only in the university catalogues and the student yearbooks. At all other times and in all other places he is known as Ben, or "Bennie."

Plays Under Yost

Ben. G. Owen, as he signs his name to checks and letters, now 40 years of age, started his football career in 1897 at the University of Kansas. He started out to make the baseball team but failed and turned his attention to the gridiron, soon becoming a star. He played two years, one of them under Fielding H. Yost, and in 1900 took charge of Washburn college team at Topeka. Two victories over Kansas that year helped some and the next season he was called as assistant coach to Michigan, whence Yost has gone. Michigan also had a big year while Bennie was sticking around scoring 550 points to 0 for all its opponents.

"[Bennie Owen drives] his team through long hours of nightly scrimmage and signal work until their tongues hang out and they are ready to drop."

In 1902 Owen journeyed to take charge of the Swedes and there he remained until 1905 when he enrolled his talents in the athletic interests of the University of Oklahoma.

Bennie Owen teaches rapid-fire, speedy football, the brand which has kept abreast of the most modern open play styles and today he undoubtedly is the greatest exponent of the entire nation in that department of the game. He teaches that style in rapid-fire manner, driving his team through long hours of nightly scrimmage and signal work until their tongues hang out and they are ready to drop. Then, barring injuries, every man is ready to play an entire game if needed. It is a notable fact that Owen in the past had made fewer substitutions than the coach of any other team which the Sooners have met. And this despite the fact that usually the Sooners are fighting teams which outweigh them heavily.

Grit and Speed Count

Sooner grit, Sooner speed, and Sooner powers, those are the winning combinations in Bennie's system. For the first few years after he went to the university he demonstrated those things by entering the scrimmages himself. He played everywhere in the line and backfield. But one winter the accidental discharge of a gun carried away Bennie's right arm; for days his life hung in the balance; the campus of the university was shrouded in gloom. When he recovered, a one-armed man was directing the two-armed work of his players especially in the forward passes, telling, not showing them what to do, but making the verbal directions very lucid and very certain to get results.

"What are you doing there, Trim? Why don't you stay with your interference and get through that hole?"

"Hap, what do you mean getting in the way of that halfback? Are you running interference or blocking the play?"

"Say, Bell, you have been playing football around here about long enough to know how. Why don't you hit that guy over there just once and see if you can stop him?"

"Lively, you've fumbled that ball about fifty-five times tonight. Better get some glue to dip your hands in."

"Don't you 'Mr. Owen' me, Balcer. You go in there and play both guard and tackle position when the line is short."

And thus it goes, every afternoon, the voice of the coach far from resembling that of a pink tea urgent, "please take some chocolates" remark. Often filled with biting sarcasm, they sting the player to a do or die determination, but just as often they are followed later by a pat on the shoulder or a whispered word that alleviates the sting but leaves the determination. It is a strictly original system but it gets results, the many victories partially detailed above and two all-victorious elevens in five years, 1911 and 1915, attesting to the statement.

It is a system which has been developed also in the teams coached by former Sooner stars, noticeably the 1915 all-victorious elevens of

> Harry Hughes at Colorado Agricultural college and Charles Wantland at Central Normal school. It is apparent in the work of the East Central normal at Ada, where Glenn Clark is in charge, Eastern Oklahoma Preparatory school, coached by Fred Capshaw, and a large number of other secondary colleges and high schools.
>
> It is a system which loyal Sooner supporters confidently believe if developed in the east with the splendid material available, would overthrow completely the famous Harvard, Yale, Princeton and all other styles of play with which it came in contact.

Owen passed away in 1970 at the age of ninety-four. So beloved is he that although the team's stadium is now known officially as the Gaylord Family Stadium, fans affectionately still call it "Owen Field."

CHARLES "BUD" WILKINSON

In the afterglow of OU's big Gator Bowl win over North Carolina State after the 1946 season, it looked as if the Sooner program was heading for some big years.

It was, but only after a strange sequence of events that saw one head coach exit through the back door and another glide in through the front.

Jim Tatum (1913–1959) was ambitious, outgoing, and a winner. "Big Jim" was also a large man with an aggressive coaching style.

The South Carolina native began his coaching career at North Carolina but enlisted in the Navy in 1942. That move proved fortuitous for his later coaching career, because he was assigned to the Iowa Pre-Flight School, where he coached football under Don Faurot.

In Iowa, Tatum helped develop the famed Split-T offense, which he would later use in other coaching stops at Maryland and North Carolina.

Following World War II, after a shattering defeat to state rival Oklahoma Aggies, OU President George Cross went looking for a coach who could win and win big. Tatum seemed to fit the bill.

> **"On the Sunday after Oklahoma beat Missouri in football in 1948, I visited Bud in the fieldhouse. He showed me movies of the game and tried to sell me on the Split-T formation. But mainly I was sold on Bud. His style and approach were so soft. He was a new type of coach for that day. You knew he was a winner."**
>
> —Billy Vessels, describing Bud Wilkinson

Under Tatum, Oklahoma went 8-3 in 1946, as returning war veterans like Joe Golding, Darrell Royal, Jim Tyree and others provided the foundation for the dynasty that began shortly thereafter.

Just days after the Gator Bowl win, rumors began to surface that Tatum, unhappy with his salary, was entertaining offers from other schools.

It is conventional wisdom today that college football coaches have only recently become obsessed with their pay scale. But Tatum proved that financial concerns played a paramount role in college coaching long before Bob Stoops, Nick Saban, and others secured lucrative, long-term, contracts from grateful universities.

On January 10, 1947, Tatum issued a statement about his future as head coach at OU. He admitted that he had entertained other offers, "as would any coach." Tatum, however, indicated that he and the other coaches were quite satisfied at Oklahoma after the school offered them a raise:

> During our first year at OU, we found the administration, faculty, students and townspeople of Norman completely cooperative and friendly. With the housing shortage and other handicaps of conversion from a wartime football team made up almost entirely of service personnel, this cooperation was a tremendous aid toward fielding a representative football team at this great state university.
>
> The administration of this university has been so generous with myself and staff at the end of our first year at OU that I don't believe there is a chance of our losing any of our staff. Several of the coaches have had attractive offers but none has asked to be released from duties here, even before the administration let us know of their splendid gesture in readjusting our contracts.

Sooner fans breathed a sigh of relief. Thus, they were doubly surprised eight days later, when Tatum was announced as the new head football coach at the University of Maryland, replacing Paul "Bear" Bryant, who had left for Kentucky.

BUD WILKINSON, who built the monster Sooner program that Barry Switzer had to feed

Originally, OU had hired Tatum to a three-year, $27,000 contract. Although the OU regents offered to boost his salary to $12,000 per year for the remainder of the contract, the Terrapins countered with a five-year deal at $12,000 annually.

Furthermore, in addition to the coaching position, Maryland offered Tatum the post of athletic director, effectively granting him near-total control of the Terrapin program. Tatum denied having any designs on the AD position at OU, which was occupied at the time by former Sooner assistant Lawrence "Jap" Haskell, who had pushed for the hiring of Tatum a year earlier. Tatum declared, "I have never made any demands on the board of regents concerning the athletic directorship. Jap Haskell is my friend. He brought me here and is responsible for the swell cooperation I have enjoyed here. I wouldn't consider staying at the university unless Jap Haskell were the athletic director."

Nevertheless, Maryland's offer was too tempting for Tatum to turn down. This left a sudden vacancy at the head of the Sooner program.

And generations of Sooner fans can thank goodness for that, because the job was filled by future Sooner coaching legend Bud Wilkinson.

Born in 1916, Wilkinson had been hired alongside Tatum as an assistant coach at OU, earning $6,800 a year. The two had coached together at Iowa Pre-Flight, before Wilkinson became deck officer on the aircraft carrier Enterprise. The hiring of Wilkinson began an OU tradition of filling head coaching vacancies by promoting assistant coaches.

Had Tatum stayed at OU, he had vowed to return the Sooners to a single-wing offense after their year experimenting with the Split-T. Wilkinson, of course, had other plans, and would soon do for the Split-T what Barry Switzer would do for the Wishbone a generation later.

Wilkinson signed a four-year contract that gave him the authority to hire his own assistants. His annual income was undisclosed.

Cross seemed happy with Wilkinson, announcing, "We are very pleased to get a coach of such high tactical ability, and possessing so many fine qualities, as Mr. Wilkinson." Haskell added, "He is well-qualified, and will do a fine job."

His tenure with the Sooners would be the only head coaching job of Wilkinson's career, aside from a brief stint with the NFL's St. Louis Cardinals in 1979–80. Since he passed away in 1994, Wilkinson has been remembered for amassing a spectacular 145–29–4 record with the Sooners, and has secured his place in Sooner history as the coach who presided over The Streak.

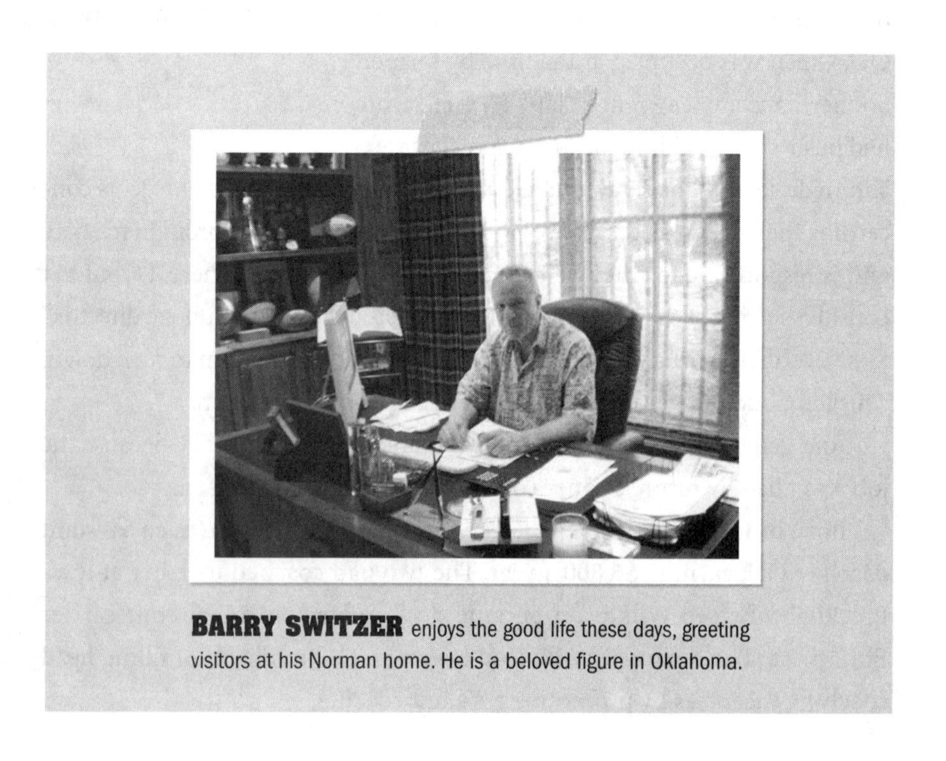

BARRY SWITZER enjoys the good life these days, greeting visitors at his Norman home. He is a beloved figure in Oklahoma.

BARRY SWITZER

Life is made up of innumerable little things that eventually add up to something big. So it was for Barry Switzer, the somewhat insecure fellow from tiny Crossett, Arkansas.

In his autobiography, *Bootlegger's Boy*, Switzer goes into some detail about his troubled upbringing, and how his father's pariah status as a bootlegger, and his mother's emotional problems and subsequent suicide, left him feeling rootless.

He grew up in southern Arkansas, a hotbed of future coaches. Paul Bryant would emerge from the same area, as would high-powered assistants like Larry Lacewell (long-time Sooner defensive coordinator, head coach at Arkansas State, and then a longstanding member of the Dallas Cowboys organization).

But the region was going through a tough spell during Switzer's youth. The South was just emerging from a terrible Depression, with many locals heading off to California, never to return.

Switzer and his brother Donnie grew up in a "shotgun" house in rural Crossett. Donnie would go on to become a successful businessman. But coaching was in Barry's blood.

Early coaching mentor Frank Broyles, for whom Switzer played at the University of Arkansas, told his young protégé once that if he hadn't landed a head coaching job by the time he was thirty-five, he should go into another line of work. Decades later, Broyles would chuckle at the memory and the generally tenuous prospect of high-profile coaching, as he reminisced about Switzer near the end of his own fifty-year tenure at Arkansas.

A series of those little things had brought Switzer to the offensive coordinator position at OU in the early 1970s. His successful and prescient experimentation with the Wishbone—and players like Greg Pruitt and Jack Mildren—had made him a hot coaching commodity.

Switzer himself would say years later that he could have coached at several other schools, but being in a place with a chance to win as head coach was his main priority.

So it was that as his thirty-fifth birthday approached, Switzer thought about his old boss's advice.

Events just after OU's sweet Sugar Bowl win over Penn State, the capstone of a great 1972 season, would sweep Barry Switzer into the position for which he had patiently waited.

Chuck Fairbanks had been installed as the Sooners' head man in 1967, after the untimely death of Jim McKenzie, who was another one of Broyles's many protégés. Fairbanks proved up to the job, taking Oklahoma to the Orange Bowl after the 1967 season. With players like Bobby Warmack and Steve Owens, the future looked bright.

It would be, but not until a few bumps in the road sparked some changes that would launch OU into its third dynasty, after those of Owen and Wilkinson.

By 1969, Oklahoma's program seemed to be waning. Nebraska was building a powerhouse program in Lincoln, while Kansas State, of all schools, was turning out some strong teams. In fact, the Wildcats' 19–14 win over OU in 1969, followed by a 59–21 blowout the following year, caused some intense anxiety among the Sooner faithful.

OU needed to rebuild after some key players finished their degrees and moved on. Deprived of the passing of quarterback Bobby Warmack and running of tailback Steve Owens, OU was looking to develop a coherent team identity, especially on offense. There had been fine individual players in the previous decade—guys like Carl McAdams, Ben Hart, Bob Kalsu, and Granville Liggins—but OU needed an infusion of talent across-the-board, along with a system that they could make their own.

The talent came in before the system did.

GAMEDAY HAUNTS

O'Connell's Bar & Grill a few steps from Memorial Stadium, has long been a traditional hang-out before and after games.

Putting assistants like Switzer in charge of recruiting great black athletes in Texas—and securing the signature of all-world quarterback Jack Mildren—Fairbanks began to find that identity. His 1971 and 1972 teams featured high-tech offense and defense, respectively.

Oklahoma's football team found itself, in the days after the win over Penn State, in a position eerily similar to that of the Tatum-Wilkinson saga twenty-five years before.

At the end of the 1972 season, Fairbanks received an offer from the New England Patriots. If not for the recent "down years" at OU he might have refused, but at the time, the prospect of coaching in the pros was too much to resist.

While sad to see their coach leave, his decision met with sympathy from Sooner players, some of whom believed his work had gone unappreciated by Sooner fans. "I don't think Coach Fairbanks owes the people of Oklahoma anything for the way they treated him in earlier years when he had some tough times," remarked senior quarterback Dave Robertson.

Dewey Selmon, sophomore defensive tackle from Eufala, said he hoped assistant coach Switzer would stay on. His sentiments were echoed by other Sooner players. On January 26, 1973, the day Fairbanks announced his departure, Sooner fullback Tim Welch circulated a players' petition stating their preference for Switzer. Other players and assistant coaches offered similar testimonials, including one from Switzer's old Arkansas buddy, Jimmy Johnson: "Nobody can do a better job and I don't care if you look all over the country."

And so it was that on the same day Fairbanks revealed he would leave, OU replaced him with Switzer.

With a certain degree of understatement, sophomore halfback Grant Burget, upon learning of the coaching change, observed about Switzer, "He knows the Wishbone as good as anybody."

Shortly before he took over the Sooners, Switzer revealed some of his thinking with regard to landing a great job:

"I haven't been looking for just any head coaching job. I've been associated with two fine football programs at Arkansas and Oklahoma and I'm not going to settle for a second-rate program. In order to have a truly great football program you have to have a great university like Oklahoma. There aren't many schools like this in the nation and that makes the Oklahoma head coaching job one of the best anywhere."

He went on to discuss the pressures of such a job.

"I don't know of any head coach who took a job and was expected to lose. They all expect you to win. The fans can evaluate the situation. They're intelligent enough to know what to expect."

Switzer had been interviewed by Southern Methodist University and Michigan State the previous year, and fans knew it was just a matter of time before he became a head coach somewhere.

Incredibly (by today's standards) Fairbanks was making a mere $28,500 per year when he left OU. One of the deciding factors for him was the restrictions the NCAA was putting on college programs, including a limit of 105 players on scholarship and no more than thirty offered in a single year.

Years later, in his typically self-deprecating way, Switzer acknowledged the keys to his success, an admission he has made many times:

"My success came because of the innovation of the Wishbone, an offensive scheme basically no one knew how to run or how to defend. And it was the emergence of the black athlete. Hell, I came along at the right time."

Many of his contemporaries understand just how bright Switzer has always been, and how he has created his own luck as much as benefited from it. Other coaches know this too, even if the media has always enjoyed portraying him as a partying, hands-off coach.

Of course, in an ironic twist years later, Switzer would cross paths with Johnson again, first in college coaching, then when Switzer succeeded Johnson as head coach of the Dallas Cowboys in 1994. The Cowboys won a Super Bowl under his direction.

Switzer, we can say with confidence, lived up to the high standards set by his predecessors, Owen and Wilkinson. He remains a beloved figure in Norman today.

BOB STOOPS

When Oklahoma Athletic Director Joe Castiglione surveyed the wreckage of Sooner football in the winter of 1998, he knew his next hire would be supremely important. Up-and-coming coaches had shunned the Sooners (Bob Davie, most notably, chose Notre Dame) and the once-proud Sooner Nation began to wonder if it were still possible to attract a great head coach to Norman.

"Joe C." moved quickly in the aftermath of OU's 3–8 record. Former Sooner lineman John Blake, three years into the job, was out. Bob Stoops, a young assistant unknown to fandom but well respected in the college coaching ranks, was in.

Stoops, a thirty-eight-year-old defensive mastermind, was busy learning at the elbow of Steve Spurrier at Florida. The former Gator Heisman winner knew what he had in Stoops, naming him defensive coordinator. That hire helped Florida win a national championship in 1996. Now it was the young protégé's turn to make good on the national stage. He had also played and coached for Hayden Fry at Iowa, then went with workaholic Bill Snyder to resurrect arguably the worst program in America—Kansas State. The Wildcats rebounded in one of the most dramatic turnarounds in college football history, becoming a power in the newly formed Big 12.

Like Wilkinson, Switzer, and Fairbanks before him, Stoops got his first head coaching job at OU.

Minnesota, Arkansas, and Texas had tried to hire Stoops before, but he turned them all down. Mack Brown had even offered him the defensive coordinator's job with the Longhorns.

SCHOOL COLORS

The school's official colors are crimson and cream, although OU is one of several teams that fans refer to as "Big Red." The colors were chosen in 1895, the first year OU played football. Mary Overstreet and Dr. James Buchanan chose the colors arbitrarily, then presented them to the student body. Originally, these colors were "crimson and corn," but "corn" was a problematic color, so the school settled on crimson and cream. There was general agreement on these colors, and they have remained with the program ever since.

From time to time, slight alterations are proposed; recently, the idea of a more classic red and white color scheme has been suggested. However, Sooner fans don't like to see any design revisions, and they're especially resistant to any revision to the famous, interlocking "OU" symbol, which has been a hallmark of the Sooners for forty years. Die-hard fans are known to grow borderline hostile when someone merely proposes such a change.

BOB STOOPS gets heavily involved in OU practices, much like Bennie Owen did

Stoops, though, had the same philosophy as Switzer: wait for the right opening. Don't jump at the first offer or even the second or third.

"I have enough patience to wait for an opportunity that would be better suited for me," Stoops said when he turned down the Minnesota job in 1997. "I didn't want to be here and then gone—ride the wave, jump on the national championship and then jump off. I just don't believe in that. I believe whatever you do, you ought to accomplish something, and you need to be somewhere awhile before doing that."

After turning down Arkansas and then Texas, Stoops remarked, "I want to be a head coach when it's the right time and the right place. My age gives me a chance to be patient. I think I've got the best assistant coaching job in America."

Stoops, a native of Youngstown, Ohio, grew up in a football family. His brothers, Ron Jr., Mike, and Mark, all became coaches. Ron Jr. still coaches at Cardinal Mooney High School, where his father coached. Their father died of a heart attack in 1988, while coaching.

Ron Sr. was a powerful influence in the lives of his children, and Bob Stoops would allude to that years later:

"I certainly have been influenced by him. Not so much as a coach, I think more as a person, how I look at life, how I handle my job and my relationships with everybody."

As a grad assistant at Iowa from 1983–87, Stoops spent a year at Kent State as a full-time assistant before Snyder came calling. He began as secondary coach with the Wildcats.

By 1995, Stoops was co-defensive coordinator and assistant head coach.

A year after Nebraska's vaunted option-I attack led by Tommy Frazier dismantled Florida, 62–24, in the Fiesta Bowl, Spurrier called Stoops. Spurrier felt an affinity with the young assistant, since he believed that

Stoops's program at Kansas State had been similar to the one he presided over at Duke.

Tracking Stoops's career after he helped turn around the Gator defense, Spurrier said, "I think he'll be a head coach within one, two, or three years. There will be an opportunity soon that he will probably go for."

As Stoops began moving toward the Sooners in late 1998, *Daily Oklahoman* writer Barry Tramel concisely summed up OU's situation:

"In December 1998, Oklahoma needs one thing and one thing only: a good coach. Young or old, head or assistant, offense or defense, right-handed or left-handed, doesn't matter. As long as he's good."

That simple, four-letter word would sum up Bob Stoops better than any flowery language from Grantland Rice or Rick Reilly. For in Stoops, Oklahoma landed a once-in-lifetime coach.

On a Sunday in December, Stoops met in Dallas with Castiglione, OU President David Boren, and regents Chuck Neinas and Eddie Crowder. He was approved shortly thereafter, at a reported $700,000 for three years.

When he was introduced as the new Sooner head coach, Stoops laid down the gauntlet in his usual, straightforward way:

"I'm not going to come in with a bunch of promises and say, 'Hey, we're going to win this year or that year,' or how many games we're going to win. I believe you go into every game trying to win, and we're going to do that. If I were to say we expect to be 9–2 next year, that means I'm giving up two games."

Indicating to his players, particularly the seniors who had suffered through the down years, that he expected to win immediately perhaps did more to cement Stoops's reputation than anything else. He also revealed some of his personal feelings in taking the Oklahoma job:

"You look at the potential here at Oklahoma and what we can do with this program . . . all of which made this an easy decision. I've never compared (the OU job) to other jobs. I've had opportunities with other schools, not just Iowa. This has always been the one that I've had my eye on for a long time, wondering if I'd ever be in the position to have a chance at it."

Luckily for the Sooners, the timing was perfect.

Approving of the new hire, Barry Switzer was present during the press conference announcing Stoops's acceptance. In typical Switzer fashion, he wisecracked before turning serious.

"Never met the gentleman. I know the women are excited because he's the best-looking candidate. That's what I've heard anyway." Switzer, though, knew what Stoops could do.

Switzer downplayed reporters' concerns about the OU post being Stoops's first head coaching job. "That's overblown," said the King, who knew something about new head coaches and success. He added, "Defensive coaches know more offense than most offensive coaches. What do they study all day long? Other people's offenses. They game plan to stop offenses. They see how people are vulnerable to what they do."

Stoops, as everyone now knows, instantly turned the Sooners into a winning team. His first team in 1999 went 7–5 with a bowl trip. This was a program that hadn't had a winning season since 1993!

Stoops's "sophomore" season is the one engraved in stone. Barely ranked in the top 25 to start the year, the Sooners performed magnificently behind passing quarterback Josh Heupel, tearing through a memorable "Red October" in which they vanquished Texas, Kansas State, and Nebraska on consecutive Saturdays.

By November, the Sooners were ranked No. 1. Capping OU's first 12–0 season with a Big 12 Championship, Oklahoma then went to Miami to take on mighty Florida State. Many felt OU was "a year away," a silly mantra rejected by Stoops and his fans. They knew better.

With Mike Stoops and Brent Venables scheming the Seminoles' high-powered offense, OU won the program's seventh national championship, 13–2.

At the time of this writing, Stoops sits atop the Big 12 and is one of the top coaches in the country. Many of his teams' wins over the years have been memorable. As he looked forward to his tenth season, Stoops recalled to the Die-Hard Fan how he viewed the Oklahoma job when it was offered to him.

"First of all, Oklahoma had the great history and tradition. Plus, the administration, Joe Castiglione, and President Boren . . . I had great faith in all of them."

The feeling was mutual.

Sooners

TIMELINE

» **1895**—Oklahoma plays its first game and loses, 34-0, to Oklahoma City High

» **1896**—OU earns its first win, 12-0, over Norman High School

» **1900**—Texas wins the first Texas-Oklahoma match up, 28-2, in Austin

» **1905**—OU beats Texas for the first time, 11-5, at Oklahoma City. This is also Bennie Owen's first year as Sooners coach.

» **1911**—Sooners have their first "significant" unbeaten season, going 8-0 under Owen

» **1915**—First conference championship (Southwest Conference)

» **1919**—First game against Nebraska, resulting in a 7-7 tie in Omaha; Cornhuskers coached by Henry Schulte

» **1939**—First bowl game, a 17-0 loss to Bob Neyland's Tennessee Volunteers, in Miami's Orange Bowl

» **1947**—Bud Wilkinson's first game as head coach, a 24-20 win over Detroit

» **1950**—Oklahoma wins its first national championship

» **1952**—Billy Vessels becomes OU's first Heisman Trophy winner

» **1953**—Sooners begin their famous 47-game winning streak, defeating Texas, 19-14, on October 10. The Longhorns were coached by Ed Price.

» **1954**—OU chalks up its first Orange Bowl win, 7-0, over Maryland, on New Year's Day

» **1957**—Notre Dame defeats OU at Norman, 7-0, to snap "The Streak"

» **1959**—Wilkinson's first conference loss after twelve years. Nebraska won 25-21, in Lincoln, and was coached by former OU assistant Bill Jennings.

» **1963**—Wilkinson coaches his last game, a 34-10 win over OSU at Norman

» **1966**—Jim MacKenzie arrives at OU, bringing assistants Chuck Fairbanks and Barry Switzer

» **1973**—Barry Switzer becomes head coach

» **1975**—Oklahoma becomes the first program to win back-to-back national championships twice

» **1989**—Switzer resigns after sixteen seasons

» **1996**—OU begins play in the newly formed Big 12 Conference

» **1998**—Bob Stoops becomes OU's twenty-first head coach

» **2000**—Sooners win the program's seventh national championship

» **2007**—Sooners win the program's forty-first conference championship

Chapter Five

THE KING

HOW BARRY SWITZER FED THE MONSTER

College football fans around the country are nothing if not narcissistic and territorial. Die-hard fans believe their team is the best program of all time, that the program's greatest coach came down from Sinai with Moses, and that the players they have cheered can shoot lightning from their index fingers.

Yet—if we lived in a perfect world and folks would really be objective—it would be difficult to find a coach more beloved by his fans than Barry Switzer.

Any Sooner fan worth his or her salt has a favorite Switzer story—or twenty. The chance meeting at a 7-Eleven, where Coach buys everybody a fountain drink; pulling up at a stoplight in Norman and looking over at the fellow on a Harley, recognizing the famous grin and shock of blonde hair... could it be? It is!

One recalls the hilarious recruiting stories, many of which Switzer himself dismisses, but that only add to the mystery. What really happened and what didn't? Did the Pearl Beer story really take place? Did Switzer really beat rival coaches to a recruit's house, only to come out of the kitchen wearing an apron and drying dishes?

Is this guy for real? How could he survive in a world of glum, tight-lipped coaches worried about their jobs?

A story that comes from cold Lincoln, Nebraska perhaps sums up Barry Switzer better than any other. Losing before he unleashed some Sooner Magic on stunned Cornhusker fans, Switzer sees an orange tossed from the stands. It signifies for the Children of the Corn that this will be their year to spend New Year's in Miami. Yes! Lobster and sun and surf!

Switzer picks up the orange—and defiantly takes a bite out of it. And just afterward, one of his streaking halfbacks crosses the goal line to send Nebraska back to El Paso.

Life is sweet. Winning is fun.

Photo courtesy of Bill Horn

BARRY SWITZER: It's good to be the King

Rival fans and media outlets have caricatured Switzer as a rogue, a guy more interested in partying than coaching. It's been said that Switzer only won because he had great players and great assistants.

It is high comedy for OU fans that Switzer himself agrees! Over the years, he's often attributed his success at Oklahoma both to the players and assistant coaches. This is another thing that sets him apart from many of his contemporaries; certain unnamed coaches believe, it seems, that they themselves are really responsible for wins on the field.

Not Switzer.

And yet, there is the paradox. This might be his public persona—a Reagan-style, hands-off figurehead. But the reality is much different, and one discovers this after talking to numerous coaches and former players who attest to the man's genius.

Switzer, in fact, is a great Xs and Os coach, one with a defensive background as player and assistant at Arkansas under Broyles, then later as the offensive mastermind of the Terror of the Prairie: the famed Wishbone.

Key proof of all this is found in the mementoes Switzer has accumulated over the years. When you stop and think about it, how many coaches never win a championship? And many of them are considered great coaches!

In Switzer's possession is a glass-enclosed case holding . . . twenty-nine championship rings. Twenty-nine! They range from a 1964 national championship ring at Arkansas to conference and national championships at Oklahoma, then to the crown—the Super Bowl ring from Dallas.

But what the coach really treasures in his heart, one can tell, are the players who won those championships for him. This sentimental attachment also came through in his colorful 1989 autobiography, *Bootlegger's Boy*, which is told in typical Switzer style, with nothing held back.

In Switzer's elegant office, he is surrounded by players from the past, players he loves and who love him. Billy Sims. The Selmons. Their photos, mostly from championship venues, are ensconced in special frames indicating their deep value to Switzer.

Switzer retired with a coaching record of 157–29–4. His 84 percent winning percentage is due as much to his own outstanding capabilities as it is to his players' abilities that he famously trumpets.

In the summer of 2007, the Die-Hard Fan sat down with Coach Switzer at his home in Norman. The discussion focused on the sixteen years he spent as head coach of the Oklahoma Sooners, when he earned a dozen conference championships and three national titles, while mentoring a Heisman Trophy winner and a host of All-Americans.

"WHAT DO I THINK ABOUT WHAT?": A VISIT WITH BARRY SWITZER

DF: Coach, you had seven Wishbone quarterbacks who each started at least one season. Give us your thoughts on each one. We obviously start with Jack Mildren.

SWITZER: We could not have gone to the Wishbone in 1970 had we not had his talents. Jack was an outstanding quarterback. He could throw and run, but probably his best attribute was that he was mentally talented. He was very smart, but he was a great runner, a Wishbone option quarterback, great speed. The premier quarterback of that day. Probably—and he would love this—we probably should have used him throwing the football a little bit more than just play action, but he led the greatest Wishbone team in the history of college football, and/or offensive team in college history, regardless of formation because those stats still hold today.

DF: Dave Robertson.

SWITZER: Dave was a quarterback who was recruited to throw the football. He was not gifted in running, but was surrounded by great players, and he was very smart. He had played a backup role for several years, and was one of those guys that if he stayed, he'd eventually play. He was not discouraged; he waited his time. He was given the opportunity in 1972 and because of his intelligence and his arm and the people surrounding him—he had a great supporting cast surrounding him after Mildren left—he was able to win for us. He didn't make mistakes.

DF: Steve Davis.

SWITZER: An unknown, but I thought he would be a good player because I watched him in a freshman game in his freshman year and I told our offensive coordinator that I believed this kid can help us in the future as an option quarterback. He too was surrounded by great talent and was a very good quarterback and came along at the right time for us.

DF: Thomas Lott.

SWITZER: Highly recruited, top option quarterback in the country probably at that time. John Jay High School in San Antonio. He was referred to as "Black Velvet." He was very smooth, fast, quick. We'd watched high school tape of him and he was a very talented, gifted runner. Had a great career. He was surrounded by good people, too. Very good option quarterback.

> **"There's only one great reward for playing the game of football, and that's winning."**
>
> —Barry Switzer, 1973

DF: J.C. Watts.

SWITZER: Probably the best at doing everything that I had in a quarterback. J.C. was the most valuable player in two consecutive Orange Bowls. That had never happened before. He had a great arm, but as our offensive dictates down, distance determines whether we throw the football or not. We were always in third and short, and my offensive coordinators knew I would fire them if they threw the ball when we controlled the down and distance variable. So we always ran the football. J.C. played eight years of professional football and took Ottawa to the Grey Cup Championship game his rookie year. He'd be recruited by the NFL today because of his arm and speed.

DF: Danny Bradley.

SWITZER: Danny was another outstanding athlete from Arkansas. They [the Razorbacks] tried to recruit Danny, but they didn't think he could play quarterback and throw well enough. Danny was here at the right time for us in 1984. When we changed, Marcus Dupree kind of took us away from the Wishbone and Danny had the ability and talents and experience enough to be able to give us an opportunity to go back to the Wishbone. Very fast, quick, had a great game when we beat Nebraska at Lincoln when they were undefeated. He was a very good player.

DF: Jamelle Holieway.

SWITZER: The best option quarterback. The best runner, best option runner, I had until he blew his knee out. He was our best; he was strong, quick, hard to tackle, he broke tackles. Very smart. He was a great option quarterback in high school. Player of the year in L.A. I knew he was special when I saw a tape of him in high school. I knew it was a matter of time before he would emerge as our quarterback his freshman year and unfortunately, Troy's [Aikman] injury allowed that to happen. He had already demonstrated in the games when we'd substitute him early on that he was special. He was the perfect Wishbone quarterback.

DF: It was ironic that he came along right when Eric Mitchel did, because I remember how recruited Mitchel was.

SWITZER: Jamelle was better, simple as that. Eric probably had more physical talent, but people gotta understand that the game is played 90 percent from the neck up. Eric—it's not that he wasn't smart. That wasn't it. Eric dwelled... he let little things get him. He would think about the bad plays instead of shaking them off and going on into the future. You gotta play the present in football. You only got thirty seconds to prepare and play for the next snap. You can't dwell on the negative and get your head down. He [Mitchel] was quick to do that. You gotta remember, in high school Eric's biggest plays were on third-and-long and if the field was scattered, he'd drop back to pass and everybody's rushing him, all of a sudden he'd take off running seventy yards for a touchdown on an undesigned play, because of his great physical talent.

DF: There's a perception today that the Wishbone is out of favor, that it wouldn't work. I heard you speak in Fayetteville a few years ago, and you indicated in some way that it doesn't work because nobody runs.

SWITZER: There are no disciples of it. Let me ask you something: Who out there other than the academies runs it? This is how I always answer that. [Former OU defensive coordinator Larry] Lacewell likes to say, "Hell, the Wishbone isn't dead, all the sonofabitches that coached it are dead!" You know, you gotta be disciples of something and today the vogue is to throw. People want to throw the football—the receivers, the skilled people—they all want to play professional football. Everyone has that dream and goal and they think they're all gonna get there. Well, everyone is a disciple in the college game today of a wide-open offense. People who are getting assistant jobs, what are they tutored in?

The question I always ask is, "Why don't the academies do that? Why don't the United States Naval Academy and the Air Force throw?" The schedules that they play, playing other state universities, the schools that they play, they wouldn't win a game because the Wishbone gives them an opportunity to force defenses to play it, and the only time they see it is that one time. The option forces defenses to be disciplined. The Wishbone neutralizes team quickness and speed because you have to play who's got deep third, who's got the pitch, who's got the quarterback, who plays fullback handoff.

It creates hesitancy, it creates indecision, it takes away the aggressiveness of skilled athletes, and if they didn't run the offense they probably wouldn't win any games. But because they do, they win five to six games a year and are competitive in the games because of the fact that they run the option and they force teams to be disciplined to play.

DF: So obviously the argument that the defensive players are bigger and faster today really doesn't. . . .

SWITZER: Nah, that doesn't have one thing to do with it. My early teams, there was nobody faster than my '73, '74, and '75 teams. Those guys in that era were just as fast, although they weren't as big. Those guys—many of them were All-American guys and went on to become high draft choices in the NFL. LeRoy Selmon is still the best player that played here. He played at 265. If he'd had a weight and strength and condition room, he'd have played at 285. That is the only difference today, the emphasis on strength and conditioning. But those other guys had great speed and quickness.

> **"He was the perfect Wishbone quarterback."**
>
> —Barry Switzer, describing Jamelle Holieway

DF: I know that when the Wishbone was being developed in Texas they had a certain style, but I noticed that as the years went on, for example, your fullbacks were faster. Was that by design, or did you fall into that because of the recruits?

SWITZER: Because I recruited the black athletes. Texas didn't and so all my guys at all positions were faster. Worster wasn't as fast as Kenny King. Kenny was 4.4 and Worster probably couldn't run 4.7. But no, it was because of the athletes I recruited. I recruited speed and quickness and the best. I recruited halfbacks. I played my fullback. All my backs were fast. And no one played the Wishbone in those days; oh, a few ran it because it was in vogue, but the backs I recruited were all I-formation tailbacks. The Billy Sims, the Kenny Kings, the Elvis Peacocks, Marcus Duprees, Mike Gaddis, Spencer Tillman—all those guys were prima donna running backs in high school and came to play the Wishbone. I'd put one of them that wasn't going to play halfback at fullback, because I wanted a runner there.

Every once in a while you recruited one that you knew was pure fullback. The Lydell Carrs, the 220 to 225-pounders that were ideal, that could run 4.5. They could take the punishment at fullback.

Kenny was a true halfback, he was a two hundred-pounder, but he was a lightening fullback. Stanley Wilson was a great Wishbone fullback. Yeah, I just recruited great speed and quickness and put a bunch of good runners out there.

DF: When you were looking at other positions, like the offensive line, was there a certain thing you looked for in a lineman to fit your style of offense?

SWITZER: No one threw the ball then, so the stances totally were different in that era. We were coming off the ball and we had tremendous quickness. We were basically a team that lines up to run the football and you're gonna have to defend the option game, you gotta defend the width of the field. You had to defend us east and west. Not only north and south with the fullback popping the line of scrimmage, but everyone had to run sideways against us because of the great speed and the playing of the option game. So, defenses had to play us laterally and that's a tremendous disadvantage for defenses because defenses want to be aggressive, they want to attack the offense, but they can't with that style of offense.

DF: Who were a few players that you can think of over the years that were underrated by the public?

SWITZER: You could name so many men. People always watched the ball and they know who carries it and who plays quarterback, but they don't know how good defensive players are or how good an offensive player is. Nobody eyeballs them but maybe their high school coach and their family. Nobody else pays any attention to them.

DF: I think about players like Wayne Hoffman....

SWITZER: He was a great player. He was gonna be a defensive player for us and would have been a good defensive player but we needed a tight-end at the time and Wayne was a REALLY good tight-end because he had great feet and he was a great blocker. He was a six-foot-five, 240-pounder that could latch on to you, because he was a good basketball player, and he could run and he could catch a ball. Good hands. He was a good player and he could play defense, but he sacrificed to come help the team and played offense. He was a good player. He was really good. There were lots of guys that you could mention that had those type of roles. You know, really good players, but no one knew that. To win and win like we did, we had to have good players at a lot of other positions that nobody knew about. Nobody was paying any attention to it, other than our competition and coaches.

DF: Now this is really an obscure thing, but in the '87 game at Nebraska, John Green was playing fullback and hit a block that sprung Patrick Collins.

SWITZER: John, he wasn't a running back, you know, he couldn't play in the competition we had. We had a better player, but he was a tough kid and he was a good blocker. He'd throw his body around and he was strong, so we just put him in that situation to be a blocker. It was a substitution for a certain particular play and that was important because he was a fresh body that knew his role and that's the play he's gonna go execute for us. [Collins sprinted sixty-five yards for the touchdown that beat then No. 1 Nebraska.]

DF: Back to the stars for a minute. How close did the Selmons come to going somewhere else? I read that they might have gone to Colorado, that LeRoy and Dewey might have followed Lucious there.

SWITZER: Well, the two brothers might have. Lucious was the key because if Lucious hadn't come to Oklahoma, the brothers probably would have followed him wherever he went. It was a close family group and they were gonna do what Momma and Daddy wanted, Momma especially. They wanted to be together. Colorado was really recruiting Lucious hard and we didn't recruit Lucious until the very end.

This was back when you could take a bunch of them. He was short, he wanted to play fullback and when you look at tape of him,

A BIG SMILE ON HIS FACE

LUCIOUS SELMON, JR.

Lucious Selmon, Jr., is the seventh of nine children. Lucious Sr. and Jessie raised good kids in Eufaula, Oklahoma: Elmer, Charles, Joyce, Chester, Margaret, Shirlene, Lucious, and then "the babies," Dewey and LeRoy.

Die-hard Sooner fans remember the days gratefully when a third of the Selmon offspring—three brothers, playing side-by-side—throttled Nebraska in Norman and wound up as football legends. And get this: each made All-American. After his senior season of 1973, Lucious was drafted by the New England Patriots, but opted instead to play for the World Football League in Canada, spent some time in a league in Memphis, then headed back to Norman to coach for Barry Switzer.

Photo courtesy of Bill Horn

LUCIOUS SELMON. The first of the three Selmon brothers to sign with OU, Lucious moved from offense to defense and became a disrupting force at noseguard, making All-American

"Playing for him and then coaching for him was thoroughly enjoyable," Lucious remembers. "Coach Switzer's personality and demeanor was a very positive way of working with young men."

Integration had already begun at Eufaula when Lucious noticed that football was a popular activity. "It was kind of a peer pressure thing," he says now. "The coach spotted me out there playing like a wild man, and since I was bigger than anyone else, he said I should play football." That was Paul Bell, "the toughest man I've ever known," Lucious says.

At OU, Lucious played through a few periods of transition. When Chuck Fairbanks exited, the players were naturally concerned about the direction of the program—that is, until Switzer came into the locker room upon being named head coach. "I remember the day he came in with a big smile on his face—we were so glad he had been hired." Lucious remembers that Switzer let the players have their individual personalities, "but he had some rules he enforced."

Lucious Selmon coached defense for nineteen years at OU and remains a beloved figure.

"I cannot remember a single season or day I didn't enjoy coming to work in Norman," he says.

As a sophomore in 1971, he played tackle in a four-man front, then shifted to noseguard when OU went to a five-man. His quickness and strength befuddled opponents for years. In a crowded field of great noseguards at OU, Lucious is the standard-bearer. Besides the Switzer hire, he says today that the most memorable moment for him was the day Dewey and LeRoy signed with OU at Eufaula High. The trio almost ended up farther north.

"My parents really like Eddie Crowder at Colorado, but in the end Oklahoma was closer to home."

Selmon exemplifies the kind of former player who fondly remembers his playing days under the blonde genius from Crossett.

he wasn't gonna be a fullback for us, but on defense he didn't play hard because he thought he was an offensive player. So therefore, when you evaluate him on defense, when you looked at him physically and knew that this guy could run a 10-flat hundred and he's a 4.6 guy, when you look how muscular and strong you say, "Well this guy can squat down and be a noseguard." As quick as he was, he could be a great noseguard or something, but he didn't show us that he would perform at that level.

But that is what coaching is. He immediately showed us that he was a difference-maker when we put him down with his hands on the ground. If we hadn't taken him we probably would have lost the other two. We hadn't seen the other two. I think there would have been no question we would have taken him right away if we had seen the other two at the same time because they were so much bigger than Lucious.

DF: I guess recruiting is probably the main answer, but what was the key to the resurgence in the early '80s? What was the key to the resurgence in about '83, '84?

SWITZER: What, the going back to the Wishbone?

DF: Well, overall. You know, '81, '82, '83....

SWITZER: Well, '81, '82, '83, I didn't have a quarterback, I didn't have my quarterbacks. It was the recruiting. I mean, we had it at kind of a dip but we lost to top people. People think, "Well during that period of time, y'all were losing." Well, wait a minute—we won eight games, you know. We lost to Nebraska three years.

DF: Their only good run at you.

SWITZER: But it was the Triplets. And I'd lost Turner Gill. They got him. I didn't have the quarterback that I wanted. I get Marcus Dupree and he runs off a bunch of backs. Then he leaves me and the cupboard's dry and bare. We got away from the Wishbone because of him in that era. Here's who we lost to in that era, this is how I defend this: We lost to Southern Cal twice; we lost to

Photo courtesy of Oklahoma Historical Society

A POSTCARD depicting Owen Field in the 1940s

Photo courtesy of Harold Keith

THE SOONERS celebrate a victory over arch-rival Texas, 1948

Photo courtesy of *Sooners Illustrated*

JAMELLE HOLIEWAY takes the snap in a game against Penn State

FOREVER NO. 20: The incomparable Billy Sims

TIM LASHER hits a field goal to beat the Huskers in the 1986 Orange Bowl (top), only to get thrown on his back during the celebration (right)

Photos courtesy of *Sooners Illustrated*

Photo courtesy of *Sooners Illustrated*

PATRICK COLLINS puts a move on the Cornhuskers

Photo courtesy of Bryan Procter

ADRIAN PETERSON greets the fans. Known to the Sooner faithful as "AD" (a reference to his ability to run "all day"), he injured his shoulder in his junior year during a touchdown run against Iowa State

Photo courtesy of Bryan Procter

Photo courtesy of Bryan Procter

^ **CHIJIOKE ONYENEGECHA** scores on an interception return to clinch a win over Nebraska at Lincoln

» **ADRIAN PETERSON** breaks away for a late touchdown against Tulsa, 2005

Photo courtesy of Bryan Procter

THE RUF/NEKS, who originated in the early 1900s and were known early on for intimidating opposing fans

Photo courtesy of Bryan Procter

"PLAY LIKE A CHAMPION" has been a Sooner tradition since the Bud Wilkinson era

Photo courtesy of Bryan Procter

SOONER FOOTBALL is a rush!

THE MAGNIFICENT MURAL, created by sports artist Ted Watts, on display in the Barry Switzer Center. This section shows OU coaching legends (left to right) Bob Stoops, Barry Switzer, and Bud Wilkinson. Chuck Fairbanks is in the lower left-hand corner.

Ohio State, lost three to Texas and three to Nebraska. Now let me ask you, should we be losing to Iowa State, Kansas State, and Missouri? Now those elite teams you should lose to because they are good or better than you, you know what I mean? They are just as good with their tradition. No, you don't have to duck your head when you lose those games, 'cause they're great opponents.

DF: You were mentioning Gill, who was a recruit that stands out in your mind as being the biggest disappointment because you lost him to Tom Osborne.

SWITZER: It was Turner Gill, without a doubt.

DF: Not Eric Dickerson?

SWITZER: Nah, nah, I had running backs. That didn't keep us from winning. Eric called me once and I asked him, "Well, do you want to transfer here?" He was dissatisfied because of the Pony Express [at SMU], you know, sharing time. Earl Campbell was a bigger disappoint than Eric. I worked hard on Earl. I thought we'd get Earl, but it came down to us and Texas and, shit, they got him. Now, Eric, you know, I recruited the hell out of Eric, but the one that really hurt is the quarterback because I had other backs. You know, we were undefeated and won the national championship when Earl was playing at Texas, so you know, he would have been another great player playing with us and made us a little better, but shit, we were still good.

Photo courtesy of Bill Horn

SOONER NEMESIS

Turner Gill. The Fort Worth native broke Switzer's heart and signed with Nebraska. He directed some of the greatest offenses in Cornhusker history.

DF: And Gill was from Texas, right?

SWITZER: Yeah, Fort Worth! Shit, two hours away! His mom and dad wanted him to come here, he was a baseball player and we had Enos Seymore. Baseball was important to him and we thought he'd commit to us, so I told him we'd go get other players. All along he told me he was coming. In the eleventh hour he switched to

Nebraska and I never understood this. Really, I've never, never... that's always puzzled me. But anyway, that's the way it works.

DF: Just like you did with your quarterbacks, give us your impression of the backs you had. Let's start with Greg Pruitt and Joe Wylie.

SWITZER: Oh, Greg Pruitt had a great professional career. Greg Pruitt was the smallest player that played bigger than anybody. He was five-foot-seven, 156 pounds when he came to the University of Oklahoma. The only reason we took him was because of Bill Michaels' persistence in saying, "Guys, we need to take this little kid. I know he looks like a pygmie, but I'm gonna tell ya, he is a great player, great competitor."

So Billy was recruiting in Elmore High School in the inner-city in Houston. He had been down there for years and recruiting, knew the coach Wendell Moseley well, and he was sold on this kid. Problem is, he is the only one. He had to come sell me and Chuck Fairbanks, and I'll tell ya, I worked him out and violated the NCAA rules. I'd take Jack Mildren who was already here, I'd take Eddie Hinton who was a first-round draft pick of the Baltimore Colts, he was on the team, I'd take Eddie and Jack out there with little Greg to work them out and I'd never seen him before.

Well, I'll never forget working him out on the practice field over here. The three of us out there. I'm having Jack throwing balls at all of them, they're running routes and Chuck asked me later, he said, "Well, what do you think?" and I said, "What do I think about what?" Chuck said, "Greg Pruitt." "Well, I think he's better than Eddie Hinton," and he looked at me and he said, "You've gotta be shitting me." I said, "No, I think he's better than Eddie. He's faster, he's quicker, he's got better hands. He's a little guy, but he is lightning. He's got everything you want. He just doesn't fit the package." And of course, he was a great pro.

I had Jim Garrett who was a scout for us [the Cowboys] and he had coached in Cleveland. He was a running back's coach at Cleve-

SWITZER with longtime assistant Warren Harper. Harper turned out a tremendous number of great linebackers.

Photo courtesy of Bill Horn

land [his son Jason Garrett was a player and coach in Dallas] and he told me, "Greg Pruitt is the best little player I ever coached." I remember pro scouts, everybody wanted the big backs. A prototype, north-south running game. You gotta be big—six-foot-two, 210. I'll never forget the pros who were always asking Greg when he'd come on the field, "Greg, how tall are you?" Finally, Greg, I'll never forget one day he stopped and looked at those guys and he says, "You know, we run this way, not that way at Oklahoma." And they all looked dumbfounded when he said that. I said, "That's a good point isn't it, guys?" You know, the hole's this way, not this way.

He proved just like today, the guys that are under six feet are the best running backs. Stop, start, go sideways. Big guys take a little longer to decelerate and start again. The little guy is just harder to get hold of. Plays underneath people's pads, and big guys are trying to tackle them, and they're playing on a different . . . their gravity levels are a little lower.

But anyway, Greg was a great, great player. He was electricity. He could bust through, he could accelerate through a gap, a crack, and he'd make you miss.

DF: And that was the start of the Hello/Goodbye thing.

SWITZER: Oh yeah, yeah. He could make you miss and then out-run you. He had great speed. He was probably a 9.5 guy. He was a hurdler. I saw him win the big indoor freshman sixty-yard high hurdles. Greg was a great basketball player, played basketball here, freshman basketball. Started at point guard. He played thirteen years in the NFL.

DF: I knew he played a long time but I didn't realize it was that long.

SWITZER: Marcus Allen was a rookie at Oakland and Greg was in Oakland. He came at the same time and I've heard Marcus tell a great story. I've heard both Greg and Marcus sit there and tell me the story. Marcus, he's the Heisman Trophy winner and you know, he got all this attention. All of a sudden he's in pro football and a rookie and they'd go have scrimmages and have games, and Greg's in there and of course, Greg had been in the league a long time. He was smart, savvy, and still could play. They'd hand him the ball and then, all of a sudden, Marcus didn't know shit. You know, I've got to beat this guy out and he thought Greg was trying to beat him out of his job.

Greg finally walked up, because he wouldn't speak to him or, you know, he'd just ignore him. Greg smarted off—he'd been in the league—that he didn't want no rookie going in and telling the owner he couldn't cut him. So, he walked up to Marcus and said, "Marcus, I'm not here to beat you out, all I want to do is return punts. But when they ask me to play, I give them what they want. I don't want your job, I don't wanna play, and I don't want you to get hurt where I have to play. I wanna finish up my career being a punt returner in the NFL." And that's what he was, a punt returner for them. Kickoff and punt returns for 'em. But Marcus thought, "This guy's beatin' me out!"

DF: Joe Wylie.

SWITZER: Joe was a straight-A, 126 hours of a graduate. Straight four-point, never made a B in college, straight four-point, 126 hours. Great athlete. He was different, but had some injury problems. He had great speed, though, and was a really good player.

DF: And then of course, Joe Washington, and then another guy who was underrated a little bit, Grant Burget.

SWITZER: Grant was highly recruited coming out of high school. Everybody wanted Grant Burget. Alabama, everybody wanted him, you know. He's a six-foot-one, 180-190 pound guy who had 4.5 speed. He was a good track athlete. He won a lot of events at state track meets and everybody wanted him. He was tough, very physically tough, a really tough back. He ended up being a good player, and the other back with Joe Washington, you know, he was just kind of a lead blocker and Grant had the ability to make a play to run the ball, but if you could hand the ball over to Joe, you gotta give it to him.

> **"He [Switzer] was definitely memorable in his energy, his coaching, his honesty. To this day I don't think he gets credit for his innovation, and as a tactician and motivator. He understands players."**
>
> —Joe Washington, 1972–75

DF: Washington was special.

SWITZER: He had a great career. He won a Super Bowl. Most valuable player on the Super Bowl team, voted by his teammates. Joe was the fourth player picked in the draft in 1976. I don't think that there has ever been a player of smaller stature picked higher. Joe was only 172 pounds, five-foot-eight-and-a-half when he came out, he's the fourth player, and they considered him the third player.

[Chuck] Muncie, the big back from California, was six-foot-four, 235, the prototype. Joe was the opposite and they're trying to make a decision on draft day which one to take. I remember being on the phone with the Chargers, and New Orleans was on the phone with them and they're trying to make a decision who to take. I had both

DID YOU KNOW?

Barry Switzer, former OU defensive coordinator Larry Lacewell, and Alabama's Paul "Bear" Bryant were all born and raised in Arkansas.

Joe and Muncie in the Hula Bowl. I had coached them—that's why they had me on the phone. I said, "You guys are going to take the big back but Joe Washington is a winner and he'll be a great player because he's just special." He played a long time!

DF: And then Elvis Peacock and Horace Ivory.

SWITZER: You know, Elvis was a great player coming out of high school. He was a stallion, boy, I mean, he was so pretty. I saw him run 9.4 in high school and I saw him at a state track meet at Miami Central High School. We went to Miami in the spring, that's when national recruiting for a long time was a free-for-all. He was the top back, one of the top backs in the country, everybody's recruiting him. Michigan, I mean everywhere, you know? He could have gone anywhere.

I recruited him hard. I was there on national signing date, no other head coach came and I think that impressed him. I came because I wanted him and he came here and started for me as a freshman and was a really good player. Big and fast, tough, smart. I remember the first day I saw him in shorts out there jogging and I said, "I wish all of them could look like that." He was six-foot-one, 215, just glided, just special. Just a gazelle. Beautiful.

DF: Horace Ivory.

SWITZER: Donnie Duncan had him down at Navarro Junior College. He was a really good player, too. He was one of those underrated backs because no one really remembers him. Hell, he played eight years in the NFL with the Patriots. He was a helluva running back. See, he was a halfback but I stuck him at fullback because I had good halfbacks, I had speed guys. I had the Joe Washingtons and those kinds of guys and Peacocks and all. So I just took Horace Ivory and put him at fullback, and I'm glad I did because he pops one against Texas in the Cotton Bowl for thirty yards and a touchdown and wins the game. He had the quickness and speed and acceleration, could run right by everybody, quick. Yeah, he was a good player.

DF: Then of course the incomparable Billy Sims.

SWITZER: Billy was the best player we ever had. Billy had it all. He had the size, the speed, the strength, the toughness. He played at five-foot-eleven, 215. Ran 4. 4. That's why he's the number-one back pick. He was NFL rookie of the year, and would have played longer if he hadn't blown his knee out. But they don't last long.

DF: Buster Rhymes.

SWITZER: Buster was a highly recruited back. Buster was probably a split receiver playing halfback. But I'm glad he came along when he did because his freshman year he made some big plays for us to help win games. He was a big back and had great speed. Six-foot-three, 200-210, could really run.

DF: Then guys like Chet Winters, Jimmy Rogers. . . .

SWITZER: Arkansas kids that were just tough, good football players that could. . . .

DF: Talented, but had guys in front of them. . . .

SWITZER: Yeah, there was someone always better than them talent-wise, but, because of who they were, their character and all, they played. Because they're just gonna find a spot. You find spots for guys like that to play. Spencer Tillman, Earl Johnson, they were good players too.

DF: Anthony Stafford and Patrick Collins.

SWITZER: Patrick Collins and Stafford, see, they were prototype Wishbone halfbacks. You know why they were? Because both of them were totally unselfish. Neither cared about their statistics, and when they were playing it was a wonderful, wonderful experience to go into a game when they played in their era with Jamelle Holieway, and Lydell Carr at fullback. If you have to worry about getting your halfback, a certain halfback named Billy Sims or a Joe Washington, twenty-five or thirty touches a game in the Wishbone, you're probably in the wrong offense.

I always wanted to design things and try to get the ball at the right places and the hash marks. Well, when you have Patrick Collins and Anthony Stafford, it wasn't any pressure to make sure they got that many touches. I didn't care if Patrick got it six times or four times or ten times, or Stafford the same because when they touched it, I knew that they had the home run ability, the great speed. I mean, talk about great speed now, both of them had it then! I saw Anthony Stafford run a 10.3, I saw him in a state track meet win a 100 meters in 10.3. Won the 200, won the 400 and would have won the 800 but they wouldn't let him enter it. He won three; he won the 100, 200, and 400 in the state track meet in Missouri. But, he had great speed and was a little compact.

Both were intelligent, great blockers, be in on ya like that [snaps his fingers], and they loved to do that. And Jamelle [laughing], coming in right behind 'em. When they got the ball pitched to them on the edge, they were gonna go a long way. You never worried about whether they'd pout about not getting it enough or you had to get it in their hands. Great blockers, they were rockets coming in there. Blocking linebackers and cornerbacks. They were special.

> **"I'm going to play it just like they deal it."**
>
> —Barry Switzer, 1973, after a Big Eight Conference hearing on alleged recruiting violations

DF: At that time there were a few other programs running the Wishbone: Alabama, Texas, A&M....

SWITZER: They were all winning. We were the only team that won 102 games in a decade. But Alabama and Texas and Oklahoma, they were all winning.

DF: So were there cases where coaches from other programs wanted to run it?

SWITZER: Yeah, there were a lot of people experimenting with the option. The option was still the best-played football. Even though everyone's in the spread offenses now, people still want options. Options still hurt a lot of people's offenses. They don't run it that hard, because they don't want to put their quarterback in jeopardy that much, but the ideal quarterback is the guy that can run and throw. Everyone looks for that guy; he's a premium.

DF: Finally, was there a particular game—and it may not have been a national championship or a bowl game—was there a certain game that was memorable to you personally?

SWITZER: Oh, everybody asks that question and everybody expects it to be a win. It was a loss. It was a loss at Nebraska. We were ranked number one in the country, and had been ranked one all year long. It was Billy's junior year, 1978. We were undefeated. I had Daryl Hunt and Cumby. I had great players like Reggie Kinlaw. Reggie Kinlaw was the last player picked in the draft and he played twelve years. Oakland Raiders' noseguard, a great player. He was six-foot-three, 245-250, but talk about quick. When you know how to play technique and you play underneath people's pads and you play under the big guys, you separate and lock out—he knew how to play underneath people's pads. You don't have to be big. A 300-pounder can't block a 245-pounder that plays great technique.

But anyway, I had a great team; we should have won the national championship. We go to Nebraska that day, we fumbled nine times and lost six of them and we only got beat 17 to14. We should have won when Billy made a great run to get the ball to the two. We're gonna be first-and-goal on the two with a minute to go in the game. We win that, we're gonna beat whoever's in the Orange Bowl. But we got to play Nebraska again. Nebraska hated it, but the Orange Bowl's job is to get the highest-ranked team in the country that's available for the Big Eight champion. Well, we're the highest-ranked team in the country that's not tied to another bowl! So we go play Nebraska in the Orange Bowl and won. But that '78 game—it haunts me. It haunts me, it haunts Billy. But we win that, we'll win another national championship. That's the one that kills me of all the games, the one I think about.

RECIPE FOR COACHING SUCCESS: BROYLED SWITZER

Legendary Arkansas coach and athletic director Frank Broyles visited with the Die-Hard Fan a few months before retiring after a glittering fifty-year career in Fayetteville. Part of Broyles's legacy will be the unusually large number of his assistants who went on to great success in college and the NFL. From his spacious office overlooking Donald W. Reynolds Razorback Stadium, Broyles reminisced about his most famous pupil and other successful assistants.

DF: Coach, Barry Switzer played for you and then was an assistant. Tell us how Coach Switzer crossed the border to Oklahoma.

BROYLES: I had an agreement with all the people on my staff that I'd help them become a head coach only if they wouldn't take anybody from my staff. Well, right before Christmas of 1965, after Jim [Mackenzie] had just taken the Oklahoma position as head coach, he came to me and he said, "You know, Barry has worked with me on defense and he's got a promotion coming with me and he really wants to come with me." I said, "Well let me ask Barry." So that was on the twenty-fourth of December. I just went to Barry and asked him about it: "Oh no, Coach, no, no, I don't want to leave," he said. "No sir, no, I'm happy to be a Razorback!" And then on the twenty-sixth he called me when I was at home and he said, "I need to see you, Coach." I knew what was going to happen. He came in and said, "You know, I would really like to go with Coach Mackenzie," and I said, "Okay, I'll make an exception."

And so he went over there and in four or five years he became the head coach, won thirty some-odd games in a row without losing and had an unbelievable career. It wasn't only my decision that we wanted him to become a coach after he captained the championship team of '59. It was a joint opinion of everybody on my staff. They felt like we'd do well to bring him into the coaching ranks and so we called him and he accepted and came back and the rest is history.

See, Barry's strength—he had many strengths as a coach—but in particular as a head coach, he had a great relationship with his players, and his players believed in him and he believed in the players, and he had a personal relationship. With that personal relationship, you have the ability to influence, and leadership is nothing more than one word: influence. That says it all, and with his caring about them and the things that he believed in that he put in practice there at Oklahoma, I think, that was key.

> **"A fair man, a great coach. He was a brilliant delegator and he surrounded himself with great assistant coaches and then let them do their jobs."**
>
> —Victor Hicks, four-year starter at tight-end, 1975–78, discussing Barry Switzer

I watched his teams play for years and years and years, envious like everybody else of how hard they played and how consistently they played at a peak performance. As much as any coach of our time, his players played with a peak performance. Normally, you get a peak performance of about six out of ten times and he must have had eight or nine or ten times of peak performance and that is the reason his record is so outstanding.

DF: Mackenzie was going to be a great coach.

BROYLES: Well, Jim Mackenzie was... we miss him. He was coaching I guess at Texas A&M junior college, the junior college in Bryan, Texas. He had played for Coach Bryant in Kentucky and he was coaching there and Coach Bryant left and went to Alabama. And so, I've forgotten how, who recommended him to me, I'll have to think about that, but anyway, we called him and brought him to our staff at Missouri, my first staff.

Mackenzie was one of those big, big, big linemen that was able to conceal how smart he was—and he was smart! I remember one time he was calling the defensive plays, obviously, as the defensive coordinator and I said to him after the season, "Jim, you know, we've got to be sure when they're running the ball or throwing deep and when they're throwing short we're defending, you know, and that's gonna be up to you studying, and being able to call the right defense at the right time. At the end of the season he said, "I've got something to show you." He said, "Here we are every time we played the gap; here's the chart. They threw one pass against us every time we were in the gap. Did I call them right or not?" I said, "You sure did, 99.9 percent you were right!" We were in a gap and they ran the ball and only one time had they thrown when he called this gambling-type of a defense.

But he was smart as he could be, smart, I mean really smart. He could conceal that by being a big lineman, but he had a football mind that I believe, if he would have lived, he would have been extremely successful and as successful as maybe anybody but Bud Wilkinson. He was a great coach.

DF: And Jimmy Johnson coached there for a time.

BROYLES: Yeah, he was on the staff there when I brought him back to Arkansas. Jimmy was a psychology major and he used that psychology in his playing and in his coaching to the utmost. He could find a reason to get you to work harder and play harder and excel. He could work on you mentally. I mean he had the ability to use all kinds of reverse psychology, any kind of psychology, and he used it all through college. I think he aced every final he ever had. I'm not sure.

He was very, very smart. In fact, I can remember as a player, he was playing noseguard on defense and playing over the nose, and we were slanting a lot to the left and the right, and I got to watching, and all of a sudden we were slanting to the left but he went to the right and made the play. And I thought, "Well, you know, he just busted the defense."

And so I confronted him. I said, "You busted too many defenses. You're getting lucky in making the play," and he said, "Coach, I'm not getting lucky, I could tell by the weight the offensive guard had on his hands they were gonna run that side and they weren't gonna run the other side, so I just went where the ball was going. That's all right, isn't it?" I said, "As long as you make the play, it's all right."

And he did. He made a lot of them. He was great, he played with his mind and coached with his mind, too.

DF: Now moving to the question of the Wishbone. Didn't Arkansas run it for a while with those great backs like Ike Forte and Jerry Eckwood?

BROYLES: We never ran it exclusively. We ran it goal line, short yardage, as an alternative. It was an unbelievable offense. I can remember the Texas/Tennessee Cotton Bowl game. Doug Dickey was on my staff; he was the head coach in that game and Texas had always flared their halfback. Tennessee worked, getting ready for that game back then when the back player at the end was going up the field and stopping the pitch play. And Texas put in for what they call the lead play—the halfback started like he was going to play and then he turned up inside as a blocker, and it was designed for the quarterback to keep the ball. And they beat Tennessee something like 42–7 with that change that they had not used before the bowl game.

"I remember our neighbor pulling into their driveway and my mother asking the neighbor what the final score was of that game (I was ten) and my mother replied, "Oh, I feel so sorry for Missouri." It was at that moment that this person inside of me came alive and I realized what OU football was all about. It was about NOT feeling sorry for your opponent and dominating everyone you played. I turned to my precious mother and said, "You don't ever feel sorry for the other team."

—Member, OUInsider.com

But the Wishbone had so much opportunity to make the big play and you had to get ready for it, and the defense had to be disciplined. What happened is, in football, when you turn and hand the ball to the tailback, who's eight yards deep or nine yards deep and you're quick and all, you can beat your blocker and have time to get to the ball. And you see which way it's going pretty early, and so everybody is pursuing toward that ball carrier. But in the Wishbone you couldn't play defense the same way. You had to give an assignment to the defensive man. One defensive man had to take the fullback and one had to take the quarterback and one had to take the pitch, and so they had to play more disciplined.

Until the Wishbone, there wasn't much option play, but more than that, defensive people just reacted to the ball and played football and weren't assigned to a particular play on offense. But when the Wishbone came in, you had to assign the person to play the fullback when he came up and one to play the quarterback and one to play the pitch and they had to be disciplined, I mean, really disciplined, and that caused a lot of sorrow for the defensive teams because they weren't disciplined for that one game. So it revolutionized defense for a good ten years.

DF: And you had great backs. I mean, you had enough running backs to run some of it, right?

BROYLES: We ran the option play out of the "I" rather than have all three backs back there. We kept a flanker but we ran the principle of the Wishbone by riding the fullback, or the quarterback keeping it, and Scott Bull was voted outstanding player of the Cotton Bowl when we defeated Georgia, and he did it with the option play.

DF: So that's a little bit of a precursor to the Nebraska offense?

BROYLES: Yeah, the same thing. Nebraska ran it later with the I-formation.

Photo courtesy of Bill Horn

MERV JOHNSON. Having coached at OU for nineteen years, Merv is now director of football operations.

"MERV, WHO'S THE BEST OFFENSIVE LINE COACH IN THE COUNTRY?"

Merv Johnson is universally liked in the Oklahoma University system. He's just a nice guy. He's also a coaching legend in his own right, having spent time at Arkansas, Missouri, Notre Dame, and, for the past quarter-century, Norman, Oklahoma.

Currently Director of Football Operations at OU, Johnson visited with the Die-Hard Fan inside the Switzer Center in early 2008. His enthusiasm for working with young men, and the lessons he learned from Barry Switzer, have earned him a self-described great job.

Johnson has had a weighty coaching career in his own right. As offensive coordinator at Notre Dame immediately before coming to OU, Johnson coached Joe Montana. "That ice game at the Cotton Bowl against Houston [an epic comeback by the Irish] was my last game there," he remembers.

Having coached at Missouri and Arkansas—part of the remarkable football coaching factory erected by Frank Broyles—Johnson was well-trained to come in and replace Gene Hochevar as offensive line coach.

When Switzer phoned in January 1979 and asked Johnson who he thought the best offensive line coach in the country was, both knew it wasn't a serious question. "I think I am, Barry," Johnson responded. That settled it, and Johnson would coach at OU until 1996.

Johnson oversaw a period transition for OU's offensive line priorities as players became heavier. The days of 250-pound guards were receding into the past, and Johnson helped build OU's unit into one of the best in the country, consistently pushing great players to even greater heights, and molding good players into champions. Of course, he had Billy Sims to run behind that first line. Johnson remains close to Switzer, and understands him and his place in history very well.

"So much of coaching is motivation," Johnson says. "He [Switzer] had fun coaching, and he made it fun for the people around him. He was the same every day."

Through the championships and Orange Bowls and All-Americans, Johnson knew that Oklahoma was a special place, and that the program also benefited from the Boss. "You won't find anyone more enjoyable. That's what's endeared him to the fans in Oklahoma—he shares that pioneering spirit with them. They don't like 'coach-speak' and Barry didn't do that. He can run into someone in Enid and see them ten years later and remember meeting them."

Johnson has been blessed himself to find stability in his career (due as much to his own ability as to opportunities he might "luck" into; Johnson is nothing if not modest). He knows the pitfalls of coaching and recognizes in Switzer the qualities that are needed to survive in a cut-throat world.

"He's as bright as he can be; he has a great football mind," says Johnson. He knows that Switzer too often is recognized more for his colorful personality than his achievements on the field. "If they underestimate him as an Xs and Os guy, they're making a huge mistake."

Johnson was at Switzer's side for some of the greatest wins in OU history. All those bright memories are still fixed firmly in his mind, but one rival in particular still sticks out.

"I'd lead off with Nebraska," he says. "It's too bad we couldn't have retained that game. It was so good for our conference, for college football."

Surrounded by photos and mementos of that era, Johnson recalls the cold days in Lincoln and the sunshine in Norman. "Every one of them was huge."

From his plum perch in the OU football complex, Johnson seems to be the glue that holds things together. In his position, he does a bit of everything, and draws on his vast experience in every area of coaching. For many years, OU fans have enjoyed his insightful analysis during radio broadcasts of the games. He clearly enjoys having had the opportunity to serve with coaching legends like Switzer, as well as the guy who currently occupies the big office down the hall.

"A lot of Coach Stoops's qualities are similar to Barry's. He has a brilliant football mind, and he's very much a 'buck stops here' guy." Johnson also shares another trait that Bob Stoops has in common with Switzer: "If a starter is out, he says, let's just go play. That gives a backup real confidence."

Johnson's plate is full every day. At any given moment, he might serve as liaison with pro scouts, log in high school video tapes and evaluate transcripts, handle the walk-on program, or book alumni speaking engagements. Johnson enjoys all of it—especially the daily interaction with the players. He also knows what Switzer knows:

"I've been fortunate enough to coach at places where you can win."

Merv Johnson—a true gentleman and coaching legend in his own right.

Sooners'

LIFETIME RECORD

BY YEAR

1895: 0-1
1896: 2-0
1897: 2-0
1898: 2-0
1899: 2-1
1900: 3-1-1
1901: 3-2
1902: 6-3
1903: 5-4-3
1904: 4-3-1
1905: 7-2
1906: 5-2-2
1907: 4-4
1908: 8-1-1
1909: 6-4
1910: 4-2-1
1911: 8-0
1912: 5-4
1913: 6-2
1914: 9-1-1
1915: 10-0
1916: 6-5
1917: 6-4-1
1918: 6-0
1919: 5-2-3
1920: 6-0-1
1921: 5-3
1922: 2-3-3
1923: 3-5
1924: 2-5-1
1925: 4-3-1
1926: 5-2-1
1927: 3-3-2
1928: 5-3
1929: 3-3-2
1930: 4-3-1
1931: 4-7-1
1932: 4-4-1
1933: 4-4-1
1934: 3-4-2
1935: 6-3
1936: 3-3-3
1937: 5-2-2
1938: 10-1
1939: 6-2-1
1940: 6-3
1941: 6-3
1942: 3-5-2
1943: 7-2
1944: 6-3-1
1945: 5-5
1946: 8-3
1947: 7-2-1
1948: 10-1
1949: 11-0
1950: 10-1
1951: 8-2
1952: 8-1-1
1953: 9-1-1
1954: 10-0
1955: 11-0
1956: 10-0
1957: 10-1
1958: 10-1
1959: 7-3
1960: 3-6-1
1961: 5-5
1962: 8-3
1963: 8-2
1964: 6-4-1
1965: 3-7
1966: 6-4
1967: 10-1
1968: 7-4
1969: 6-4
1970: 7-4-1
1971: 11-1
1972: 11-1
1973: 10-0-1
1974: 11-0
1975: 11-1
1976: 9-2-1
1977: 10-2
1978: 11-1
1979: 11-1
1980: 10-2
1981: 7-4-1
1982: 8-4
1983: 8-4
1984: 9-2-1
1985: 11-1
1986: 11-1
1987: 11-1
1988: 9-3
1989: 7-4
1990: 8-3
1991: 9-3
1992: 5-4-2
1993: 9-3
1994: 6-6
1995: 5-5-1
1996: 3-8
1997: 4-8
1998: 5-6
1999: 7-5
2000: 13-0
2001: 12-2
2002: 12-2
2003: 12-2
2004: 12-1
2005: 8-4
2006: 11-3
2007: 11-3

Chapter Six

THE CHAMPIONS

SPOTLIGHT ON OU'S SEVEN NATIONAL CHAMPIONSHIP TEAMS

In this chapter, we'll profile the five quarterbacks who have led OU to national championships: Josh Heupel, Claude Arnold, Jimmy Harris, Steve Davis, and Jamelle Holieway. With these remarkable athletes at the helm, Oklahoma went 10–1 in 1950; 11–0 and a 20–6 Orange Bowl win over Maryland in 1955; 10–0 in 1956; 11–0 in 1974; 11–1 in 1975; 11–1 in 1985; and a perfect 13–0 in 2000.

The Die-Hard Fan had a special day when we brought Claude Arnold to OU to pose for a photo with Josh Heupel—the first Sooner quarterback to win a national championship with the latest one. During the visit, Heupel said to Arnold admiringly, "You started all this!"

The day before OU's Red-White game in the spring of 2008, Arnold stood on the field where his great passing skills had produced one of the legendary comebacks in Sooner history: the 1950 free-for-all against Texas A&M. It was the same field upon which Heupel threw magic passes to upend then number one Nebraska in 2000.

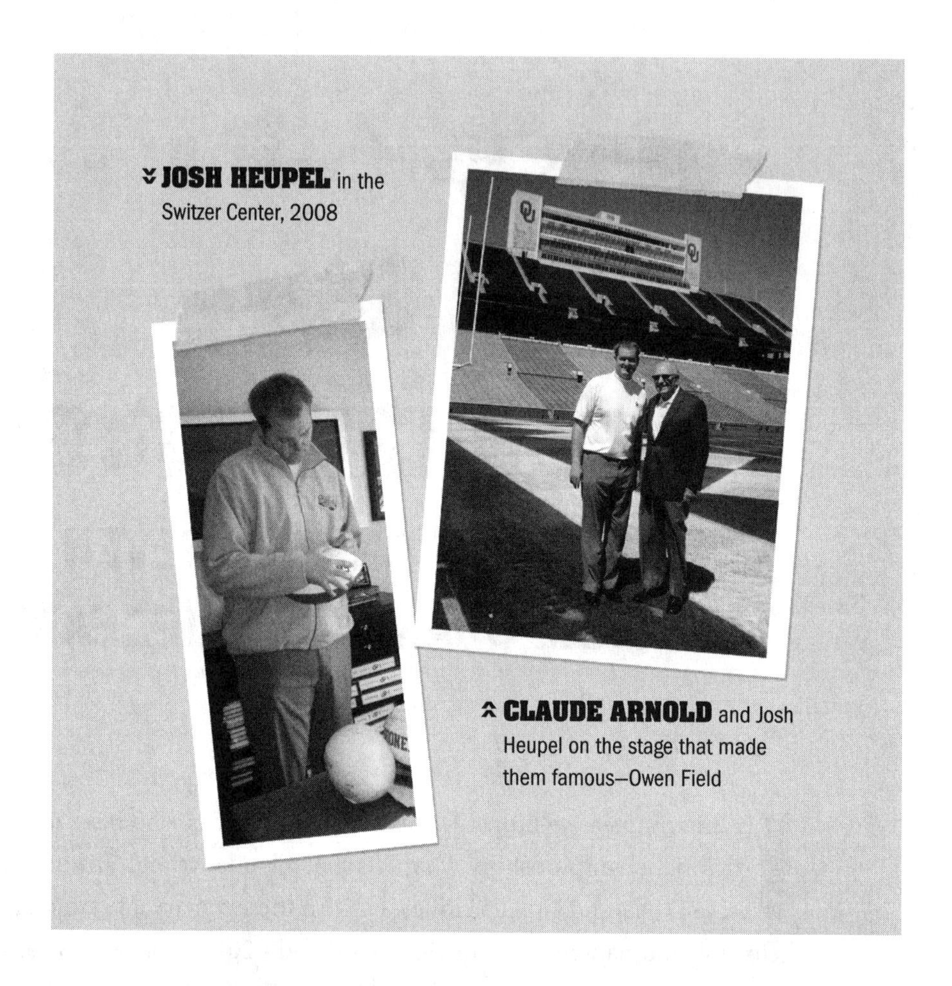

JOSH HEUPEL in the Switzer Center, 2008

CLAUDE ARNOLD and Josh Heupel on the stage that made them famous—Owen Field

Jimmy Harris was in town, too. These guys were the leaders of the greatest teams in OU history. Really, was anyone better?

A better question is: Who cares? As Heupel said to Arnold, "It's all relative." He meant that the old-time players who returned from winning World War II were tough, skilled, and lion-hearted—just like the guys who won it all in 2000 (or 1974–75, or 1985).

Driving past the shadows creeping over Owen Field, the Die-Hard Fan asked Arnold about Jack Jacobs, a truly great player at OU just before the war.

"If he was nationally known in those days, if he was so good and could have gone anywhere in the country, why did he pick OU?"

"Because he was an Oklahoma boy," Arnold said softly.

Thus, he revealed the key to Oklahoma's champions: homegrown boys who wanted it bad. They were players who knew it meant something to put on the Crimson and Cream.

JOSH HEUPEL: OU'S FIRST CHAMPION OF THE TWENTY-FIRST CENTURY

Josh Heupel is from South Dakota, but today he is an Oklahoma boy: he works as an assistant coach at OU. He was adopted as a bona fide Okie at some undetermined point in his college career in Norman. Maybe it was when he hit Andre Wolfolk with that acrobatic catch.

Or maybe it was on that cloudy day in Dallas that still plays over and over in Sooner minds like some fantastic Christmas present: "Time Life Presents Epic Victories: Oklahoma Destroys Texas."

But it could be that Heupel became an Okie during his recruiting visit in the winter of 1999. He was playing at Snow Junior College when OU assistant Mike Leach contacted him, sensing that the blonde passer could be something special.

"It's true that I asked Coach Stoops two questions when we met on my recruiting visit," Heupel remembers. "I asked him if we could win a Big 12 championship and a national championship. He said yes to both questions."

Heupel made this comment as we walked toward the football offices, past Heisman Park. He should really be immortalized there, with his own bronze statue. But walking past the frozen Billy Vessels, Jason White, Steve Owens, and Billy Sims, Heupel was lost in his thoughts about what mattered to him most from his playing days. He's too humble and too kind to comment on Florida State's Chris Weinke, who beat him out to win the 2000 Heisman Trophy. One senses Heupel truly doesn't care about that and has no hard feelings.

Why?

He has a ring. Winning is what mattered to him, both then and now.

Heupel came in with a reputation as a cerebral coach's son who could read defenses. He also had a pretty good arm. In 1999, he led OU back to

> **"If anyone has produced a super-human performance in what has been a marvelous and memorable season, it's [Josh] Heupel."**
>
> —*Tulsa World* writer Dave Sittler, describing the Sooner quarterback in the national championship season of 2000

respectability with a 7–5 record and an Independence Bowl berth. Disappointing close losses to Notre Dame and Texas fueled the team's determination in the off-season.

In 1999, Heupel threw for 341 yards in the opener against Indiana State, then had back-to-back 429-yard games against Baylor and Louisville. For the year, he threw for almost 4,000 yards. Suddenly, OU fans began getting used to this innovation known as the forward pass.

No one thought OU was special at the beginning of the 2000 season. Early games didn't inspire much confidence that they could win the Big 12 championship that Heupel and Stoops wanted so badly.

Then came October. In a three-game span, the Sooners blew out Texas, 63–14, defeated Kansas State at Manhattan, 41–31, and toppled No. 1 Nebraska, 31–14. Heupel's outstanding talent was particularly spotlighted in the KSU game, when he threw for 374 yards, accounting for all but eleven yards of OU's total offense.

An arm injury hampered the quarterback's effectiveness down the stretch—"I actually got hit twice on it against Kansas State, but you just shake it off and go play," he says. But he still led OU to the Big 12 championship game against Kansas State in Kansas City. On an icy, bitter night, OU came out on top, 27–24, for the school's first-ever twelve-win season.

Few gave the Sooners a chance against mighty Florida State in the Orange Bowl, but Stoops and Brent Venables devised a masterful defensive game plan that led to a historic 13–2 OU victory. Heupel had his championship.

It's obvious that he still treasures the ring today.

THE GREAT CLAUDE ARNOLD

Claude Arnold has a ring, too—from the 1950 season. His championship and Heupel's are separated by fifty years. Now eighty-three years old, Arnold still remembers his games as a Sooner as if he played them yesterday. The Die-Hard Fan sat down with Arnold and reminisced.

DF: Claude, *Sooners Illustrated* ran a great story about your time at OU in the December 2007 issue. But not as much is known about your Canadian pro career. Can you tell us about that?

ARNOLD: Funny story. Quite a few years ago, we were in Baja, California, at a friend's house down there on the coast. I was sitting out there one day reading Frank Gifford's book, and he writes about the year he graduated. He graduated the year after I did and he was playing the year I was working for Humble Oil out on the West Coast. He was originally the draft choice of the New York Giants, but they couldn't get it together, so he was about to sign with Edmonton for $8,500. Then, the Giants came back and offered him $500 more. I went inside and said to my wife, "Nancy, Nancy, this is when Edmonton started calling me!" Edmonton thought they had him and then they didn't, so they were kinda desperate! That's how I happened to go up to Edmonton.

DF: So when you graduated did the old NFL draft like they do now?

ARNOLD: Yeah, but I was twenty-seven and I wasn't a very high draft choice, so I didn't even consider playing.

DF: Business was more attractive?

ARNOLD: Yes, I was working in the oil business. Pro football wasn't anything I considered doing, and even when Canada called me I didn't consider it until they just kept calling. I actually went up there just to get a free trip to Canada. Nancy couldn't believe it when I came back and said we were moving.

DF: You had a reputation at OU for being a pretty good passer, right?

ARNOLD: Yeah, that was one of my talents.

DF: That didn't really fit the Split-T but they took advantage of your skill anyway, didn't they?

ARNOLD: Well yeah. We had to do something to come from behind a lot in 1950. We didn't work on passing a whole lot, but a lot more than they did in '46 and '47 and '48. We weren't strong

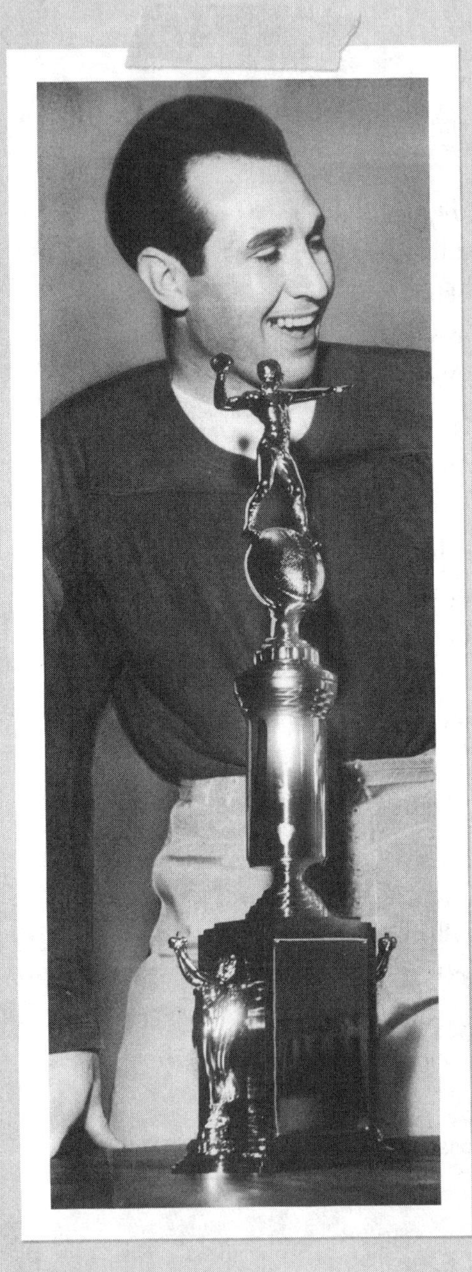

CLAUDE ARNOLD poses with OU's first national championship trophy

physically, as far as overwhelming everybody with the Split-T, and we had to throw. [Arnold threw for 1,200 yards in 1950.] You wouldn't think it was very many pass attempts, but it was about twice as many times as the year before and the year after.

DF: Who was your position coach?

ARNOLD: Bud [Wilkinson].

DF: So back in those days the head coach was that involved?

ARNOLD: Yeah, he ran the drills for the backs. There were only about five coaches on the staff.

DF: What was it like playing for Wilkinson? I mean, what stands out in your mind about him?

ARNOLD: Oh, he was just a unique guy. He was head and shoulders above the other coaches at that time. He was so articulate, such a gentleman, and his looks, the way he spoke, he was just a class act, and very brainy. Offensively he was very ahead of everyone.

DF: What do you think of Stoops now?

ARNOLD: Oh, I'm crazy about him. I think he's terrific.

DF: What was it like to be part of the first national championship at OU? What was it like in those days and what has it meant in the years since?

ARNOLD: Well, it meant a lot, but it's almost meant more afterwards than we realized it was going to at the time.

DF: When you were declared national champions, what happened?

ARNOLD: It was not what it would be now. We got some publicity for it. We got trophies.

DF: Did they give you rings then?

ARNOLD: No, we got a tall trophy. In 2000, the fifty-year anniversary, when we won the last one, they gave us the ring I'm wearing today. They gave us really nice rings.

DF: So how did they name you national champions? Did they just award it at the end of the season?

ARNOLD: Well, they had teams, you know, 1, 2, 3, just like they do now all through the season. We had been number one probably for several weeks, and in those days they named you after your last game before the bowl game, which was probably unfortunate for us because I don't think we were nearly as ready to play at the bowl game against Kentucky as we should have been.

DF: There was a letdown?

ARNOLD: We didn't play very well and they beat us 13–7, but they had a good team. I don't think we were as mentally ready to play like we were some other times, because we had already been named national champions.

DF: What happened on the field?

ARNOLD: We had a really good defense and our line wasn't like it was the year before. We had guys in there that weren't nearly as experienced as the '49 team. The Kentucky players were right in the middle of our handoffs a bunch of times. We had several fumbles. Then we got down to the goal line and lost five yards. See, in those days we called our own plays.

DF: Is that right?

ARNOLD: Yeah, and I had a brainstorm. It was third down and Vessels would have walked across the goal line, but one of our linemen failed to pull and the guy came across. Caught him for a five-yard loss.

DF: Was it in high school where you developed your passing skills? Did you guys throw much then?

> **"My mouth would get so dry I'd be sucking the sweat out of my T-shirt so I could call a play."**

ARNOLD: Well, yes. I weighed 127 when I was a junior. I weighed 142 when I was a senior, and OU still recruited me.

DF: And what were your height and playing weight at OU?

ARNOLD: About 180, six feet.

DF: And so you came to OU and they were running that Split-T. What were your impressions of that offense?

ARNOLD: Well, it was a great running offense, but I really didn't fit in.

DF: The Split-T is a little bit similar to the Wishbone. Did you run much option yourself?

ARNOLD: Oh we did, yeah. We either handed off or kept it and optioned off at the end, kind of like the Wishbone—very much like the Wishbone.

DF: And did you personally run much as a quarterback in high school or was that something you had to learn when you got to OU?

ARNOLD: Well, I was a halfback in high school, so I did run in high school.

DF: So the option wasn't that big of a deal. Even though you were known as a passing quarterback, you still ran.

ARNOLD: Yeah, yeah. I had 132 yards against Colorado. They had their defense set up to take the pitch, but I was just keeping it.

DF: So with the speed and conditioning emphasis, they ran you guys pretty good in practices, right?

ARNOLD: Oh yeah, they didn't give you any water. I can remember losing eleven pounds in one practice, and you know, we were just lucky we didn't have heat strokes. My mouth would get so dry I'd be sucking the sweat out of my T-shirt so I could call a play. And they wouldn't give you a sip of water. They thought that was the way to do it in those days.

DF: Amazing.

ARNOLD: Oh, it was just crazy! Just amazing.

DF: Who are some players you remember from those days?

ARNOLD: The guy that I was most impressed with was Jack Jacobs.

DF: Indian Jack?

ARNOLD: People don't know that today, but man, he could kick that ball. He was unreal. I think he still has the single-season punting average record.

DF: He was from Muskogee, right?

ARNOLD: Yes. I remember in high school, he was five years older than I was. I was just a kid and remember seeing him play against Okmulgee; he was a huge national star. He was written up in *Time* magazine.

DF: It sounds like he could have gone anywhere to play ball. Why did he pick OU?

ARNOLD: Because he was an Oklahoma boy. He was a good friend.

DF: And he played pro football for several years.

ARNOLD: Yeah, he played in the NFL for one or two years, and then he got lured to Winnipeg in Canada. I played against him those three years.

DF: What happened to Jacobs after his playing days?

ARNOLD: Jack died at fifty-two. He had a heart attack. I couldn't believe it. One of his relatives called me the day he died, and I went over to Muskogee. But he had played football until his forties. Couldn't get him to quit. He was such a good player—He was a fine defensive player too.

DF: Claude Arnold, thanks for speaking with us.

ARNOLD: Thank you.

JIMMY HARRIS: UNDEFEATED AT OU

The next Sooner quarterback won two championships, in 1955 and 1956. He also never lost a game—think about that. At the Red-White game of 2008, the Die-Hard Fan sat down with Jimmy Harris, OU quarterback from 1954 to 1956.

DF: What was it like to win back-to-back national titles?

HARRIS: Well, publicity is much more now than it was at the time, but of course everybody was conscious of what we'd done. I had played in high school and we had won the state championship and AAs in Texas. The reason I came to Oklahoma was because it was essential for winning it all and being a national champion. I mean, you kinda set your goals, so I was thinking that from the get-go, I guess.

DF: Those were remarkable teams that you played on.

HARRIS: I will tell you something interesting. For the first time, in 2006, when we had the fifty-year reunion, I saw the highlights for the '56 season and got a copy. They gave everybody a copy.

DF: That must have taken you back.

HARRIS: I am very proud of it. I mean, after my sophomore year, I was still young and naïve and of course you couldn't play as a freshman at that time, but we won them all and part of that was just the polls at that time. I guess Ohio State maybe won it, but we felt like we were as good as anybody. I felt like we were probably the best team, and you look back and we did have some great players. We had some great second-string players and some third-string players who were great. One of the guys I was talking to last night, Bob Derrick, hell, he was an extremely fast, great athlete. He played third-string most of the time as a running back. He was a 9.8 runner and he weighed 195 pounds, but he didn't start.

DF: Who else?

HARRIS: Oh, Billy Pricer. I mean, he kinda fit in like I did. Of course, quarterbacks got a little more publicity than a fullback did, but the two guys on each side of him his senior year made All-American—Clendon [Thomas] and Tommy McDonald. Billy's blocks, I mean, he could get out there and cut people down, and they wouldn't have made probably half the yardage had he not been that good. Most people don't realize that he played for the Colts for about five or six years. You know, he wasn't the star in the pros, either, but he was a tremendous athlete.

DF: And then of course, there was The Streak.

HARRIS: It is one of those things that makes you feel good, and it's like when I had to root for Texas when they were playing USC [in the 2006 Rose Bowl, to snap the Trojans' 34-game winning streak]. I love the fact that we went undefeated.

DF: What offense did you run in high school?

HARRIS: We ran the Single Wing and I was the tailback.

DF: So by the time you got to OU, you hadn't thrown much, right?

HARRIS: The only time we really threw would be right before a half. One of the longer passes was to Tommy McDonald at the OU-Texas game and that was right before the half. Of course Tommy's

JIMMY HARRIS is still wildly popular with OU fans

philosophy was, "It was a great catch—it wasn't a great throw." But that's just Tommy's demeanor.

DF: And so again, it's incredible that you had so many talented athletes on those teams.

HARRIS: It was discussed at that time that maybe the first two teams were the best in the nation. Some of the second-stringers always said they could have played just as well as the first-stringers, and I said, "Yeah, but Bud didn't have a first and second string; he had a starting unit and a follow-up unit, and I said I wanted to be on the starting unit."

DF: And you relied on speed and quickness.

HARRIS: Right. It's not the same game now. We didn't lift weights, either. Once I started pumping weights after I got out of college, I gained about twenty pounds.

DF: What was your playing weight at OU?

HARRIS: About 180, and I'm a little over six-foot-one. And again, they didn't start pumping weights until '61 or '62. And that was like running the 40 [yard-dash]. Nobody ran, you know? They can all talk about what they want to talk about, but I didn't run a 40 until I was with the Dallas Texans in 1960 and the Cowboys in '61. Before that, nobody did it. I could run 4.5, though, and that was after I had three knee operations.

Switzer has told the story about going to look at the old bunch from my era. He said they had films of, I guess, the '56 highlights, and they were going to look at them and laugh about how little and how slow the old guys were. But he said they thought they had it on high-speed. He couldn't believe it. Everything on the Split-T was just [claps his hands] and it was all over. All you wanted was just a little bit of an angle.

Jakie Sandefer, who is one of my good buddies, was a good hundred-yard-dasher. In the hundred, I was always about a 10-flat, but one day I ran against him. I couldn't run the hundred well—I'm short-legged—but I could outrun a bunch of people for the first twenty to forty yards; very seldom do you ever need more than forty yards. That's why they started doing the forty-yard dash

DF: Some make the mistake of comparing eras and claiming one team is better than another team, but I've heard Josh Heupel say that it's all relative. He acknowledged that your teams were gifted.

HARRIS: Oh yeah. Well, Heupel, I've got to brag on him. He is such a knowledgeable, interesting person. He came up to me early on—when they played in the bowl game down in Shreveport. I was out on the field visiting with one of the other coaches and he came up to me. He already knew who I was! He had been to the College Hall of Fame; he had already been up there, he had read everything that I had done and I was highly impressed with him. I've visited quite a bit with him since then and he's a very sharp guy. He is truly a great athlete. He could make things happen. Man, he could do it.

DF: You played in the secondary in the pros, right?

HARRIS: Yeah. I never got to throw the ball and never got to take a snap. I was in the league five years, but I was drafted as a defensive halfback and I was the forty-ninth guy drafted. I went down to Florida and played the North-South game, and I played fullback because I was the best guy down there. The pros saw my speed and agility, and I could hit, so it was one of those things.

In 1957, the Rams in the off season traded for me. In '58 I went out and played with the Rams and made $9,200—part of that was because I got $100 for every interception, up to four. We had a guy that was a substitute defensive back, but he was making $10,000. The next year, they sent me the same contract for $9,000 and I said, "I want $10,000." The Rams said they'd go to $9,500 and that was it, and I said, "Well I'm not coming back." I coached under Wilkinson as a defensive halfback coach, and got my degree in geology.

Later, I was going to Dallas to work as a geologist and at the same time, the Dallas Texans came into being. The same bunch that wouldn't pay me $10,000 had gone to the San Diego Chargers, and they called and asked, would I come play for them? I told them no, I'm through with pro football, I'm going to Dallas. And the Chargers said, "You know, we'll pay you $13,000 now." I said, "What? You wouldn't pay $10,000," and he said, "Well, things have changed. We now have competition, we've got two leagues."

So I go in and see Lamar Hunt and Jim Beavers. They were excited because I had two years of experience and they were trying to get anybody who could move or do anything. Beavers said, "How much do you want?" and I stupidly said, "Thirteen thousand dollars—that's what I've been offered." So they asked what I wanted up front. I mean, they were excited. So I ended up getting $3,000 up front and then the other $10,000 later, and then of course the Cowboys came in and the Rams [makes quotation signs with his hands] "traded me" to the Cowboys. They didn't have the contracts written, so I ended up going to the Cowboys and playing the next year.

After that I told Tom Landry that was it. When I was leaving he said, "What do you want, a no-cut contract?" I said, "No, I'm quitting. I can make as much money in the oil business. Maybe not quite as much, but they'll give me a car, they'll give me an expense account, and I'm not getting any younger and I don't want to be crippled like so many people are." So I quit. The only reason I went to the pros was to see if I could and once I realized I could play with those people, I wanted to go do something else because there wasn't any money in it.

DF: You had quite a career.

HARRIS: I had a good career—I didn't make All-Pro, I didn't make All-American but you know, I was always in the hunt. I guess I'd have loved to say, "Hell, I made All-American," but I never even came close.

DF: But you've got that winning streak.

HARRIS: Yeah, I'm proud of that. I'm also proud I got a couple of degrees and have been fairly successful. You know, I don't know if they could have done it without me, but they probably could have [laughs].

STEVE DAVIS: TWO-TIME NATIONAL CHAMPION

Steve was a three-year starter at quarterback—1973–75. In that span, Oklahoma won thirty-two games, three Big Eight championships, and two national titles.

DF: You're from Sallisaw.

DAVIS: Yeah.

DF: Were you originally from Muskogee?

DAVIS: No, no. I was born in Louisiana and raised in Sallisaw. My parents were from Sallisaw. My mom and dad were high school sweethearts.

DF: So how did you come to be born in Louisiana?

DAVIS: My father was in the Air Force. I was born at Barksdale Air Force Base in Bossier City, Louisiana.

DF: And at Sallisaw, did you play quarterback from the beginning?

DAVIS: In my early years, junior high school, I was a quarterback, defensive back, kicker, and punter. Sophomore year I was a defensive back. My junior year I was thrust into the position of tailback due to an injury. I think I learned how to run the football my junior year. I had a wonderful junior season and was actually competing on a statewide level with Grant Burget on scoring touchdowns, and Grant eventually became my teammate.

DF: So high school was a good time for you.

DAVIS: I had a lot of success in high school. Then my senior year I was quarterback and ran the option play and you know, did a lot of things that Oklahoma was doing.

DF: Okay, so you had a little bit of that background.

DAVIS: Oh yeah, yeah. Absolutely.

DF: Who was your high school coach?

DAVIS: Perry Lattimore. And Perry, my senior year at OU, died of a heart attack, and I had to go back to Sallisaw and preach at his funeral. So I lost my high school coach, but he was also a dear friend of our family and a mentor and just a good human being.

DF: So you arrived at OU in the fall of 1971?

DAVIS: Yeah, that was my freshman year. I was in the last freshman class that was not eligible to play varsity football. The '72 freshmen became eligible to play varsity. So I was a member of the last Boomer freshman football team.

DF: You were kind of buried on the depth chart early on.

DAVIS: I was, I was. I was not heavily recruited.

DF: Who did recruit you from the staff?

DAVIS: Leon Cross was the recruiter in that area. He had kind of a northeastern quadrant and then Larry Lacewell—Leon was north of I-40 and Larry Lacewell was south of I-40. There were an incredible number of guys that became starters at OU that played in the same 2A conference. You had all three Selmon brothers at Eufaula, you had Terry Webb who played at Muskogee, you had Wayne Hoffman and Rod Shoate at Spiro and me at Sallisaw, and we all ended up starting at Oklahoma. We all came from a little 2A conference.

DF: What was the recruiting experience like for you?

DAVIS: Like I said, I was not heavily recruited. I got a little bit of a soft look from Arkansas. OSU really didn't have an interest in me. I visited Baylor because I was a Baptist kid. I was a Boys' State Governor my junior year and went to Boys Nation, an American Legion program, and I had opportunities to go to one of the academies. My father really wanted me to go to an academy, so I had looked very seriously at going to West Point, but I wanted to go to OU. It was my dream. It was my high school dream.

When I got to Oklahoma, fortunately they were recruiting a lot of quarterbacks. They had a lot of scholarships and they recruited eight quarterbacks to try to find somebody that could imitate Jack Mildren, and I was one of those eight. I was the bottom of the eight but I was one of those eight, and through early fall drills I started out as number eight quarterback. My roommate was Larry McBroom from Ada. Larry was very, very talented but the first day of practice, Don Jimerson, my freshman coach, told all of us, "Don't worry about the depth chart, we had to slot you somewhere."

So we go in the dressing room after that first practice, and I look at my name and I'm number eight. That didn't bother me, but Larry McBroom was number seven and he was my roommate, and Larry had hurt his shoulder in the All-State game. He had shoulder surgery so he couldn't even practice, but he was number seven. I called my dad and I said, "Dad, I've got good news and bad news. The bad news is, I'm number eight on the depth chart. The good news is, I'm pretty confident I'm going to move up pretty quickly!" And that's how it started. [Former Oklahoma quarterback] Bobby Warmack was one

STEVE DAVIS TODAY. The winningest quarterback in Oklahoma history used the same competitiveness and skill he showed on the football field to become a successful real estate developer.

of the freshmen quarterback coaches and he had been my idol in high school, and I just picked up the offense faster than everybody else. Because I'd been a running back, I was able to take a hit, and I really loved running the offense and it was perfectly suited for my abilities and my talents. So that's how I ended up at that time, and I had a wonderful freshman season.

I got disenchanted my redshirt year, got overweight, slow, and seriously thought about leaving OU. Then over the Christmas holidays, going into that '73 spring, I really kind of dedicated myself to getting in shape and competing. Then lo and behold, we find out we're on probation. Kerry Jackson's suspended and I find myself earning the number one spot and then I wasn't going to turn loose of it once I got it.

"I wanted to go to OU. It was my dream. It was my high school dream."

DF: They describe you guys as real green coming into that season.

DAVIS: Yeah, we were. We were young and there were a lot of unknowns. A new coach, a new quarterback. Our defense was kind of small but pretty talented. And we were starting a freshman quarterback that had no reputation whatsoever and no real legacy. Think of the guys that they'd had. They had Jack Mildren, they had Bobby Warmack. OU had had great quarterbacks, guys that were pegged to be really great players, and I was not that kind of guy, but that's how I got started.

DF: So in 1973, as the season's going along, was there a particular point at which you guys thought, "Man, we could be really good?"

DAVIS: Probably when we played Southern Cal in the second game of the season. I think when we matched up with them the way we did, we knew we'd be okay. They were the defending champions of college football, the best in the country. They were big, they were strong, they were fast, they were seasoned, they were experienced, they were a veteran team with all the legends and all the lore attached to that program, and we went out there and fought them for sixty minutes and should have won the ballgame. We had plenty of opportunities to win the game, and I remember after that game I cried because I knew we should have won. It hit me just how passionate I needed to be as a player.

I think that was a launching pad for us that got us to realize that we can go compete. Coming back in the Miami game and winning that game late in the fourth quarter was big, and then when we massacred Texas, then I think there was no doubt. I think the program recognized that we were young, but that we were talented, that all the big question marks were now gone. You had a quarterback who was performing, you had young players that could make big plays, and the defense was getting better and better and better, and it was really fun.

DF: And I guess Switzer, as a motivator, was a big factor. What are your impressions of playing for him?

DAVIS: I think his greatest skill has been his ability to relate to players. He never forgot what it was like when he was a player, and players don't change a whole lot. There are a lot of outside influences that mold the perspectives and viewpoints that you have as a player, but I think he always had that very vital connection you have to have. I think he's believable, he's truthful, he'll look you in the eye and tell you what he thinks. You never felt that he was hyping you or giving you something that you couldn't handle. He treated us like young men. He expected us to perform. He was fair-minded. He was passionate. He was also compassionate, and I think that was probably the thing that was endearing.

And he made it fun. I mean, the old cliché that we're gonna go hang half-a-hundred on somebody—that came from his ability to look at a team and say, "There's no reason why we can't dominate this team, and I expect you to go out there and hang half-a-hundred on 'em and let somebody else play." And we did it, and did it week after week after week and Switzer would tell us, "There is no reason why this game shouldn't be over early. You know, let's let somebody else play."

DF: He had a different approach than a lot of coaches.

DAVIS: Yes, and I never felt like things were tight. I never felt any pressure. I never was nervous before ballgames. I was always excited—the bigger the game, the bigger the opportunity, and I think it just gave you a cool, calm confidence. You thought, "Hey, I'm prepared, I deserve to be here, now let's go out and play and go have fun." And that is what we did.

DF: So playing on that stage was not really pressure for you?

DAVIS: If you think that a game is pressure, then you don't deserve to be there because it's not that way at all. I mean, that's the grandest stage of college football and that's where you find players who are prepared and have dreamed all their lives to be on that kind of stage. That's what you live for. I never felt nervous or anxious. I mean, I just couldn't wait to get out there and go play, go match up, go see who's better. I never got tight. I was an excitable player, but I think I played within myself, and just knowing that I was going to go compete in front of 70,000 or 80,000 people and go find out who's best—it was great. If you're well prepared and you really have done your homework, there's no reason to feel pressure. Every player is different, though—I saw guys throw up. But I just couldn't wait to go play. I couldn't wait for Saturday to get here.

DF: When you guys ran the Wishbone, was most of it true read option or did you do a lot of predetermined stuff?

DAVIS: A lot of it was predetermined and certainly my junior and senior year we got more into the true read. Most defenses would tell you what they were going to do, and we felt like we were the dom-

DID YOU KNOW?

Bud Wilkinson was a friend of John F. Kennedy. In 1961, JFK named Wilkinson "Special Consultant on Youth Fitness to John Kennedy, President of the United States."

inant team in most cases, so we didn't need to take the risk of quarterback/fullback exchange and fumbling the ball. So a lot of our stuff was predetermined.

DF: In your three-year run there were so many huge plays, but what are a couple that really stand out to you?

DAVIS: I think probably the touchdown pass to Tinker Owens late in the Miami game my sophomore year was critical. Any one of the touchdown passes in the Texas game just broke their back. We had a real fun play against Colorado where we handed the ball to Joe Washington. Joe threw it back to me then I threw it to Wayne Hoffman. I mean, that was a fun game. That was my sophomore year. There were a couple of big plays in the OSU game. There were just all sorts of big plays that you can remember clearly.

"Switzer would tell us, 'There is no reason why this game shouldn't be over early. You know, let's let somebody else play.'"

The one my senior year against Texas, the Horace Ivory play, was big simply because I read the defense and changed the play and it made all the difference in the world. You know, there were just so many of them. Of course the Missouri game my senior year where Joe breaks it for the touchdown and then the extra point play was big. That was a critical, critical big play. In the Nebraska game, I guess it was my junior year up in Lincoln, there were several big plays. It was kind of tough sledding. Elvis Peacock fumbled the kickoff and we had to come back. There were several big third-down plays when I had big runs.

The things that I'll remember for the rest of my life are the great moments and great efforts by my teammates. I can remember Jimmy Littrell as a fullback and I remember many big plays that he made and incredible runs that Joe Washington made and being able to have the best seat in the house to watch what I think is the greatest football player that has ever played, you know, as a running back. So those are the kinds of things that will always be special to me.

CATCHING UP WITH

JIMBO ELROD

Elrod, as OU fans know, was an All-American defensive end from Tulsa East Central and played on two national championship teams (1974–75). The Die-Hard Fan visited with him after his radio show at O'Connell's.

DF: What was it like to play for those national championship teams? Obviously it's still meaningful. Those were special teams.

ELROD: To be fortunate enough to play on a team like that doesn't happen very often. You have Kansas in basketball, you know, Bill Self just did it. It might not be another ten years before you catch one, who knows? Bob Stoops won one in 2000. How long has it been, eight years? So when you're on a team that has a run like we did, just losing one and tying one in four years, it's just amazing. You're in awe as a player. As a player it is just a privilege to come here. And you really didn't think "I'm gonna be a starter," but when that happens you realize that you're there and it is just an amazing feeling.

We have the alumni functions. I've always come back except when I played in the NFL. I never miss them. I love coming back, and Coach Switzer, he always comes back, too. You won't find that every place, but he's tied to this university because of what he did here. He moved to Dallas and coached the Cowboys. Won a world championship, but where is he living now? Norman. All of his players mean so much to him that he just loves it here.

So it is really just a big family and we all love each other, we still do, and that is what I try to emphasize to these young players coming out now. You better enjoy your time here and take it all in and never forget it, because there are so many things that can happen from an experience at a place like this—especially for the Oklahoma kids that have a national powerhouse right down the street from them. I don't know why'd they want to go anywhere else.

DF: What was it like playing those series against Texas and Nebraska?

ELROD: Well, that's one thing I can say: we never lost in a four-year run against them. With Nebraska, it was nothing but *pure fun*! Pure fun and respect. Texas was Roosevelt Leaks and Earl Campbell and Marty Akins and all those guys—Brad Shear. I mean, you could go on and on, All-Americans on both sides of the ball just pounding the heck out of each other. Fortunately, we came out on the good end of that stick every year that I played here. I can always smile about it.

DF: Some of us remember that hit on Campbell in '74, when he fumbled late and you guys won, 16–13. Did you cause it or recover it?

ELROD: No, I caused the hit; I didn't recover the fumble. When Texas was running the Wishbone, Larry Lacewell was just a genius. He was one of the best defensive coordinators ever, and he just knew how to defend the Wishbone. We all had our assignments—take the fullback, take the quarterback, whatever the assignment was. On that particular play, Earl Campbell and I just happened to get to him right when the ball got to him and the rest was history.

JIMBO ELROD flashes some rare jewelry. Elrod was an All-American defensive end on two national championship-winning teams in 1974–75

DF: The post pattern to Tinker Owens against Michigan in the Orange Bowl—Elvis Peacock picks up a block to protect your blindside.

DAVIS: Absolutely. You know, I don't know how good those teams are compared to history. I know that we have two national championships to show for it, but I know that that was a three-year stretch of some pretty darn good football. Then how that '75 team evolved and how we came together; even the Kansas defeat represented a turning point. I mean, had we won against Kansas, I think we would have lost to Missouri the next week. That would have been devastating and we would not have had the chance to win a national championship. That was the wake-up call. That was the time when we began to realize that we need to go back to work, and maybe we need to think differently about the way we play. I think we did, and I know I did personally, and so some great things happened.

The other thing that is rarely mentioned in these types of books is that the things that really make for a great team are the things that happen away from the game events. It's the practices, it's the travel, it's the meetings, it's the off-season, it's the social time, it's those things that bind the team and cause a kid that might be an overly conservative small-town kid from Sallisaw to run around with a wild and crazy outside linebacker from Tulsa. Those are the kind of relationships, along with our relationship with our coaches, that helped to forge the greatness of those teams.

DF: You mentioned that three-year run. Do you think about it differently now than you did then? I mean, are you surprised now, looking back, that you guys never lost to Texas, Nebraska, or OSU?

DAVIS: Oh, I don't know. I know I didn't want to lose to any of those son-of-a-guns. I think when you're eighteen, nineteen, twenty, twenty-one, you don't have a clue of the gravity of how it affects you and will impact your life forever. You know, I will never get away from the fact that I was an Oklahoma quarterback. I will never get

“When you’re eighteen, nineteen, twenty, twenty-one, you don’t have a clue of the gravity of how it affects you and will impact your life forever. You know, I will never get away from the fact that I was an Oklahoma quarterback.”

away from the fact that I only lost one game. All of those things are a part of my legacy and my history.

I am very thankful for what happened. I don’t know that I would trade my career for any other quarterback that has ever played at OU. I really wouldn’t. I’ve had a chance to be a part of many more games than any quarterback that has ever played at Oklahoma and it’s not because I quarterbacked them, it’s because of the teams that I played on, and I think over time you start to learn and appreciate more what the team represented.

I think there were times in those years because we were so talented that we got a lot of attention. There were the stars and the non-stars, and I think some of that got kind of old. I can understand where kids get this sense of entitlement and I think I probably got wrapped up a little bit in that. As time has tempered my perspective and my experience of what really happened, I realize I was a part of a very special time in Oklahoma football history, and I’m very proud of my teammates and their journey and their experience and our collective efforts to do something that hadn’t been done in a long time. We always looked back to those teams of the ’50s as the guys that really were the standard. Our teams, ’74 and ’75, they kind of represented the new era of college football in terms of that next generation of players, and so, I think we did okay.

DF: And tradition breeds tradition.

DAVIS: Oh, absolutely. Absolutely. That’s the thing about great football traditions. I was at Oklahoma because of guys like Bobby Warmack and Steve Zabel and Steve Owens and Kenny Mendenhall and Granville Liggins—guys like that. Guys that I saw play when I was impressionable in my junior and senior years of high school, and that’s the way it works. Then guys like J.C. Watts will look to the teams that I played on, and we were the teams that impressed him as a youngster out of Eufaula and got him to come to Oklahoma.

So, this overlap of several generations or several years creates this tradition, and I feel like I had a part in some of the guys that came to Oklahoma because of the years that I played, just as Bobby Warmack and all those other guys of the '60s did for us, and that continues to go on and on. So, we are part of a very unique football family, and I think as you grow older you begin to think less about your own accomplishments and more about the collective whole. You carry the banner for a period of time and then it's time for you to pass it on to someone else, and I left it in better shape than I found it and I did my part. To go back to Owen Field and Memorial Stadium and know that two of the years that I played are memorialized on that press box and that those were some of the greatest years of Oklahoma football... my teammates and I did our part.

DF: Do you go back much?

DAVIS: I go back occasionally. I'm a businessman and my career really requires a lot of time and effort and I stay very busy, so I don't get to go back very often. But I do enjoy going back; it's good to see the younger generation do what they're trying to do to create their own legacy.

DF: Talk a bit about a guy like Dave Robertson.

DAVIS: The thing about Dave was that he was so outside his element. To me, that showed what an athlete he was, to be able to fit in an offense that was absolutely contrary to his ability. He was a passer, and to do what he did was absolutely great. There's a guy that's kind of an unsung hero in the sense that he waited, always in the backup role. He waited until his senior year and took full advantage and did something with it. Dave was solid, dependable, and made plays. I mean, he was a California, pro-style quarterback. I was a redshirt on that team, I was third-team quarterback behind Dave and Kerry, so I spent a lot of time with both of them.

DF: You talked a little bit about Jim Littrell, another unsung guy who was actually a great player.

"Jimmy would come out from a play and he'd be spitting blood."

DAVIS: The thing about Jimmy was, Jimmy was a tough, physical, passionate player. I mean, because of his running style, he would take serious hits. As a fullback he was probably a little undersized. Sticking it in there in that five hole the way he did, Jimmy would come out from a play and he'd be spitting blood and everything else. I just loved the way he played; he just ran hard, he gave it great effort and he was just one of those kids that I had such confidence that he was gonna do the right thing, make the right play, make the call, make the block, sacrifice his body, do all the things that you have to do as a Wishbone fullback. He was my favorite fullback, my favorite player in a lot of ways. He personified everything that you want in a football player at Oklahoma, and he was from Muskogee, which is tradition-rich in terms of what they produce and send to Oklahoma.

DF: Tinker Owens and Billy Brooks, split ends in the Wishbone—were they unselfish guys?

DAVIS: Yeah, they were. It upsets me that I was not a better thrower than I was, that I couldn't take advantage of their skills, but the thing is that we knew that we were prolific at running the football. That is what we were destined to do, and those guys could make big plays, and we did a fairly good job of utilizing them. They were a real threat out on the perimeter. I mean, who knows how much of a headache it caused the defensive coordinators, just knowing that they were out there? I was just efficient enough at throwing the long ball to cause them to think about it.

Those corners and safeties, they couldn't just fly to the ball. They had to be aware of where Tinker or Billy was, and that is the dynamics of the Wishbone. If you've got a quarterback that can occasionally hit the big ball, then that causes that defense to straighten up, and we did that a lot. We had a lot of success throwing the ball deep.

DF: Talk about some of your offensive linemen.

DAVIS: Oh, Kyle Davis [at center] my sophomore and junior year was a special player and another proud Oklahoma kid from Altus. Physical and tough and had my back all the time. I love Terry Webb, John Roush, Jerry Arnold; of course Wayne Hoffman, Karl Baldischwiler, Buck Buchanan my senior year, God rest his soul. Good players that were unselfish. It was incredible walking into that huddle knowing you got those big bodies in front of you. You could look at John Roush and say, "John, you're gonna have to make the block, you're gonna have to make the block here, John." I had a special relationship with those guys because I could look them in the eye on a critical down and tell them, "Guys, we need three and we've gotta make a play. Nobody jumps offside, let's concentrate on what we're doing, let's go get three," and that's what we'd do.

DF: The great Joe Washington touchdown run against Missouri in 1975—you guys decided to go for it on fourth down on your own 29.

DAVIS: Well, we had to. There wasn't any doubt we were gonna go for it. We were not going to get the ball back, probably, and the thing is, I was a little bit surprised at the call because we were only fourth-and-one. But running that offense, you could make a big play. I knew as soon as Joe made that break, I was headed to the sidelines because I knew he was gonna score. I'm over standing next to Switzer, talking about what we're going do for the extra point. I literally went to the sidelines because I saw him break and I said, "Okay, he's gone."

The main thing was, we knew we were going to get the ball to Joe and that was the critical part. We wanted to make sure in getting it to him that we didn't force the ball to him because if you force it to him early, then there is too much pursuit and he can't make the play. So the critical part was getting down the line of scrimmage, letting the defense react to me and then get the ball to Joe and let him go make it happen. And that's exactly how it played out.

DF: Was there some secret to your durability? Did anybody else take that many hits for three years?

DAVIS: Well, Jack [Mildren] played three years. Jack was a three-year quarterback, and I think Jack....

DF: He was a tough son-of-a-gun.

DAVIS: Jack's tough. Jack was tough. I know I never missed a start. I don't think Jack missed a start. I took a lot of hits, but you know, I was from Sequoyah County. I was a running back in high school. I was fairly tough and I could take a hit. I got bumps and bruises and I got hit a lot, but the thing is, that's just part of it. Again, I was perfectly suited in my skills and my physical abilities to play that offense and it was my time. Any other decade I probably wouldn't have made a difference, but on that stage, at that moment, that was my time.

"We knew that we were prolific at running the football. That is what we were destined to do."

I enjoyed the competition. I enjoyed the contact. It's a contact sport and the bigger the player—I wasn't gonna run out of bounds—I'm gonna take you on. As a quarterback in the Wishbone, you have to be almost built like a fullback. You've got to think like a quarterback, and you've got to run like a halfback. That's kind of the way it is. Again, the offense, the style of play was perfectly suited for my abilities. It was the right match for me.

JAMELLE HOLIEWAY: SEIZING THE LIMELIGHT

In 1985, Oklahoma was trying to run a kind of hybrid offense. Famous for the Wishbone, OU also faced a dilemma in that quarterback Troy Aikman was a very rare talent. The Henryetta star was six-foot-four and 220 and could run fairly well. But passing was his real forte—Aikman could really air it out. Barry Switzer decided to bring an NFL-talent passer into the offense with which he'd had so much success. With Aikman in the limelight, few noticed his small, freshman back-up from Los Angeles.

In the 1985 opener against Minnesota, Oklahoma couldn't have looked more ordinary. OU took a quick 10–0 lead, but couldn't score any more points aside from a field goal in the final quarter. Gopher quarterback Rickey Foggie threw a touchdown pass with four minutes left to whittle OU's lead down to 13–7. The Sooners, however, gained possession at their own 30 at the end of the game and ran out the clock.

The victory didn't inspire much confidence among Sooner fans. But the OU coaches knew what they had. The defense was strong, and it looked like they were in for a good year, if only they could bring Aikman and the offense along.

The next game, against Kansas State, gave cause for hope. OU's offense got untracked and Aikman looked sharp. The Sooners gained over 500 yards total offense, with fullback Lydell Carr running for 136. In the second half, back-up quarterback Jamelle Holieway had a 47-yard gain on his first carry as a Sooner, which turned out to be the longest run of his career.

As usual, Texas was the first real test. An OU fumble close to the goal line was returned by the Longhorns for a touchdown. That play paved the way for an old-fashioned defensive battle. Texas's defense was very good, but OU's was phenomenal. The Longhorns didn't threaten on offense at all, and the game ended with future NFL pro Brian Bosworth throwing Texas quarterback Todd Dodge around like a rag doll. OU won, 14–7, after Aikman pitched perfectly on the option to Patrick Collins, who ran forty-five yards down the sideline for a touchdown.

The following game, against Miami, proved the turning point in the season. In a play that effectively ended his playing career at OU, Aikman was sacked and broke his leg. The crowd fell silent as trainers attended to Aikman on the field. On the sidelines, the freshman Holieway threw on his helmet and began feverishly talking to OU coaches. After Aikman was helped off the field, Holieway ran into the huddle, welcomed with an ovation by appreciate but apprehensive Sooner fans.

Holieway's career got off to an inauspicious start that day. OU had trouble moving the ball, while the Hurricanes' Vinnie Testaverde put on a passing clinic, leading Miami to a 27–14 win.

OU bounced back against Iowa State the next week, as Holieway gave fans some hope that the season could be a good one despite the loss of Aikman. Early on, Holieway optioned for seventeen yards and a touchdown, then threw a 77-yard TD pass to Derrick Shepard. Notably, in the course of OU's 59–14 victory, backup quarterback Eric Mitchel ran for 135 yards on fifteen carries. This provoked some speculation among Sooner fans that a new battle might be looming over the team's quarterback position.

However, Holieway established his dominance in the following game against Kansas, running for 162 yards and throwing a 42-yard TD pass to Keith Jackson in a 48–6 victory. Despite being a mere five-foot-nine, Holieway was already well known for his passing ability. His high school coach once told him in passing drills to hit a wide receiver running forty yards downfield. "Over which shoulder, coach?" Holieway asked.

Any remaining doubts about Holieway were extinguished during the following game, against Missouri. Jamelle broke the game open with a 34-yard touchdown run after a fumble recovery by Paul Migliazzo. This led to a crushing 51–6 victory in which Holieway broke Jack Mildren's single-game offensive record.

The next victim was Colorado. Showing the Buffs how to run their new Wishbone—in Norman no less—Holieway led OU to a blowout 31–0 win. The quarterback ran for two touchdowns, while the Sooner defense throttled the Colorado offense, yielding only 109 yards and six first downs.

The Nebraska game is one that still lives in the hearts of Sooner fans. On an overcast day, Holieway put on a Wishbone clinic, running for 110 yards on twenty-five carries. This was Keith Jackson's celebrated "tight-end reverse" game, resulting in a 27–7 Sooner victory.

In the famous "Ice Bowl" the following week, OU lined up against Oklahoma State in Stillwater. Sub-freezing temperatures and heavy sleet made for a tough game for both teams, as linemen had to chip footholds in order to

OU'S FRESHMAN phenom, Jamelle Holieway

Photo courtesy of *Sooners Illustrated*

block, while backs slithered and fumbled. But Holieway kept his cool, and the offense recovered all six of its fumbles. Most important, the defense put in an outstanding performance, leading the Sooners to a 13–0 victory in a game no one will ever forget.

OU's last game of the season was against SMU. The match-up was originally slated as the season opener, and Barry Switzer's agreement to change the schedule proved fortuitous; by the end of the season, the Pony Express was beat-up and distracted by accusations of NCAA violations. They met a surging OU team in Norman. Holieway ran for 126 yards and threw a 38-yard TD pass to Lee Morris. OU won, 35–13, and headed for the Orange Bowl to face Penn State.

On New Year's Day, 1986, Holieway and his teammates came in confident, even behind a rebuilt offensive line reeling from injuries. Penn State's defense, though, proved tougher than expected. The Nittany Lions blitzed and stunted their way to an almost-even game. At halftime, the Sooners were up 16–10, thanks largely to a fine performance by field goal kicker Tim Lashar. OU's offense struggled, managing only twelve first downs for the game. However, Holieway threw a 71-yard strike to Jackson for a TD, and Lydell Carr ran sixty-one yards for a late touchdown to put the game away, 25–10.

Holieway thus became the only freshman to lead OU to a national championship.

"BOOMER SOONER" LYRICS

In 1905, Arthur M. Alden, a student in history and physiology whose father was a Norman jeweler, wrote the lyrics to the OU fight song, borrowing the tune from Yale University's "Boola Boola" but improvising the words. A year later, an addition was made to it from North Carolina's "I'm a Tarheel Born" and the two combined to form the university's fight song as it stands today. Though the tune was first made known at Yale, it was the everlasting success of Sooner squads that took the melody to national fame:

Boomer Sooner, Boomer Sooner
Boomer Sooner, Boomer Sooner
Boomer Sooner, Boomer Sooner
Boomer Sooner, OK U!
Oklahoma, Oklahoma
Oklahoma, Oklahoma
Oklahoma, Oklahoma
Oklahoma, OK U!
I'm a Sooner born and Sooner bred
and when I die, I'll be Sooner dead
Rah Oklahoma, Rah Oklahoma
Rah Oklahoma, OK U!

Chapter Seven

THE PLAYERS

REVERED OR NEGLECTED, THEIR LEGEND ENDURES

We all remember the stars of every era: Billy Sims. J.D. Roberts. Quentin Griffin.

But the discerning fan knows that a dynastic program like Oklahoma's only reaches the top with the help of key players who don't generate as many headlines. And you need a lot of them to reach the rarified atmosphere that the Oklahoma Beast breathes.

In this chapter, we will detail the Sooner superstars. But first, let's look at several players who didn't get the recognition they deserve. As Claude Arnold put it colorfully, "I was on teams with linemen who couldn't carry Leon Manley's jock strap." That's a strong endorsement from a superstar who knows what he's talking about. Arnold pointed out that the players with outgoing personalities usually got all the ink. Reporters and media-relations folks just naturally gravitate toward them.

Of course, there were a lot of players who deserved more attention—every Sooner fan will have a different list of them. Our collection here is

Photo courtesy of Oklahoma Historical Society

JACK JACOBS, quarterback and punter extraordinaire, 1941

incomplete, to be sure, but we hope it will capture the broad sweep of the history of Sooner football players. We love them all.

So without further adieu, let's take a look at some guys who were flat-out good, who made significant contributions to their teams, and who deserve to be remembered.

It seems fitting to start with **Leon Manley**.

A 207-pound tackle on OU's great unbeaten team of 1949, Manley had the same experience many fine players have had at Oklahoma: he played with stars. Yet Manley's teammates remember the Hollis native as a tough boot. "When we split into teams for practice, the first thing everyone did was see which team Manley was on," Arnold remembered years later. Manley later followed former teammate Darrell Royal to Austin, where he coached.

Mike Phillips was an undersized but quick defensive end from Galveston, whose playmaking ability bailed OU out of numerous tough situations. Remember his fumble recovery against Texas in 1975? Phillips was overshadowed by the Selmon brothers, Rod Shoate, and other great Sooners, but he was pretty danged good himself.

With the great Sooner teams of the mid-'80s featuring all-world tight-end Keith Jackson, head-hunter linebacker Brian Bosworth, and other big names, it's kind of easy to overlook the great punting of **Mike Winchester**. The young man from Marietta, Oklahoma, spent his youth kicking the ball in a field. Those long hours paid off on New Year's Day in Miami, 1986, when he helped the Sooners win their sixth national championship.

In the 1940s, football was put on the backburner for a half-decade due to a certain sneak attack in the Pacific. Americans were justifiably more concerned with winning a world war than dissecting the plays on the gridiron. But neither world events nor the subsequent Sooner dynasties should allow us to forget the incomparable **Jack Jacobs**. A full-blood Creek Indian, Jacobs remains perhaps the premier punter ever to wear an OU uniform. His passing ability was also stellar, and he went on to play for many years in the pros.

Someone always has to follow greatness, and in rare occurances, a man will play between superstars. Such was the case with **Gene Calame**, a fine Sooner quarterback in the early 1950s. He followed Eddie Crowder and was the predecessor to Jimmy Harris. Calame, a five-foot-ten, 165-pounder from Sulphur, was a solid player and a key part of the team that started OU's legendary forty-seven-game winning streak. In his senior year of 1954, he shared time with sophomore Jimmy Harris. A good runner and passer, Calame often saw heavy duty, including eighteen carries in a game against Oklahoma A&M.

Victor Hicks and Keith Jackson were well-known tight ends and four-year starters in the Wishbone. But the bridge between their OU careers was **Forrest Valora**, perhaps the finest blocking tight-end Barry Switzer ever had. At six-foot, 230 pounds, the athletic Valora notched two of the greatest catches in OU history: a 58-yard TD against Nebraska, and a two-point conversion to beat Florida State in the 1981 Orange Bowl. Both passes were delivered by J.C. Watts.

Anyone who saw **Jim Grisham** and **Carl McAdams** play would say it's ridiculous to have to include guys of their stature on a list of under-appreciated players. Still, time unjustly relegates some great players to the shadows. That fact, however, doesn't diminish the contributions they made to Oklahoma

> **"It [being part of the 1975 incoming class] was something you truly had the opportunity to hang your hat on. All the All-Americans and the All-Big Eight guys. . . . Several went to the NFL. What, four total Big Eight championships and a national championship? Hey, need I say any more?"**
>
> —Victor Hicks, incoming class of 1975

football history. Grisham was a fine runner in the early 1960s, while McAdams would rate among the best linebackers OU ever produced, even though he didn't wear earrings.

Roger Steffen wouldn't dominate ESPN's coverage of the NFL draft or cause a photo-finish Heisman race, but the Oklahoma native was a key linebacker for the 2000 national champions. He personified the dependable, unheralded players who complemented OU's stars on the road to the teams' championships.

As with every other position, OU has had its share of great centers: Jerry Tubbs, Bob Harrison, Tom Catlin, and Tom Brahaney, to name a few. But were any more valuable than **Jody Farthing**? The squat lineman from Midwest City started as a sophomore in 1976, didn't play in 1977, then returned as a starter in 1978 when Paul Tabor, a member of the heralded 1975 recruiting class, broke his hand and was shifted to guard. Farthing worked quietly and effectively, helping to block Billy Sims to the Heisman and proving himself to be one of OU's best-ever centers.

THE GREATEST RECRUITING CLASS IN OU HISTORY?

Which Sooner recruiting class was the best? That question is subject to endless debate. However, with its Schooner-load of star players, the 1975 cohort was a historic haul that Texans consider to be one of the greatest raids of all time. Seven class members made All-American, and half of the entire class went to the NFL. But what made this class really remarkable is that even the lesser-known players put in stellar years at OU.

Linebacker **Barry Dittman** and defensive end **Greg Sellmyer** didn't make the cover of *Sports Illustrated*, but they provided the nucleus of an outstanding defensive squad. **Woody Shepherd** spent his career behind speedier backs, but is immortalized by his 47-yard halfback pass to Steve Rhodes that helped beat Nebraska at Lincoln in 1976. **Mike Gaither** was set to be a great fullback in the mold of Leon Crosswhite, but had the misfortune of coming to OU at precisely the moment when the Sooners transitioned to smaller, faster fullbacks.

Those who signed with Oklahoma in February 1975 will be long-remembered:

- » **Tony Antone**, six-foot-three, 180 pounds, Lawton Eisenhower
- » **Mike Babb**, six-foot-two, 190 pounds, Ada
- » **Kent Bradford**, six-foot-three, 230 pounds, Putnam City
- » **Greg Byram**, six-foot-three, 190 pounds, Norman
- » **George Cumby**, six-foot-two, 195 pounds, Gorman, TX
- » **Barry Dittman**, six-foot-one, 205 pounds, Houston, TX, Clear Lake
- » **Mike Gaither**, six-foot-two, 207 pounds, Tulsa Memorial
- » **Bud Hebert**, six-foot, 187 pounds, Beaumont, TX, South Park
- » **Victor Hicks**, six-foot-four, 230 pounds, Lubbock, TX, Estacado
- » **Daryl Hunt**, six-foot-four, 200 pounds, Odessa, TX, Permian
- » **Ken King**, six-foot, 190 pounds, Clarendon, TX
- » **Reggie Kinlaw**, six-foot-two-and-a-half, 212 pounds, Miami, FL, Spring Branch
- » **Thomas Lott**, five-foot-eleven-and-a-half, 180 pounds, San Antonio, TX, John Jay
- » **Doug Morgan**, six-foot-two, 205 pounds, Baton Rouge, LA, Capitol
- » **Bill O'Gara**, six-foot-three, 230 pounds, Shawnee Mission, KS, Bishop Miege
- » **Wayne Pettis**, six-foot-three, 205 pounds, Monahans, TX
- » **Greg Roberts**, six-foot-four, 212 pounds, Nacogdoches, TX

- **Ron Ross**, six-foot-five, 235 pounds, Tulsa Memorial
- **Greg Sellmyer**, six-foot-two, 190 pounds, Amarillo, TX, Palo Duro
- **Woody Shepherd**, six-foot-one, 180 pounds, Odessa, TX
- **Billy Sims**, six-foot, 194 pounds, Hooks, TX
- **Paul Tabor**, six-foot-four, 200 pounds, Houston, TX, Spring Branch
- **John Trest**, six-foot-five, 235 pounds, Altus
- **Uwe von Schamann**, six-foot-two, 175 pounds, Ft. Worth, TX, Eastern Hills
- **Mark Wilson**, six-foot-five, 220 pounds, Dallas, TX, Highlands

There are some great players on this list, but there are also a lot of less-heralded guys who contributed immensely to the great Sooner teams of the late 1970s. Uwe von Schamann's game-winning field goal against Ohio State at Columbus in 1977 is remembered by all Sooner fans—beating Woody Haye's Buckeyes is still a jewel in the OU crown. But we should also recall that without **Mark Lucky**'s perfect snap and **Bud Hebert**'s sure hold, we wouldn't be celebrating at all. Lucky was as reliable as von Schamann, while Hebert, also in the secondary, intercepted three Florida State passes in the 1979 Orange Bowl.

Intercepting three passes in an Orange Bowl is no small feat, but Hebert shares that distinction with **Tony Rayburn**. The rangy safety played in an excellent secondary that also had Rickey Dixon, David Vickers, and Ledell Glenn. Rayburn's turn in the sun came in the 1986 Orange Bowl, when he picked off three Penn State passes to keep the Sooners close. OU pulled away in the fourth quarter to win 25–10, and the game remains a special moment for Rayburn.

"You know, Al Eschbach uses the story about those interceptions to talk about me," says Rayburn. "But in the Kansas State game that year, I think I had about five hit me in the hands, and I didn't catch one of them. Later, against Penn State, it was just one of those things. You concentrate. Plus, I was not going to be denied that year. The experience from playing Washington the year before [a 28–17 Orange Bowl defeat] was, mmmm... [grimaces] and so, you know, you just concentrate a little more. We'd studied them [the Nittany Lions] quite a bit, and so when we saw the sets, we'd just move into our positions and it was just one of those things."

In 1975, linebackers **Bill Dalke** and **Jamie Thomas** were thought to be less talented than predecessors like Rod Shoate. Truth be told, they weren't. Perhaps they didn't elicit the kinds of swoons that would greet future stars Daryl Hunt and George Cumby. But then again, they started for the national champions. Who can forget the photo of Dalke and Thomas sweating and grinning on the sidelines in the 1976 Orange Bowl, counting down the remaining seconds in an epic win over Michigan? They were instrumental in shutting down the vaunted attack of the Wolverines that night, led by Rick Leach and Gordon Bell.

Oklahoma's program has had an embarrassing number of superstars; finding one in a starting lineup is like closing your eyes and running your finger down a phone book listing. OU has had a particularly large number of great defensive tackles. We all know who they are. But has any of them ever been more valuable to a champion than **Ryan Fisher**? The Arlington, Texas native played on some pedestrian teams before Bob Stoops came along. But Fisher was rewarded in the national championship season of 2000. The big redhead was like one of those cement barriers in front of the White House: no one got past him. Strong and determined, he helped the Sooners form a truly great run defense. He is the classic "good" player who was really a great player.

Imagine this: you're a pretty good high school player and you get recruited by the great Oklahoma. Wow. As Navin Johnson would say, "Now I'm somebody!" But then imagine that you get to school and sitting at the dining table are the Selmon brothers, with Reggie Kinlaw later joining the party. That's the situation faced by defensive tackles **Anthony Bryant** and **Richard Murray**. But we can say with some justification that OU needed

Photo courtesy of Bill Horn

PAUL FERRER, all-purpose offensive lineman who contributed mightily to the national championship season of 1985

them badly at times. Both were very good players overshadowed by Mount Rushmore-type legends.

The same can be said for noseguards **Glen Comeaux** and **George Walrond**, from Port Arthur, Texas, and Lake Charles, Louisiana, respectively. They were fine players who just happened to play at the same time as Lucious and Dewey Selmon.

The 1985 national championship team was loaded with All-Americans. It was the year of Keith Jackson's 88-yard TD run against Nebraska. It was the season Jamelle Holieway broke Jack Mildren's single-game total offense record—as a freshman. A little-known player named Brian Bosworth also became a legend that year. But that team also needed the talents of guys like defensive ends **Mike Aljoe** and **Mike Mantle**, tight end **Darin Berryhill**, linebacker **Evan Gatewood**, O-lineman **Paul Ferrer**, and center **Ric Uhles**. Most of them spelled All-American starters, but each was a good player in his own right, possessing talent that would have ensured them a starting position at many other schools. Berryhill's blocking was vital, while Uhles, although perhaps undersized, still stopped Penn State cold on the road to the national title. Aljoe and the others could

> **"You need a lot of good players to complement the great players if you're going to be successful."**
>
> —Barry Switzer

be counted on to come in and hold their ground when the great Darrell Reed and Troy Johnson needed a breather.

As a senior in 2003, **Gayron Allen** was never going to sniff the NFL, much like teammates Lance Mitchell and Teddy Lehman. But when he replaced an injured Mitchell late in the season, incredibly, he graded out higher than anyone else on defense. A teammate the year before, **Brad Davis**, was a fireplug at offensive guard, but more gifted players kept starting ahead of him. Davis seemed destined for real anonymity. Then he stepped in his senior year and, coincidentally, Quentin Griffin wound up with one of the great rushing totals of all time, almost 1,900 yards. Davis's tenacity helped pave the way.

When Jimmy Harris singles someone out for praise, you know the guy must have been good. Such was the case with Woodward halfback **Robert Derrick**. "He ran third team and played at 195 pounds, and ran a 9.8 hundred," Harris remembers. "That's the kind of talent we had at Oklahoma then." Derrick and Harris played in an era when OU put up astonishing offensive numbers. In his senior year, Derrick got quality minutes, averaging seven yards per carry against Oklahoma A&M. He also played well on special teams, participating in the convoy that sprung David Baker on a 57-yard punt return against Kansas State

Billy Pricer was the guy who followed in the OU fullback tradition from players like Leon Heath and Buck McPhail. Harris still recalls Pricer's fine play today. Unfortunately, the Sooner Nation has lost all three of these fine men in the last few years. Heath and McPhail were stars and great athletes, while Pricer is part of Sooner immortality, having played during The Streak.

GAMEDAY HAUNTS

Hideaway Pizza, located at the famous Campus Corner (at the corner of Boyd and Buchanan) is a favorite of families on gameday.

"MR. HEISMAN IS CALLING!"

In this section, we'll spotlight the four Sooner players—three runners and a quarterback—who have won the highest individual prize: the Heisman Trophy.

BILLY SIMS: NOW YOU SEE HIM, NOW YOU DON'T

Sadie Sims knew her grandson was a good boy. That's why he'd left the tough neighborhoods of East St. Louis to start over in a little Texas town, Hooks, and have a chance at a better life.

Billy was always hard-working and responsible. Thus, it came as a shock to everyone when he went missing in the final days of the 1975 recruiting season.

> **"There was nothing like him for generating excitement. When Billy [Sims] played here people would be in the stands by 4:00 p.m. for a 7:30 p.m. game."**
>
> —Charlie Phillips, superintendent of schools, Hooks, Texas, 1978

Billy was—and still is—one of the greatest running backs to come out of the tradition-rich Lone Star State. At Hooks High, Sims ran for 7,738 yards and seventy-eight touchdowns. During his recruitment, OU assistant Bill Shimek greatly added to the Texas economy, essentially camping out in the Lone Star State for months in an effort to land Sims. Famously, Barry Switzer, at halftime of what ended up as a 49–14 blasting of Colorado at Boulder, phoned Sims to tell him he was thinking about him.

But now, in the recruiting excitement of the fateful winter of 1975, Billy Sims was missing. Checked out. Ran away in more spectacular fashion than he did from defenders on the field.

On the Sunday before signing day, Sims was at OU on a visit, but he disappeared sometime that night. Sims's friend and Hooks teammate, Charles Gurley, said that he had dropped Billy off at a gas station, where his car was parked. "That's the last time I saw him," he reported. On Tuesday, an anonymous caller told Mrs. Sims that Billy would return on Wednesday.

And indeed he did. It turns out that the pressure of recruiting got so intense that Sims just needed to get away from it for a little while. So he hid out at a friend's house, resurfacing on Wednesday. And much to the delight of Barry Switzer and his staff, Sims signed with OU.

In his freshman year, playing behind a slew of All-Americans, Sims saw some action, running for ninety-five yards on seventeen carries and scoring against both Iowa State and Nebraska. By 1976, he was primed to start.

A broken collarbone put the halfback out of action, however, and he redshirted. But he came back in 1977, starting the season in great fashion. A counter play the staff had put in for Ohio State proved deadly effective in the first half of that game, with Sims running for sixty yards and a 15-yard TD. OU scored seventeen points in the first quarter and took a 20–0 halftime lead.

Sims, though, injured an ankle and had to watch as OU gave up the lead, then came from behind to bang out a thrilling 29–28 victory. He returned in subsequent games and ran for 406 yards that year.

Interestingly, *Athlon* magazine profiled Sims for the 1978 season. No one could have known then that he would win the Heisman Trophy that year. No

Heisman Trophy winners (left to right): Steve Owens, Billy Vessels, and Billy Sims

Photo courtesy of Bill Horn

one, that is, except for Barry Switzer, who back in 1975 pointed to Sims and remarked, "There goes the 1978 Heisman winner."

The 1978 season began modestly for Sims. Lined up in a deluxe Wishbone backfield with David Overstreet, Kenny King, and Thomas Lott, Sims ran for 106 at Stanford, saw limited action in a blowout of Rice, then had a solid 131 yards in a 31–10 win over Texas.

Billy then went on a tear, running for 200 yards in three consecutive games. At Nebraska, he ran for 153 yards and nearly unraveled the Cornhuskers, despite nine fumbles by the Sooners, who recovered only three of them. Sims's fumble at the Nebraska 3, late, ended the Sooners's comeback hopes, but he rebounded with 209 yards on thirty carries in a 62–7 rout of Oklahoma State at Norman. Fate smiled on Sims and his teammates, as OU received an invitation to a rematch against Nebraska in the Orange Bowl.

Sims ran for 134 yards and two touchdowns as OU eclipsed Nebraska, 31–24. For the season, he ran for 1,762 yards on 231 carries—an average of 7.6—and scored twenty touchdowns. Although Sims was a Wishbone halfback, the coaching staff "broke the bone" for much of the year, lining Sims up in the I-formation.

As a senior in 1979, Sims was pitted against USC's Charles White for the Heisman. A *Sports Illustrated* cover story showed the two good-naturedly tugging on the trophy. It seemed almost pre-determined that White would win, and he did, but Sims put his stamp on the end of the season with monster games back-to-back against Missouri and Nebraska.

Approaching 1,000 yards for the year, Sims exploded for a career-best 282 yards on thirty-six carries against Mizzou, including a 70-yard TD run, in a 24–22 win. Against the Cornhuskers, Sims had a highlight-reel run of seventy-one yards to put the Sooners into position for the winning score. Photographs show Switzer leaping into Sims's arms at the conclusion of the game.

In the Orange Bowl against Florida State, Sims ended his career at OU with 164 yards. He was chosen first in the NFL draft and played five seasons with the Detroit Lions.

Today he remains a fan favorite and has a series of "Billy Sims BBQ" restaurants around the state.

BILLY VESSELS: THE FIRST BILLY

Long before Billy Sims strapped on a helmet for OU, the Sooners enjoyed the services of another franchise runner. At six-foot-one, 195, Billy Vessels attracted plenty of recruiting attention, representing a rare package of power and speed in the early 1950s. Bud Wilkinson later said that Vessels was the toughest player he'd ever seen.

Vessels virtually raised himself in Cleveland, Oklahoma. Locals would help the youngster out, of course. But Billy was toughened by those days, and grew up to be a personable, successful person.

Vessels also benefited from excellent support. Like all three of OU's Heisman-winning running backs, he played with great fullbacks: Leon Heath and Buck McPhail. Linemen like Kurt Burris and Tom Catlin, both of whom made All-American at center, paved the way.

Vessels started as a sophomore with the national champion Sooner team of 1950. In 1951, he tore up a knee against Texas in the third game of the season. The Sooners went 8–2 that year, ironically winning their last seven games after the halfback's injury.

Vessels threw himself into his rehab as if it were the Orange Bowl. The spring following his injury, he ran with the Sooners' cross-country team, and in May entered the school's intramural meet. Vessels also rehabbed by running barefoot in the sand at the Arkansas River. "By August the sand was hot and dry, and it was difficult to navigate but great for my knees," he recalled.

In the Varsity-Alumni game, he scored on an 85-yard kickoff return.

His comeback year of 1952 was the one that everyone remembers. OU was dominating save for two games, including a 21–all tie against Colorado in the opener. Ironically, it was during OU's only loss of the season, a heartbreaking 27–21 defeat to Notre Dame at South Bend, that Vessels put in a performance that probably won him the Heisman.

In front of a national television audience of 20 million, Vessels ran for 195 yards on seventeen carries and scored all three Sooner touchdowns.

After catching a 28-yard TD pass from Eddie Crowder, Notre Dame tied the game at seven. Vessels then took a handoff from Crowder and burst into the secondary, cutting to the sideline and running sixty-two yards for a touchdown. Four minutes before halftime, Vessels took a pitch and received a "crushing downfield block" from Merrill Green, before finishing a 47-yard TD run.

Vessels later remarked about his 62-yard run, "I was a ten-second man in high school, but I never was faster than on that touchdown run."

That the Irish came back late to hand OU a disappointing loss. Nevertheless, the Sooners went on to blow out eight opponents, including a 49–20 drubbing of Texas. Vessels ran for 106 yards in that game, as OU walked over the Longhorns for four touchdowns in the first eleven minutes.

The day that he was presented with the Heisman, Vessels argued that Eddie Crowder and Buck McPhail, or even Larry Grigg on defense, could have won it as well. "They are responsible for 90 percent of my success," he claimed. Vessels also had some interesting comments about his own sports heroes:

> This may sound silly, but I am twenty-one and my sports hero is Mickey Mantle, who is only twenty. I met him for the first time this fall when our planes were grounded after the Notre Dame game. Before Mickey, my hero was Joe DiMaggio, but when DiMaggio quit baseball and Mickey took his place, I switched. Now I have a hero one year younger than myself.

Vessels was the second player picked in the 1953 NFL draft and opted to play in Canada for Edmonton. He later played for the Baltimore Colts in 1956.

STEVE OWENS: "YOU ARE THE WINNER"

Steve Owens played at OU between the Split-T days and the Wishbone, becoming a classic I-formation tailback. The six-foot-two, 215-pounder from Miami, Oklahoma, set himself apart, though, with a record of endurance that is remarkable for any era.

Owens made All-Big Eight three consecutive years, 1967-69, and was All-American his junior and senior years. He was also named Big Eight Player of the Year his last two seasons.

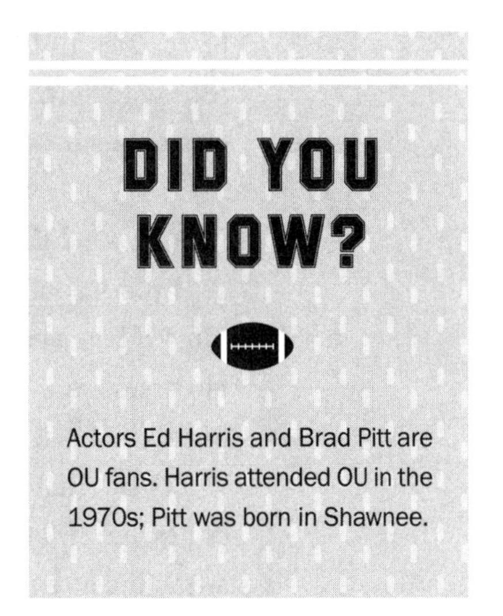

In three seasons, he ran for 4,041 yards and fifty-five touchdowns.

As a sophomore, he ran for 813 yards and twelve touchdowns, scoring against Tennessee in OU's dramatic 26–24 Orange Bowl victory. His top rushing totals came as a junior, when he had 1,536 yards on 357 carries. His season highlight came when he scored five touchdowns in a 47–0 massacre of Nebraska.

Head Coach Chuck Fairbanks remarked: "Steve is the greatest inside runner I've ever seen. He is remarkable at diagnosing defenses and finding holes. He has tremendous durability and strength."

At noon on Tuesday, November 25, 1969, a member of the Heisman Trophy Committee called University of Oklahoma President J. Herbert Hollomon. Initially a maid picked up the phone and was promptly informed that Owens had won the Heisman. Confused by the message, the maid summoned Hollomon and told him that Hollomon himself had won the Heisman.

Notified about the call, Owens raced with his wife, Barbara, across campus to take it. "You are the winner," the voice on the other end said.

Writer Katherine Hatch described the reaction of Oklahomans to the announcement that one of their own was a Heisman winner: "Even folks who had thought all autumn that a tailback was a new model Volkswagen were talking about Steve Owens and the Heisman Trophy."

Owens had some pretty solid help on a strong OU team, particularly from tailback Ron Shotts and fullback Mike Harper. After Owens won the Heisman, he attributed much of his success to Harper's legendary blocking.

Owens's durability is the stuff of legend—he once carried the ball fifty-five times against Oklahoma State. For his career, he registered a staggering

850 carries. In 1970, Owens was drafted by the Detroit Lions, playing five seasons in the pros. He later served as athletic director at OU and today is a successful businessman.

JASON WHITE: THE BLUE-COLLAR SUPERSTAR

Even Jason White would admit that the prospect of a bronze statue of himself being erected outside Oklahoma Memorial Stadium—what is called Heisman Park—was unlikely and maybe even laughable when he was growing up in Tuttle.

It's not that he wasn't highly recruited—he sparked a good deal of interest, especially at Miami. It's just that White's personality isn't geared toward attracting attention. He wasn't going to be at the Playboy mansion or chatting with network college football analysts. He just liked to play football.

As a freshman in 1999, he was in an uncertain quarterback mix. The situation seemed resolved, however, when Josh Heupel emerged as an All-American and national-championship winner. So White bided his time. In 2001, he competed with Georgia transfer Nate Hybl, with Hybl getting the nod. As a competitor, White was disappointed, but he waited some more.

Toward the beginning of the season, Hybl led OU to an electrifying 38–37 win against Kansas State. But the Wildcats defense pummeled the young quarterback. Although he finished out the Kansas State game, lingering injuries from the beating forced Hybl to bow out early from the following game, against Texas. White came in and led the Sooners to a 14–3 win. It marked a coming-out party for wide receiver Mark Clayton, who would make a ton of memorable plays with White over the next three years. Against Texas, White ran for thirty-eight yards and threw for 104. He quickly became known as a dual threat.

Later in the year, against Nebraska, White's knee buckled on a pass attempt as he was pushing away from an onrushing lineman. He crumpled to the turf with a torn anterior-cruciate ligament that would ruin his season.

White plunged into rehab the way he approached working for his father's concrete business: with relentless hard work.

BRENT VENABLES TALKS THE ★★★ UNSUNG PLAYERS

Brent Venables, current OU defensive coordinator and part of the staff since 1999, shared his thoughts about the players who toil in the shadow of stars.

DF: Coach, you guys have had stars here. The great linebackers who got a lot of ink, like Rocky Calmus and Teddy Lehman. But there were some pretty good players around them, too, right?

VENABLES: Oh, worth their weight in gold. First of all, this program has had guys that never had any sense of entitlement. You never had to ask them to do anything more than once. You have to have guys ready to have their bag packed and ready to go to come through when you need them. Roger Steffen and Gayron Allen are two classic examples. You know, it's something that Roger played here on the national championship team and beat out a four-or five-star recruited guy. That's a guy that has started for the San Francisco 49ers now for the last, I don't know, seven years maybe. Roger beat him out. He was changing positions, too, and hadn't been playing, but was just a team guy. Wasn't special at anything but was solid at a lot.

Gayron, it took two guys to go down in front of him [Lance Mitchell and Wayne Chambers]. He was a third-team linebacker and ended up starting on two back-to-back national championship-contending teams. And those couple of times when we weren't good—we lost once in '04 and once in '03—when we didn't play good in those two games, it wasn't because of him, man.

Not only that, but Gayron is on my linebacker drill fundamental board probably more than anyone else outside of Teddy Lehman. We have more clips of him

JAMES HALE, left, of OUInsider.com, interviews OU defensive coordinator Brent Venables, 2008

using the right technique of linebacker play, the fundamentals of the game, and my players all embraced that. They embrace him and really respect him, like they do with a lot of these guys that work hard here. When we watch the tape they see that it isn't always about your 4.5 speed and your four-hundred-pound bench press. Those things help, but if you don't have technique and fundamentals, you have nothing. If you're not in the right position and executing your responsibility, you have nothing. And when you just bind to the system, do what you're supposed to do, good things will happen for you and it happened for them as players. It also happened for them as young men contributing to this team, being a part of an experience of a lifetime and creating those memories and the legacy they've left for others to follow. You'll never be able to replace that.

By the time the 2002 season rolled around, he had beaten out Hybl. Sooner fans licked their chops, as they'd already seen enough of White's big arm and feet to know that he was a special talent.

Against Alabama, after tossing a 30-yard TD pass to Antwone Savage, White was running an option-keeper when his *other* knee buckled. Same injury, different knee.

He missed the rest of the year, and had to watch as OU fielded its first Rose Bowl team.

When the 2003 season approached, White was part of a quarterback battle featuring Paul Thompson, Noah Allen, and Brent Rawls. The highly recruited Rawls looked terrific in the spring Red-White game, while White tossed two interceptions.

As usual, though, the coaches knew what they were doing, and White earned his job back. As the season progressed, it became clear that White had reinvented himself as a dropback passer. He no longer relied on his rebuilt knees.

JASON WHITE'S
Heisman-winning performance of 2003 is immortalized at Owen Field

By the time of the Texas game, White had earned a reputation as an emerging star. Against the Longhorns, he established himself as an All-American candidate, throwing for 290 yards on 17-of-22 passing. His deep passes were incredible.

After the 77–0 slaughter of Texas A&M at Norman, in which White threw for five touchdowns in the first half, the national media was abuzz about the bionic quarterback.

White won the Heisman after throwing for 4,000 yards and forty touchdowns, against just eight interceptions. He decided to return for his senior season in 2004 and proved his greatness again, although by now it looked almost routine: White drops back, throws long to Clayton/Jones/Bradley, touchdown! In his final year as a Sooner, his key touchdown passes to Bradley, against Oklahoma State and Texas A&M, sent OU to the Orange Bowl as Big Twelve champions.

White today is part of OU royalty and makes many public appearances with fellow Heisman winners Steve Owens and Billy Sims. His statue stands alongside theirs in Heisman Park.

THE GREATEST "FORGOTTEN" PLAYER IN

★★★

OU HISTORY IS...

In a completely subjective, totally biased, and thoroughly unscientific poll, the Die-Hard Fan sifted through mountains of research—the books, the newspaper archives, the interviews—to discover the most underrated Sooner ever. At a place like Oklahoma, there are so many good players that they're stacked up like cordwood at each position. Yet, we found one player who really stands out for being sensational in his era, but largely obscure today. Like a comet, he streaked across the sky briefly and then faded from view. But we should remember...

Joe Golding!

Joe "Junior" Golding, a running back from Eufaula, came to OU in the fall of 1941. Shortly thereafter America was drawn into World War II. Golding went off to fight, but he returned to Norman amidst a confluence of factors that would transform Oklahoma's football team into a dynasty.

Golding had the privilege of playing with Jack Jacobs in 1941. But, as it turned out, Junior was just getting his feet wet back then. In 1946, he really got the chance to showcase his skills.

Jim Tatum worked the Sooners into shape in the spring and summer of 1946. He had a good nucleus of players returning, and a lot of them were coming back from real battle. They were mature men. Buddy Burris, Dee Andros, Jack Mitchell... guys who would lay the foundation for OU to become the winningest program in the modern era.

Junior wore No. 30 long before Greg Pruitt and Kenny King made the number a staple at OU gift shops. He weighed 185 during the war, but after returning to OU, got down to his playing weight of 171. (By contrast, his center, Max Fischer, was six-foot-four and weighed 174!)

George Brewer, freshman Darrell Royal, and quarterback Jack Mitchell rounded out the backs. Running from the "T" formation, Oklahoma's backfield was set; that is, until Golding was kicked in the knee during two-a-days, which had begun on September 1.

Tatum and Wilkinson held Golding out of practice for two days, anticipating an opening-day matchup with the mighty Army team. The defending national champions, Army was playing at home—and this was in the days of Glenn Davis and Doc Blanchard.

Golding was put in for the game but had a modest outing, gaining seventy-five yards on twelve carries. Although OU was handily defeated, 21–7, the team seemed to play better than the score indicated, giving rise to some optimism among the coaching staff.

In Game 2, against Texas A&M, the Sooners scratched-out a 10–7 win. It was in the next game, against Kansas State, that Golding broke loose, running for 164 yards and three touchdowns on seven carries (scoring runs of 43, 12, and 81 yards).

OU followed with a 63–0 dismantling of Iowa State at Ames, then held on in a driving rain the next week at TCU to win, 14–12.

A setback in Week 6 against Kansas at Lawrence still saw Golding pop for 130 yards, including a spectacular 65-yard TD run in which he ran over the right tackle, then cut back across the field.

Golding was nothing if not versatile. Like many players of his era, he played both offense and defense, usually in the same game. Once, playing defensive back against the Missouri Tigers, Golding intercepted the ball and returned it seventy-five yards for a score in a 27–6 home win.

After beating Nebraska at home, also by a 27–6 margin, Golding helped OU win a grudge match, 73–12, against Oklahoma State. Having been pounded by Oklahoma State in a 47–0 loss the previous year, his last year as OU coach, Dewey "Snorter" Luster came into the locker room after the 1946 win to thank the players for getting some payback against the team's cross-state rival.

In his final game at OU, in the Gator Bowl against North Carolina State, Golding went out in style. After the Wolfpack had tied the score at 7, Junior took the kickoff to his 35, then flipped the ball to Charles Sarratt, who galloped the final sixty-five yards to paydirt.

For the year, Golding rushed for 912 yards. Today, he would probably give a lot of credit to his offensive line. Incredibly, three O-linemen made All-American that year for OU: guards Plato Andros and Buddy Burris, and center John Rapacz. The offense was further solidified by tackles Wade Walker, who made AA in 1949, and Homer Paine, who played with his brothers, Charles and Clarence, and was a valuable lineman at OU his entire career.

The elusive, fast, and tough Golding later went on to play defensive back in the NFL for five years.

We salute Joe Golding!

Will Justice Prevail Today In Sugar Bowl?

NEW ORLEANS, Dec. 31—(AP)—The Sugar bowl football teams came to town Tuesday night, ready to show 73,000 observers Wednesday the comparative merits of Georgia's T-formation featuring all-American Charlie Trippi and North Carolina's single wing starring the sensational freshman, Charlie Justice.

There was scant hope, however, that the field and weather would be in condition for the triple-threat Charlies to display their best dipsy-doodings.

The U. S. weather bureau hints at heavy clouds and temperatures in the high 40's. There has been no sun yet to soak up all the rain which fell on the field the last couple of days.

Bulldogs Have Edge

Georgia's Bulldogs, unbeaten, untied co-champions of the Southeastern conference, are generally rated two

Probable Starters

Photo courtesy of the *Daily Oklahoman*

JOE GOLDING (on right) clowns around with Plato Andros before the Gator Bowl, 1946

Chapter Eight

THE FANS

THE BOND THAT CAN NEVER BE BROKEN

When one undertakes to write a book about OU football ("Aw, what do you want to write another book about Oklahoma football for?"—Larry Lacewell, June 2007) one quickly discovers that the coaches belong to an exclusive club. And the players belong to an exclusive club. In fact, pretty much anybody associated with The Program is, well, envied, if we're being honest.

"You clean the Sooners's locker rooms? Seriously? Cool!"

We like to see our champions on TV, but we also like to rub elbows with them if we can. That's why writers, when interviewing Bob Stoops, sheepishly ask the coach for an autograph for their own children. It's why we troop down to Norman just to watch a scrimmage. It's why we needlessly drive by the 7-Eleven, just in case the King is gassing up.

But one also realizes that for pure love and camaraderie, it's hard to beat the Fan Club. You don't have to donate any money or attend meetings. But on Game Day, we all stand together, whether we're at hallowed Owen Field, checking cattle on a Lawton farm, or huddled by a radio overseas.

SUPER-FAN Cecil Samara exhorts the Sooners

Photo courtesy of Bill Horn

We're part of the Sooner Nation. We have our own club. It's made up of folks from all walks of life. Middle-aged guys wearing game jerseys. Moms who know more football than their husbands and sons combined. Kids at recess who reveal their secret alter-ego as Adrian Peterson.

Occasionally, we are a guy who dresses all in red and drives a red Model-T to every game. That was Cecil Samara, the famous OU fan who got countless high-fives and thumbs-up as he rolled through a good chunk of Sooner history. The Die-Hard Fan remembers being a kid at the 1976 Varsity-Alumni game, looking to his left, and seeing an older fellow shouting and grinning, decked out all in red. When Samara turned to say something in his gravelly voice to the boy, the startled lad could see "Go Big Red" enameled on Samara's teeth.

Most of us fans are rank amateurs compared to the great Cecil. When he passed away in 1994, he was buried wearing plenty of Sooners gear, according to his wishes. Cecil, may you rest in peace, friend, knowing that your spirit lives on at every Sooners game.

For this chapter, the Die-Hard Fan solicited fan memories. And boy, was it fun. We are all the same if we love the Crimson and Cream. The Die-Hard Fan recalls his own grandmother, born and raised at Wetumka, settling in Oklahoma City. When she was eighty, she knew who was playing left halfback and who was playing right halfback in Oklahoma's Wishbone. She sat intently by the radio, a cigarette perched with its long, long ash too near her fingers. Somehow, despite her excitement, she never got burned, even if her "boys" were lighting up some hapless opponent to the tune of half-a-hundred.

Many thanks to the fans who contributed to this chapter, especially Randy Horn, whose dad, Bill, was quite a character and a fixture on the OU sideline for many years. Bill finagled his way onto the field by carrying a camera and, well, let's let Randy tell the story.

BILL HORN, "SOONER PHOTOGRAPHER"

—by Randy S. Horn

This is the story of one the greatest Sooner fans I have ever known—my father. His name was Bill Horn and he lived in Okmulgee. Born in August 1922, Dad grew up in Oklahoma during the Depression years. My grandmother had two large pecan trees in her yard. As I cracked and shelled pecans during cold winter days for her, she told me how they used to sell coffee cans full of shelled pecans during the Depression for five cents, and how Dad used the very same pecan cracker I was using.

The family moved around the state. They lived in Okmulgee, then moved to the Kiamichi mountains near Winding Stair Mountain, where they ran a family grocery store at Muskogee. They eventually made it back to Okmulgee.

As a kid, Dad hunted arrowheads and hopped trains, riding through Oklahoma, Arkansas, and Missouri. After fishing, his biggest passion was hunting rattlesnakes. He took me on a drive from Okmulgee to the Kiamichi Mountains when I was young, just to show me the exact spot where he caught his first rattler as a kid. It must have been a great way to grow up (except for the snake-hunting part).

Dad played high school football in Okmulgee and Muskogee. He was a running back. He was very small, but he was fast. When I was growing up, if I got in trouble there was no running from him. When he was about fifty years old, I saw him running sprints against workmates half his age. It wasn't even close!

I'm not sure when he became a Sooner fan. He talked a lot about the Bud Wilkinson years and "The Streak." I suppose he grew up a Sooner fan just like I did.

My first memory of OU football was the OU-Alabama Orange Bowl. I remember Dad being so upset he was cursing (he was good at that) and he even punched the wall. He had a great passion for

> **"A tremendous part in building our football program at the University of Oklahoma has been played by the officials of the University and the people of this state in lending their whole-hearted support and creating a favorable situation for intercollegiate football. The belief of these people in the value of our athletic program has at all times been evident."**
>
> —Bud Wilkinson

Sooner football. He didn't really start attending games until the Wishbone days, around 1976 or 1977. He never missed a home game and went to as many road games as he could.

In 1983, I was in the Air Force stationed in South Korea. I got up about 3:00 a.m. to watch the OU-Nebraska game on the Armed Forces Network. I had just gotten married, and my wife had never met my father. But she'd seen his picture, and suddenly during the game she pointed at the TV and yelled out, "There's your dad!" Sure enough, there he was. It was raining and cold, and he looked miserable (probably because we were losing). I will never forget that.

He was good, or perhaps just lucky, at being seen on camera during the games as he spent most of his time roaming the sidelines. When Marcus Dupree scored his first TD at Owen Field, a little guy came running into the end zone, jumped up and slapped him on the shoulder. Yes, it was my dad! During one of Barry Switzer and Tom Osborne's pre-game talks, Dad walked to the center of the field and listened intently to their conversation. After they were through talking, as Coach Osborne walked away, Dad asked Coach Switzer several questions which he cordially answered, probably thinking Dad was some kind of reporter. After a few minutes, he realized something wasn't quite right and asked, "You're not supposed to be here, are you?" Dad said, "I guess not," smiled, and calmly walked to the sideline.

He had a system at first. He learned the patterns of the security guards, the way they patrolled the sidelines. He would always move in the opposite direction and blend in with people who were supposed to be there. He brought his camera, which made him look like he belonged on the field, and he took lots of great pictures. After a few years went by, I guess they got used to seeing him and paid him no attention.

He spent most of his time after that around the Sooner bench. He became good friends with Billy Sims—at least, that's what he told me. At the time, I took the stories he told with a grain of salt. For me, being that close to the Sooner players and coaches was a fantasy. These were the guys I watched on TV and heard play on the radio every Saturday during high school while I was working at Hall's Bait Shop in Okmulgee.

Those days seem like a lifetime ago. Dad spoke of the many conversations he had with players and coaches, and the many friends he made at the games. He spent the famous OU-Texas tie on the sidelines under an umbrella with Bob Losure, a Tulsa news anchor who went on to work for CNN. They became very good friends and wrote each other often.

Dad said when David Overstreet, Billy Sims's roommate, was killed in Miami in a car accident, Billy asked if he had any good pictures of him. Dad said that he did and asked where he should send them. Billy said to just send them addressed to Billy Sims, Hooks Texas, and he would get them. So, that's what Dad did.

I got a sideline pass to the OU-OSU game in 1987 while I was home on leave. During the game Dad came up and wanted to introduce me to someone. When I turned around, there was Billy Sims extending his hand to shake mine. He was on crutches. This was during the time he was playing for Detroit and had injured his leg. I was surprised and very honored to shake the hand of such a great Sooner. I don't know if he still remembers Dad today, but I hope he does. I never doubted Dad's stories after that.

After Dad retired, he never missed a game. He would have never taken Mom to Hawaii if OU hadn't traveled there to play. It was his excuse not to miss a game—he gave Mom a trip to Hawaii, and he got to see the game and the USS *Arizona* memorial.

BILL HORN, OU's unofficial sideline photographer, poses with super back Greg Pruitt at a Varsity-Alumni game

He served in the Navy Armed Guard during WWII on merchant ships. He wouldn't talk about the war much, so I think he must have seen a lot of action. He did talk about the Kamikazes some. He was a 40 mm anti-aircraft gunner. This is part of what made him the man he was, I guess. He was tough as nails and wouldn't back down from anyone or anything.

During one of the games a new security guard started hassling him about being on the sidelines and told him to get off the field. Dad raised his camera, put it close to the guy's face, and "click." The guard asked why he did that and Dad told him he would need something to use for toilet paper when he got home, only he used much more colorful language. To some, that may be distasteful and vulgar, but I don't care who you are, that's funny! That was my dad.

One particular Saturday he and my mom were taking friends out to dinner to Jamil's steak house in Tulsa. Upon arriving at the restaurant, the OU game was still on the radio and dad was not about to go inside until it was over. Mom didn't think much of that plan and protested, but to no avail.

Dad was a huge Barry Switzer fan. He thought he was the greatest coach of all time and could do no wrong. I have never seen anyone as upset as Dad was when he resigned. Dad recorded the press conference and sent the tape to me in Florida. He said it would be the end of Sooner football as we knew it. I guess he was right, as it was the end of the Wishbone era. He continued to go to the games through the bad years, never giving up hope that Sooner football would once again be on top.

Dad was the happiest man I have ever seen during the 2000 season. After every game, or sometimes during them, I would call from Florida. All he wanted to talk about was football. I asked him after the third game what he thought about the team. He said we would be No. 1 and win the NC. I had my doubts, but Dad turned out to be right as usual.

Dad had a heart attack in 2002 and was close to dying. I took leave and went home to help out for a couple of weeks while my brother and I got things in order for him and my mom. The first thing Dad told me was, "There I was, about to die, and all I could think was that I would never get to watch OU football again!" If that's not a true Sooner fan, I don't know who is.

When I retired from the Air Force in 2003, I moved back to Oklahoma to take a job in Tulsa and help take care of my dad, whose health was failing by that time due to cancer. I watched every game with him until his death in the spring of 2005. I will always cherish that time. Dad, my older brother David, my two sons Jeremy and Jason, and I spent those games together cheering for OU. Three generations of die-hard Sooner fans going through the jubilation of the many wins and the bitter disappointment of the losses, all together with Dad for the last times in our lives.

When Dad passed, he was buried with the same OU jacket he is wearing in many of his pictures, and with his favorite OU cap. His eulogy was mostly about his passion for OU football and his love of photography, which has left us all some fantastic Sooner memories. He was a great fan and a great man.

Please raise a glass and toast one of the greatest Sooner fans of all time. I can still hear him saying "He's gone" when I watch games today, and I still see the wide smile on his face when he talked of all the great times he had in Norman attending football games—Sooner football games. He was proud to be a Sooner fan, and I was proud to call him Dad.

THE GOSPEL ACCORDING TO LUKE

—by Luke Neighbors

Let's begin with a little background. I was born at Norman Memorial and a few years later my family moved out to California, where my dad took on a position as pastor of a church. We both are die-hard OU fans. Being out in California, you get all the USC mumbo jumbo, but even out there my faith and fanhood never wavered.

Living in California made me realize that Sooner football is not something you acquire a taste for. You don't wake up one day and say, "Wow, they are good. I think I'll become a Sooner fan." It's something you are born and bred into. (I'm not trying to steal from "Boomer Sooner," but that's why the song was written that way.) A true Sooner fan is, from the day he or she is born, indoctrinated into the life that is Sooner football.

Photo courtesy of Luke Neighbors

LUKE NEIGHBORS' son, Tyson Alan Burr Neighbors, shows off his superb taste in headwear.

Living or dying on every win or loss, standing up to those (especially here in California) that harass you after a loss—that's what Sooner football is about.

You have to be there for the team in the good times and the bad.

My earliest memories of Sooner football date from 1990–92. My first OU game was the UCLA match in the Rose bowl. I also remember around that time, as an eight- or nine-year-old boy, crying my eyes out when we missed the field goal against Texas. And since 2000, I've been to at least one home game a year and every bowl game they've played in California. My wife, a California native, learned real quick that during those three to four hours on Saturday, she has to give me a kiss and a Dr. Pepper, and celebrate with me after a win or prop me up after a loss. She has now given me a wonderful son who I hope will one day play for OU.

OU football is a lifestyle that begins the moment you are born and ends... well, it never really ends.

My family's love for OU goes back several generations. My great uncle was a Rufneck back during the Bud Wilkerson days, and while he was at OU the team never lost. He is now up there in age, and was told by his doctor not to watch OU games due to his heart condition; the stress and excitement could provoke a heart attack. Well, you know that won't fly, so he came up with the idea of taping the games and watching them after they end. But he still cheats a little—his wife watches the games live, and if OU has a big lead, he joins her in front of the TV.

REMEMBERING THE MARSHALL

—by Levi Coe

I have been a Sooner fan since I was about five years old, and I remember watching my first game with my dad. My favorite Oklahoma memory is the 2000 season. In the lead-up to that season I told Dad, along with everyone else that would listen, "If Oklahoma can beat KSU on the road, then they'll be National Champions." My prediction drew a lot of laughs—our opponents for part of the schedule were known collectively as "Murderers's Row." But we beat KSU, and then we won against Texas. It started to look like my prediction would come true.

But we still had to face Nebraska in a game billed as "The Game of the Century, Part Two," as the sequel to the titanic OU-Nebraska match of 1971. As I'm sure you remember, NU jumped out on us early. I remember everyone in my house being down in the dumps. You could just see it on everyone's face—they thought it was all over. I told them to hold on, reminding them that we had a great quarterback who, I defiantly declared, would lead us to victory. And he did just that, with a lot of help from the OU defense.

I remember feeling pretty good going into the Texas A&M game; that is, until I watched ESPN's Gameday. I saw the Aggie crowd was going to be crazy, probably louder than anything these Sooners had ever heard. I was worried as the game got underway—Oklahoma looked a little flat and fell behind early. It was obvious they were going to be tested. I literally got down on my knees and began praying for something to turn the game around.

The Sooners started coming back in the second half, but I wondered if it would be enough. Would this be the end of the perfect season? It sure seemed like it might be—until "The Play." As I was still kneeling, Torrance Marshall got ready to make the play of his life. I remember it like it was yesterday—Torrance dropping back into coverage and making one heck of an interception on a quarterback who obviously never saw him. The sight of Torrance striding down that sideline with the ball was awesome; seeing him score was unbelievable. I ran through the house screaming like a madman.

Later, I went to the Big 12 championship game, which is the greatest game I've ever attended. After our victory we celebrated with the players, knowing Oklahoma was back. What a feeling to see my prediction come true, and what a season for a die-hard eighteen-year-old Sooner fan!

WAITING IT OUT IN THE LAND OF LINCOLN

—by Christopher Nickel

I'll tell you about my fondest OU memory: the 1986 Nebraska game in Lincoln. My parents were watching the game with friends, and the

THE CUTEST OU cheerleader ever, Lauren Spurlock, just happens to be the Die-Hard Fan's niece.

neighborhood kids were all playing football in the big yard on our street. We stopped to watch the OU game at a house across the street from mine.

With OU behind, none of the kids stayed past halftime, although they came back a few times in the second half to see Nebraska holding on to a 17–7 lead. Even though they'd given up on the Sooners, I stayed glued to the TV all by myself. My friends kept coming in and telling me to give up and come play so the teams would be even. I wasn't going anywhere, though, because I knew Jamelle was gonna pull us through.

In the fourth quarter, we narrowed the score to 17–10, then tied it with a touchdown. A friend finally sat down and watched the remainder of the game with me. When Lasher hit the winning field goal, I didn't say a word to anyone. The game ended, and I just went out and started playing football with the other kids. They asked if I enjoyed wasting my time watching OU lose. I nonchalantly told them I watched us win. Not one of them believed me until later that night when our game broke up. But I didn't care, because I sat through every second of it and they didn't.

I learned my lesson that day: I WILL NEVER stop watching an OU game until the last second ticks off the clock.

LONG RUNS, LONG MEMORIES

—by Roger McGee

I wrote this the evening I returned from my mother's funeral, Christmas Eve, 2004. It was posted on OUinsider. At the time I was single and living alone. There was a snowstorm that weekend that stranded most of my family in Tennessee. I felt quite alone, but the writing of it and the responses were quite therapeutic. Just thought it shows how deeply being a Sooner can affect one's life.

A SOONER MOM

Imogene McGee passed from this earth 3:30 a.m. Wednesday morning, December 22, 2004. She was 75 years old, and she loved watching the Sooners. My mother was 13 years old when her mother died from diabetes at the age of 38. Mom was forced to quit school and become the woman of the house, tending to the housework and raising her three-year-old sister, Meta, while their father worked to support the family. Married to a drunkard and gambler, Mom got divorced three months before I was born. I never met my father, nor did Mom ever remarry or even date. I had two brothers and a sister.

Not having a high school diploma, Mom was forced to work menial jobs for less than minimum wage, never receiving a dime in child support. We never had any money, but she always took care of us kids; she was a hell of a cook and we ate like kings (you just can't beat good ol' country cookin').

During junior high I began watching the Sooners. Who wouldn't get enamored with a team boasting players like Pruitt, Little Joe, and the Selmons. Mom always watched with me and loved watching the long runs the Wishbone was churning out during the 1970s.

In the military, I spent two years stationed in Greece from '77 through '79. Mom was working in a curtain factory as a seamstress the week before the Ohio State game. For the first time ever, she put a dollar down in a pool on the game, and Uwe won her $50 with the last-play field goal—one of the most famous plays in Sooner history. I smile every time I think of that. The next day in church the sermon was on the evils of betting on sports and gambling in general. But it was the only football pot Mom was ever in, and she had won. I received a long letter in Greece telling me all about it. After I'd left home in '75, Mom kept watching games, even by herself, up until Wednesday morning.

Mom's baby boy has grown up and has been following the Sooners around the country since Stoops arrived. She'll be at Joe Robbie

Stadium next Tuesday night with me, watching. If I could have one wish, I'd wish everyone could have as great a mother as I had. I've truly been blessed. I love you, Mom.

Sooners Rock! "Never Underestimate Tradition!"

BOOM, BOOM!

—By Lynn Rainwater

Upon exiting the Orange Bowl after beating Florida State for the national championship, I realized that my group of Sooner fans was walking alongside some Florida State fans. Showing some class, I restrained myself from digging them on the fact that their offense, #1 in the nation at the time, hadn't scored a point, and that we, of course, had to score their points for them.

After a minute or two (which almost seemed like an eternity because of my exuberance), an attractive lady in her mid-twenties turned and asked me, "Why are you people yelling 'Boomer/Sooner' back and forth? And what exactly is a 'Sooner,' anyway?"

I told her that we yell this back and forth across the stadium in Norman whenever a group of Sooners are together, and then briefly explained to her the history of the land runs in Oklahoma and the stories of the "Sooners" going in before the actual "BOOM" of the guns to signal the start.

She nodded and we continued walking alongside each other for a bit when she turned again to me and said, somewhat shocked, "You mean to tell me your team name is from someone who actually broke the law?" And so I replied, simply, "Yes." We walked about ten more steps and she blurted out to me, "Well, you still kicked our butts today."

Of course, everyone already knew that, but I was still a little surprised to hear her confirm it. I then wished her a safe journey home. She indicated morosely that it was going to be a long trip due to the outcome of the game.

TIMING IS EVERYTHING

—By Jody Manning

I have been a long-time Sooner fan beginning in earnest in 1985, when one night my dad told me we needed to watch Oklahoma play in the Orange Bowl. I had no idea what that meant, but after the game I was hooked. Watching a team representing the state win was just what this Oklahoma boy needed.

Fast forward to 1995, when I was a junior at Oklahoma Baptist University. Growing up with a family that was lukewarm to sports, I had not had the opportunity actually to witness a game firsthand.

My roommate at the time (and to this day my best friend) shared a similar fascination with OU football. It was a bit of a transition year for the team, but a friend of my roommate who attended OU said that she could get us a couple cheap tickets to the OSU game. While the team was struggling and neither of us was really enamored with the hiring of Schnellenberger, we loved our Sooners and did not want to pass up the chance.

To our dismay, we awoke game day morning to find that a winter storm had blown through. With each of our vehicles bearing tires equally unsuitable to the slick roads, we were in a dilemma as to whether it was worth driving from Shawnee to Norman in the icy conditions to watch our beloved, though struggling, Sooners.

We sat around our dorm room for the better part of the morning discussing what to do. Finally, we decided that there was no guarantee we'd get an opportunity in the near future to watch a game live, so we decided to go.

"Everyone has things that help them get through difficult things; mine is God, family, and OU football."

—A fan on OUInsider.com

We dressed in our warmest clothes and made our way out of the dorm. As we stood at the side exit, we stared at the ice and debated our decision one last time. Having agreed that we would not be swayed by a little inclement weather, we took our first steps outside.

I remember that I told my roommate that I hoped this would not turn out to be a bad idea. No sooner had the words escaped me than I heard a commotion behind me. I turned around only to witness the midstages of my roommate doing a most impressive scat dance, trying to avoid falling to the icy ground. He was unsuccessful and quickly kissed the sidewalk. He lay there and looked at me in a sheepish, yet contemplative, pose. While I admit that I cannot recall his exact words due to my excessive laughter, I do remember him relaying how worried he was that this was a sign that we should go back in the dorm.

After helping my wounded (mostly pride) friend to his feet, we made our way to Norman. Unfortunately, his fall was a bit of a foreshadowing, as OU lost that day. I can remember sitting in the north endzone, sixty-three rows up, taken with the sheer size and grandeur of the stadium and the beauty of the field, while being equally disappointed by the play on that field. We left the stadium cold and disappointed. To this day, though, I would not trade a moment of that game, as it was the truest introduction to live Sooner football. If I was not an addict before that game, I certainly was afterward.

As a sidenote, my buddy who was attending OU as a grad student called me just after John Blake was dismissed to ask if I would be interested in buying two season tickets. We had gone to two or three games during the Blake era and witnessed the team lose each time. At that point I was really wondering if winning football in Norman was a thing of the past. My friend talked about the team's possibilities if the administration could find the right coach. "Who knows, maybe in a few years they might at least be competitive," he said. I reluctantly agreed.

And since 1999, from our perch nine rows up in the same section every year, we have witnessed Coach Stoops and his teams once again dominate at home. Sometimes timing is everything.

NOW THERE'S A REAL

DIE-HARD FAN

Bryan Procter runs the website SoonerFever.com, where he has kept a diary of some of his experiences as an OU fan. How big a Sooner fan is he? This big:*

October 20th 2006 Well I just wanted you to know that I threw out my sacred lucky poker underwear that have been worn during every single game OU has played since Bob Stoops arrived. They were on during Red October run, they have been to Dallas, College Station, Lincoln, Stillwater, Boulder, they even made that hell trip to Miami in 2005 where my brother's car blew up and we left it in Birmingham, Alabama, only to be completely stripped on the way to the game. (My underwear screamed from the suitcase that it was a sign but I didn't listen). EVERY OU game since 1999 they have been on me. However, they ripped during the Oregon game. For the past three games I carefully hand washed them to ensure that they would stay intact. I wore them to the Middle Tennessee game even though my goodies were hanging out.

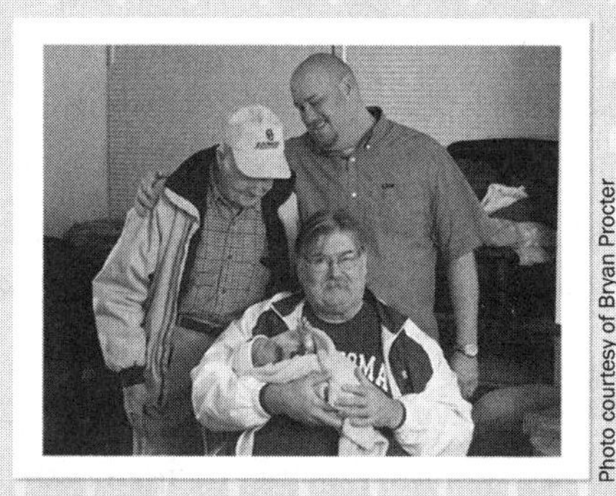

Photo courtesy of Bryan Procter

FOUR GENERATIONS of Sooners fans: Bryan Procter (standing, on right, hopefully not going commando) with Great-grandpa Lewis Procter (in cap), Grandpa Tom Procter, and baby Carter.

I thought about retiring them, locking them in the safe and bringing them out when my son was old enough to hear OU stories...you know, let him hold them while I reminisced about the good old days those undies had post-John Blake. I thought about having grandma sew them up, knowing that they would last another six years if she laid her hands on them. Then I thought about the fact that this has been the season of hell, with Bomar being a screw-up, the mishap at Oregon, Peterson's season-ending injury, the fact that I could probably start on the defensive line if I was in shape, and now finally Reggie Smith getting a hairline fracture on his foot and being doubtful for the next game. I finally realized that they had seen enough, there was no more luck in them, so I just wadded the sacred underwear up and threw them in the trash.

I will not wear another pair of underwear for game days the rest of the season. I will be commando for game day until next year, when I will then carefully select another pair to be my sacred game day underwear. It will be hard shoes to fill, these were extremely cool, with "feeling lucky" inscribed on the waistband and they had a special flap in the front for easy access. . . . But I digress. I don't know what exactly this means for myself or the state of Sooner Football but I thought I would share. . . .

Sincerely,

SoonerFever

PS: We are going to the Texas Tech game, I will have my camera in hand and I will be commando!

*Reprinted with permission, SoonerFever.com

A FAMILY AFFAIR

—by Grant Huffman

My mom and dad grew up in Medford, Oklahoma. My older brother and sister were born in Edmond, but I, along with my younger brothers, was born and raised in Kansas. I always felt I should have been born a Sooner! Every Thanksgiving, at least all the ones that I remember, was spent in Medford at the grandparents', Bill and Minnie Eulberg. As we drove down there from western Kansas, and later from Wichita, after we moved there, I would always make a sign out of cardboard and tape it to the side of the station wagon. Of course, like all good OU fans, I would always predict an OU victory over the 'Huskers. The best part, besides watching the game, was a spirited game of football afterward. I was lucky enough to have aunts and uncles that would get out and play with us.

One Thanksgiving in particular. My second-cousins from Minnesota had made the trip down. We must have had twenty people between the ages of twelve and thirty-five. That year we were lucky enough to go up to the high school and play some football on the field. I felt like I was playing for OU. We ended up having about ten on ten—pretty good for a family get-together. Some thirty years later, I still remember it like it was yesterday. It was during those Thanksgiving trips that my love for OU football got started. From an early age I remember my aunts and uncles jumping up and down, screaming in celebration, and listening to Boomer Sooner.

I went to my first game with my aunt and uncle, along with another aunt and her husband. I couldn't wait. It was the ISU game in 1977. I remember the colors; red and yellow. Thomas Lott wore his traditional bandanna, I believe yellow with red polka dots. It was a cold, rainy October day. We parked south of the stadium, and I clearly remember walking to the stadium in wet, soggy grass. I have since returned for many games, but that field where we parked isn't there anymore.

We had a small cooler with us—back then, it was still okay to bring them into the stadium, as long as there was no alcohol. As we got closer to the stadium, my uncle stopped to move the top row of pop over to cover the beer below. I got to carry the cooler so it wouldn't get inspected too closely. Can't say I wasn't nervous, but we passed through without a problem. I had my pop, they had their beer. I don't remember much of the game except for climbing up a ton of steps. OU won easily, though, 35–16. That was my first game and it was so much better than watching on TV!

As I grew older, I became the biggest OU fan in the family. I routinely received OU clothing and other memorabilia for my birthday and Christmas. I would always talk to my grandpa about the upcoming season. An old farmer, he forgot about his worries by immersing himself in OU football.

As with most fans, the success of the program just fueled my fervor for the team. It has been a great ride. My son now inherits the OU clothing and, hopefully, the passion I received from my family. Sometimes I look at him and my daughter and think, "Maybe they'll attend Oklahoma University some day."

THE THRILL OF VICTORY

In the early 1980s, Oklahoma's economy had taken some hits. People needed something to help them feel good again, to make it to the next day, the next month.

In 1985, the Sooner football team began to have one of those special seasons. In the 1986 Orange Bowl, Switzer's Sooners met Joe Paterno's Penn St. Nittany Lions. Just before kickoff, we learned that Tennessee had upset Miami in New Orleans. The setting was eerily reminiscent of the 1976 Orange Bowl, which was also for all the marbles.

We know of course that OU won that night, sealing the deal with Lydell Carr's 61-yard touchdown run late in the game.

A few weeks later, a handsome commemorative edition of *Sooners Illustrated* chronicled that magical season. One article in particular captured the moment:*

No. 1—It meant so much. . . .

Gerta Payne is a widow in her late 60's who lives in a mobile home west of Tulsa. She is not a football fan. She doesn't dislike the game. She's just never gotten involved in watching the game.

On New Year's night of 1986 Gerta Payne watched the end of her movie and, while looking for something else to watch, came across the telecast of the Orange Bowl Classic. The Oklahoma Sooners were playing for the national championship. She knew that much from talking to her daughter Caryll and son Jimmy.

So Gerta Payne watched for a while.

By the time Lydell Carr made his 61-yard run to start the celebration on the Sooner sideline, Ms. Payne was clapping her hands, shouting "We're No. 1" and walking through her lonely mobile home with the index finger of her right hand held aloft.

Cori Peterson has never been an OU fan. The 16-year-old sophomore at Jenks High School has never had any reason to dislike the Sooners. She has simply never gotten involved.

On New Year's night of 1986 Cori Peterson watched the celebration of Oklahoma's 25–10 triumph over Penn State with tears in her eyes. Tears of happiness.

Gary Jelinek and his brothers, Joey, Roger and Ronnie, are OU fans—BIG Sooner fans! They suffer with every loss. They suffer from January 2 through the start of the next season.

Gary had a little Orange Bowl "Watch Party" on New Year's night. He and his brothers and fifteen or sixteen friends got together in Gary's home near Mannford and moaned and groaned and cursed

---

*Reprinted with permission, *Sooners Illustrated*

and cheered and stomped some feet and got downright involved. There was plenty of shrimp and lobster and other snacks. Even a little liquid refreshment.

When Carr crossed the end zone to clinch the victory, the champagne bottles came out of the ice and the corks were popped. The celebration began in earnest. Except for Mike Cady, one of those fifteen or sixteen guests. Cady refused to begin his celebration until he saw OU head coach Barry Switzer being carried off the field on the shoulders of his new national champions.

National champions.

Has a nice ring to it. And it couldn't have come at a better time for Oklahomans.

It's been a tough two or three years in the state. It's not really getting much better. And holidays almost always make life tougher for those who are struggling.

New Year's night was one holiday that was worth celebrating. Oklahomans forgot about unemployment, layoffs, problems in school, a lean Christmas, and bills that were due the next day.

Their Sooners were hanging in there against Joe Paterno and his Nittany Lions, holding off one challenge after another and refusing to let that national title slip away. And Jimmy Johnson and his Aggies . . . oops . . . his Hurricanes . . . had already folded their tent in the Sugar Bowl and gone back to their hotel in New Orleans with absolutely nothing to say about the final ratings.

There wasn't much suspense on January 2. Oklahoma was named national champion in both the Associated Press and UPI polls. It wasn't a surprise. But it still had a nice ring to it.

National champions . . .

Members of that 1985 national championship team had no idea, of course, that their accomplishment in the Orange Bowl—or at least climaxed in the Orange Bowl—carried such an impact throughout the entire state of Oklahoma. Or that Sooner fans from Maine to

Southern California (and those in between in Pennsylvania!) were carrying their heads a little higher and smiling a little more often the next few days.

There was no way for them to know. Those 1985 Sooners had been dedicated all season long to winning the national championship. They did everything they could to do so. They got some help along the way. And they got their national championship.

It was not until those players and coaches returned home to Will Rogers World Airport in Oklahoma City at noon Friday, January 3, that they began to see just how their hard work and success had affected the state they represented.

The airport was crowded with fans who wanted to show their appreciation. Fans who wanted to get a look at their heroes, who wanted to have another memory to carry with them for years to come.

And there was the bus ride, with a police escort, from the airport to downtown Oklahoma City and Kerr Park for a massive celebration organized by the Oklahoma News Network (KTOK radio) and KTVY-TV (Channel 4 in Oklahoma City). During that bus ride the players watched as people pulled their cars off to the shoulder of the road, got out, and waved and shouted and cheered.

And there was the pep rally in downtown, where men, women, and children piled into Kerr Park, waited and waited for their team—some climbing trees or utility poles or hanging out of office windows—so that they, too, could see those national champions and let them know they loved them.

And the celebrations continued. On January 14 the city of Tulsa honored Lombardi winner Tony Casillas with a prestigious luncheon at the Summitt at the Fourth National Bank Building. The program was hosted by Tulsa attorney Larry Oliver and Oklahoma City businessmen E. W. "Dub" Giles. The invitation list was shorter than the number of actual guests. But no one seemed to mind. Casillas was given the Key to the City by Tulsa Mayor Terry Young. And Governor George Nigh was on hand to declare the day in honor of the Sooner All-American and to emphasize once more to the crowd of more than 200 just what the national championship meant to the state.

But no words could tell the story as well as the sight of Gerta Payne getting giddy over a football game . . . or Cori Peterson crying as OU players hugged each other and jumped with elation on the sidelines in Miami . . . or Gary Jelinek trying to talk Mike Cady into that glass of champagne before the final gun.

Ha-a-p-py New Year from the Oklahoma football team, Oklahoma!

THE RIVALS

THE ACCURSED TEAMS OF TEXAS AND NEBRASKA

OU has its share of despised opponents, but two stand out in their ability to get Sooner blood boiling—we're speaking, of course, of the University of Texas and the University of Nebraska. But we should really feel, on some level, grateful toward these teams for giving us several lifetimes of great moments on the field. After all, the Longhorns and Huskers enabled the Sooners to give us fans countless thrilling plays and rapturous OU victories. So this chapter is dedicated to our worthy rivals in Texas and Nebraska. To them we say: may your programs last forever—so we can beat you some more.

DARRELL ROYAL GOES INTO THE BELLY OF THE BEAST

In 1939, history's greatest comedy team had another classic hit on their hands. Laurel and Hardy's "Way Out West" followed the adventures of the goofy pair as they battled injustice in frontier America. At the same time, way

Sooners Pick Up Two Fresh

Pokes May Turn Speed Into

—Daily Oklahoman Staff Photo

Darrell Royal . . . packs the mail for Sooners.

Razzle-Dazzle Pioneers Face Cowboys First

By OTIS WILE

STILLWATER, Aug. 31.—Denver university's Sun bowl team, the defending champions of the Mountain States (Big Seven) conference, tip off the football season in Stillwater September 21, just three weeks hence.

Tulsa will be playing in Wichita for its opener that weekend and Oklahoma will be awaiting its trip to meet Army, leaving the state's big three field to the Cowpokes and Coach C. W. "Cap" Hubbard's boys from Denver.

This is a good schedule break for the fans interested in seeing what Coach Jim Lookabaugh's re-built Sugar Bowl champions are coming out with. It's being rumored about that Lookabaugh may lean more heavily toward the "T" this year, but Jim's devotion to the single-wing is well established.

Pioneers Play T

If the Aggies have even more speed this year than last, a factor now being argued frequently, it might swing them to more "T" formation stuff and more open play.

Denver is strictly "T" and the more wide-open the better. Hubbard began throwing razzle-dazzle to the Denver fans the day he took over at the Mile-High city and they love it in the Rockies.

Showmanship being a Hubbar characteristic DU, has given th Aggies the impression the last tw years that it would rather run wi flip a lateral and gain five yards th pick up an orthodox first down in dull charge through left guard. (Hubbard has been with Denver since 1932, head coach since 1939).

Dangerous Backs

While considerable has been made of fast John Karamigios, the galloping Greek of Denver who will duel Aggi Bob Fenimore again this year, it possible Denver's Bob Hazelhurst is more dangerous back. He runs fro the righthalf position, opposite Kara migios.

But the polished lad of DU's line up this year may be an end, Gregg Browning, a man they feel in the Rockies may make a serious all-America bid this year. Browning was all-Pacific Coast servicemen's end while performing with the San Diego NTS eleven and last season played with the Pearl Harbor all-stars. He was last at Denver in 1942. He's 6-1, 190, and does 9.9 in the century.

43 Lettermen Return

Browning is one of 43 returning lettermen at Denver, which means Hubbard has back most of his aces from the last four seasons.

Denver met New Orleans in the Sun Bowl last New Year's, losing 24-34. That score is indicative of the typica ... game. The Aggies and Denve ... a 33-21 game in 1944, wit ... wns all over the place. ... lly. Denver is one of fiv ... on the Aggie schedul ... gia from the Oil Bo ... Pres...

Hot Hurricane Sessions Melt Grid Squad to 85 Candidates

TULSA, Aug. 31.—(Special.)—Hot pace set by the University Tulsa football squad to make up for missing a summer practice d to be ready for the opener three weeks hence had reduced Hurricane from a record-breaking roll call of 130 players to Saturday as Coach J. Q. "Buddy" Brothers sent his charges ... the fourth day of

... Jay Francis, is closing in on ... ranks second to the

Chiefs Swing To High Gear

Head-man, super-chief Coach Bo Rowland will open the gridiron gates at Oklahoma City University Tuesday morning for the late arrivals and will devote the afternoon hours to the first autumn foot... ...ice, it ...nounced

Photo courtesy of the *Daily Oklahoman*

out there in western Oklahoma, in the tiny town of Hollis, Dick Highfill's most famous football player was running plays in his front yard while his family listened to OU broadcasts on the radio, which they'd place on the porch on Saturday afternoons.

Highfill, the high school football coach at Hollis, ran his own pipeline of players to Bud Wilkinson's Sooners. After World War II, guys like Leon Heath and Leon Manley followed the frontyard quarterback to glory at OU.

Darrell Royal vividly recalls those days.

"I was an Oklahoma fan when I was a little kid," Royal remembers. "We'd play out in the yard, listening to those games on the radio."

Oklahoma came calling early.

"By the time I was in high school, I was getting a lot of attention from recruiters. If I'd grown up in Texas, I'd have been a Texas fan. But I was from Oklahoma. If that doesn't make you loyal, you can't be had."

Royal could do it all: run, pass, kick, and of course, he excelled as a defensive back. He remains one of OU's greatest punters—observers of the time say he could put the ball wherever he wanted on the field. His versatility was a key asset to the Sooners, who had him replace the graduated All-American Jack Mitchell at quarterback his senior year. Plenty of fans consider that team, in 1949, to be the greatest of all time.

Royal played at 170 pounds while at OU and made All-American in 1949.

A coaching stop at Mississippi State led to a stint in Canada, where he coached many former OU players for the Edmonton Eskimos. Former teammates like Claude Arnold and Leon Manley remain wonderful friends, as does Royal's long-time golfing partner, former Arkansas head coach Frank Broyles.

It was a black day in Sooner history in 1957 when Royal signed on to coach OU's arch-nemesis, the Texas Longhorns. Royal held the job for two decades, retiring in 1976. Despite his long service to the enemy, however, Royal still feels a certain nostalgia for his Sooner days.

"I still have some loyalty to the University of Oklahoma," Royal says today from his home in Austin. "After all, that's where I got my start. I was a big fan of Oklahoma until I came to Texas. Then they became another opponent you

« **DARRELL ROYAL** as a freshman at Oklahoma, 1946. Royal, from Hollis, made All-American and excelled as a defensive back, punter, and quarterback.

had to prepare for. It's one experience as a player, but a coach's experience is totally different."

As Longhorn coach, Royal amassed an impressive record against the Sooners. After dropping his first game against OU, 21–7, he went on a tear, winning the next eight. (Mike Vachon's leg saved OU in 1966.) In twenty seasons at Texas, Darrell Royal beat his alma mater twelve times, against seven losses and one tie (his final match-up against OU ended at 6–6). His record against the Sooners was remarkable—that is, until Barry Switzer arrived; Royal never figured out how to beat Switzer, going 0–3 in head-to-head match-ups, with one tie. There is a myth that there's a lot of antipathy between the two former coaches to this day, but that doesn't appear to be true. Both men are secure in their own legacies, with little reason to resent other successful coaches. In fact, as the Die-Hard Fan left Norman one day, Switzer said of Royal, "Tell Coach I said hello."

Despite his regrettable stint in Texas, for true OU fans, Darrell Royal remains a big part of the glorious tradition built by the hard work of countless players and coaches.

Royal's service to Oklahoma has provoked many wonderful tributes from Sooner fans. Here's an excerpt from a particularly good one by Wann Smith that appeared online at CollegeTeamBoards.com:*

Darrell Royal, Sooner Legacy

> After Bud Wilkinson resigned following the 1963 season, there was a groundswell of support for the idea of bringing Darrell Royal back across the Red River. Royal was inundated by calls from old schoolmates and friends urging him to take the OU job.
>
> But Royal wasn't interested in returning to his home state. He had made it clear from the start that he had no interest in the Oklahoma coaching vacancy. However, Royal's decision to stay in Austin had nothing to do with any enmity for either the State of Okahoma or for his Alma Mater.

---

*Reprinted with permission, CollegeTeamBoards.com

"I had been searching for something," said Royal. "And I found it in Texas. Also, I didn't want to follow Coach Wilkinson. He'd have been a hard act to follow."

Royal also knew that had he returned to Norman he would have been eternally looked upon as one of Bud's students . . . a perpetual assistant. Also, considering the path that the nomadic Royal family followed in the six years following his college graduation . . . Norman to Raleigh . . . Raleigh to Tulsa . . . Tulsa to Starkville . . . Starkville to Edmonton . . . Edmonton back to Starkville . . . Starkville to Seattle . . . and finally Seattle to Austin . . . it should have come as no surprise that, after spending seven continuous years in Austin by the time the Oklahoma job became available, Darrell Royal would want to remain in Texas. He had established himself there. It was home.

"I haven't been back to Norman in years," said Royal. "But they've always treated me great when I did go back. There's a lot of emotion involved in the OU—Texas game but it shouldn't separate you from your home state or your friends, and it hasn't. My being down here has never affected any of the friendships I had with my OU teammates."

In 1996, Darrell K. Royal was afforded a rare honor. "The president of the university, Logan Wilson, phoned me," recalled Royal. "I thought, 'What in the world is he doing calling me?' I was pretty sure I hadn't done anything wrong, at least not intentionally. And he said 'I need your permission to do something,' and I couldn't imagine what that might be. So I asked him, 'What is it?' And he said, 'We've decided to put your name on the stadium.' There was a long silence and then he said 'Well, we have to have your approval.' And I said, 'Oh my goodness! You're asking for my permission to put my name on the stadium? The answer is yes, yes, yes!'"

Over the past half century, Darrell Royal has become more than the man who restored the pride and tradition of the University of Texas; he has become an institution. Royal, the boy who once played football with a tin can on the unpaved side streets of Hollis, has become larger than life. The teenager who once hitchhiked from

California to play football in Oklahoma now includes presidents and celebrities as well as teammates and colleagues in his circle of close friends.

But his days as a Sooner have not gone unappreciated, nor have they been forgotten by his native state.

We claim him, too.

THE OU-TEXAS GRUDGE MATCH: A BRIEF HISTORY

Many OU-Texas games over the years have become classics. Played annually at the Cotton Bowl in Dallas, Sooner-Longhorn match-ups have often been decided in low-scoring, defensive games, while a few were blowouts. Here we'll look at just a small number of the best games between these two powerhouse programs.

1947

In Bud Wilkinson's first season, there was explosive controversy at the OU-Texas game that, for some, continues to this day.

Texas, with Bobby Layne at quarterback, finished the season 9–1, beating OU 34–14 along the way. But it would be a call by a referee, Jack Sisco, that would go down in infamy in Norman that year.

As time ran down in the first half in Dallas, the teams were locked at seven each. Texas man-

SOONER SCHOONER

The "Sooner Schooner" is very familiar to OU fans. Introduced in the 1960s, it was officially chosen as the football program's on-field mascot in 1980. The Schooner, pulled by ponies "Boomer" and "Sooner," is reminiscent of the old covered wagons popularized by pioneers on the American prairie in the nineteenth and early twentieth centuries.

Photo published according to the GNU Free Documentation License

THE SOONER SCHOONER rides again.

An ugly controversy broke out over the past decade when the university debuted costumed mascots, also named Boomer and Sooner, whom disgruntled OU fans have derisively nicknamed "The Horse Pigs." The mascots are now being reconsidered.

aged to move to the OU three, where it appeared Randall Clay had been stopped and the clock had run out. However, Sisco came running in, claiming the Longhorns had called timeout with three seconds left. The officials gave Texas time for one more play—and the Longhorns scored.

Truth be told, the Sooners didn't help their own cause with their lost fumbles and numerous penalties. But that didn't mollify visiting Sooner fans, who sent cushions and bottles raining onto the field as time expired for the second time. Sisco was hustled away by security, but only after decking a charging Sooner fan.

1948

After an opening defeat at Santa Clara, OU didn't lose another game all season. In the third week, Wilkinson got his first win against Texas, 20–14. Junior Thomas scored twice, Leon Heath once, and OU held off the Longhorns late.

1958

A historic day, as it marked the first win by Darrell Royal's Longhorns against his alma mater, with OU getting edged out, 15–14. Texas scored first on a 10-yard pass on fourth-and-four, and Royal ordered a successful two-point attempt.

Bobby Boyd scored, but the Sooners' two-point try failed midway through the third quarter. Early in the fourth, the Sooners' Jim Davis scored on a 24-yard fumble recovery, but quarterback Bobby Lackey threw a 7-yard TD pass with three minutes left.

1966

It had been a long, long dry spell for Oklahoma when Jim Mackenzie's first team went to Dallas. Although Royal's Longhorns were down by their standards (after a 1963 national championship, they would finish 7–4 in '66), they were still Texas. But OU kicker Mike Vachon knocked through four field goals to seal an 18–9 Sooner win.

1972

OU's stout defense, overhauled and much more potent than the previous team's, shut out Texas, 27–0. Lucious Selmon, Derland Moore, and linebacker Rod Shoate led the way, as the Longhorns never really threatened all game long.

1982

After three straight losses in the series, it looked like some Longhorn fan had put a hex on the Sooners. Texas was good in 1982, but OU unveiled Marcus Dupree, who ran sixty-three yards for a TD the first time he got the ball. Weldon Ledbetter added 144 yards at fullback, and Switzer celebrated a 28–22 win.

1984

This is the "Jack Sisco" game for a new generation, as Barry Switzer ended up chasing officials down the field after the game. With OU clinging to a 15–12 lead late in the rain-soaked Cotton Bowl, a sliding Keith Stanberry intercepted the ball in the Nebraska endzone. The official, however, waived the play off, calling Stanberry out of bounds. On the next play, the Longhorns kicked a game-tying field goal as time ran out.

1993

In a troubled decade in which OU would only win twice against its chief rival, Gary Gibbs's Sooners won one for the Gibber. Gibbs had never lost to Texas as a player, and as a coach his superb defenses usually throttled the Longhorns. In this one, the Sooners trounced the Longhorns, with OU quarterback Cale Gundy throwing for 111 yards and running for two touchdowns. OU totaled 275 yards on the ground to win, 38–17.

2003

After OU decimated Texas, 63–14, in 2000, some in the Lone Star state consoled themselves by dismissing the game as a fluke. So Texas fans were still chomping at the bit for revenge in 2003. From the beginning of the game, however, Texas just could never get any momentum going. Cornerback Derrick Strait got OU off to a great start with an interception on Texas's first possession. Later, defensive end Jonathan Jackson picked off a Vince Young fumble and ran for a touchdown. Quarterback Jason White threw for 290 yards while OU finished things off on the ground in a 65–13 dismantling of the Longhorns.

ENTER THE CORNHUSKERS

If there's one rivalry that could match OU-Texas, it's OU-Nebraska. While some Sooner fans prefer the natural antipathy of the Red River Shootout, others can't help but dwell on the "Sooner Magic" that broke Husker hearts so many times. Those games in Lincoln sure were fun, as OU under Barry Switzer in particular made a habit of pulling a prairie jackrabbit out of the hat at the last possible moment.

Nebraska has been no pushover; outstanding coaches Bob Devaney and Dr. Tom Osborne won five national championships between them.

Oklahoma fans old enough to remember the simple red "N" on the white Nebraska helmets will also recall the great names from the series: Reynolds, Tagge, Rozier.

Great talent and superior coaching made Nebraska arguably the hardest team to beat in the 1970s and 1980s. The Cornhuskers were always so superbly prepared that it was a rare day when OU could blow them out. It happened a few times: 1973, 1975, 1977, 1985, 1990, and 2004. But the discerning fan will notice that those games were all in Norman. In Lincoln, the Sooners always seemed to have to fight just a little bit harder.

Let's take a look at some of the more memorable games played in both cities.

LINCOLN, 1947

This was Bud Wilkinson's first season as head coach. The Sooners played in cold, 25-degree weather on November 22. Early on, Nebraska's Cletus Fischer

NEBRASKA COACH Tom Osborne, exhausted after another dose of Sooner Magic

picked a Darrell Royal pass and raced sixty yards to paydirt, juking Royal at the 20. Thankfully for OU, Dick Hutton missed the extra point.

Junior Thomas and the Sooners answered immediately, with Thomas gaining thirty-six yards and a 10-yard TD on the drive. Amazingly, on a play that was unplanned, the Sooners recovered their own second-half kickoff after a short, high kick by Buddy Burris. Thomas scored again, from the two. On the extra point, which would prove critical, Dave Wallace hit it a bit under the ball, but it sailed through and OU took a 14-6 lead with less than three minutes gone in the second half.

The Cornhuskers countered on the ensuing drive, with quarterback Dick Thompson throwing a 27-yard strike to Alex Cochrane to pull within one point of the Sooners. After that, what had looked like a real shootout turned into a defensive struggle the rest of the way.

Late in the game, OU's defense came up big. It was at this point that Royal's almost mythic punting ability came to the forefront. Royal put the ball on Nebraska's 18, but according to Oklahoma City sportswriter Volney Meece, Royal "asked his field captain to take a penalty so he'd get another shot at coffin corner." Incredibly, Royal dropped this one on the 10, and shortly after, OU took home a 14–13 win.

NORMAN, 1950

Bobby Reynolds put on one of the greatest performances ever seen against the Sooners. Reynolds, an elusive, smallish back, ran for almost a hundred yards in the first half, sending Nebraska to the locker rooms with a 21–14 halftime lead. But in the second half, the OU offense really turned on the juice, led by sophomore running back Billy Vessels, who rushed for 208 yards on the day. Claude Arnold scored on a 16-yard run and later scored again from the one, and also threw a touchdown pass to fullback Leon Heath. Vessels scored on a spectacular 69-yard run, and was helped in the touchdown department by John Redell. In the end, the Sooners catapulted to an improbable 49–35 come-from-behind victory.

LINCOLN, 1959

OU's sheer dominance at the time provoked shock in Oklahoma when the Sooners lost their first conference game in twelve years. Bud Wilkinson suffered his first-ever loss in the conference this day, as Nebraska scored on a 61-yard punt return and held off OU late. Bobby Boyd's Hail Mary was intercepted in the endzone with twenty-five seconds left, leaving Nebraska with a 25–21 victory.

Oklahoma's superiority was beginning to fade in the lead-up to the game; the previous week, the Sooners had barely eeked out a 7–6 win against Kansas in Norman. OU still had some great athletes, but other teams were starting to come on strong. In a comment afterwards that seems almost quaint today in light of the titanic egos of many head coaches, Wilkinson remarked: "I must not be doing a good job of coaching or the team wouldn't continue to make the same type of basic mechanical errors so repeatedly in every game. I have always believed they were controllable if a team had the morale and discipline which results from proper leadership."

NORMAN, 1964

Gomer Jones never gets enough credit. Wilkinson's long-time assistant had taken over after the Man left OU to enter politics. Jones, a line coach for most of his career, was the bridge between the Wilkinson and Switzer dynasties who guided the Sooners for two years in the tumultuous 1960s.

After a rough 1–3 start to the season, Jones's Sooners were bound for the Gator Bowl. The team still had plenty of talent: quarterback Ronnie Fletcher, one of the finest passers in school history; fullback Jim Grisham; Ben Hart, who would catch a 95-yard TD strike from Fletcher in the Gator Bowl; linebacker Carl McAdams; tackles Ralph Neely and Bob Kalsu; and receiver Lance Rentzel. Also, perhaps fittingly, OU was buttressed in that difficult year by a sophomore fullback from Ponca City named Jon Kennedy.

This excellent lineup beat up Nebraska for a 17–7 win.

LINCOLN, 1972

Dave Robertson did what his superstar predecessor never did: beat Nebraska. He did it with his arm, passing to Tinker Owens for numerous completions that set up touchdowns. With ten minutes left in the game, Lucious Selmon recovered a fumble at the Nebraska 27, and Rick Fulcher kicked a field goal to win the game, 17–14.

NORMAN, 1975

Two weeks after a stunning upset at the hands of Kansas, OU's senior class came in against second-ranked Nebraska with a determination that would cement their status as Sooner royalty for all time. Steve Davis ran the Cornhuskers into submission, and the defense played great in a surprising 35–10 blowout. The Sooners would go on to defeat Michigan in the Orange Bowl for their second national championship.

LINCOLN, 1980

Trying to cope with life without Billy Sims, OU's Wishbone had regrouped behind Stanley Wilson and J.C. Watts. Freshman halfback George "Buster" Rhymes ("Buster rhymes with Luster," the Miami punster liked to say) had a 43-yard run with a little over two minutes left to get the Sooners into position, then he did the honors himself, going over from the one with fifty-six seconds left. The 21–17 win sent OU to Miami again, and Nebraska moved on to a scintillating Sun Bowl victory against Mississippi State, 31–17.

LINCOLN, 1982

Despite Sooner touchdowns by Marcus Dupree and Stanley Wilson, Nebraska's famed Triplets—quarterback Turner Gill, tailback Mike Rozier, and wingback Irving Fryar—led the Huskers to a 28-24 victory. Nebraska would enjoy one more win in the series in 1983 before OU took off on another tear.

LINCOLN, 1986

This is one that Sooner fans still talk about today. A vintage OU team headed north to meet an outstanding Cornhusker squad. Much to the delight of the hometown crowd, Nebraska took a 17–10 lead late. OU looked finished—that is, until Jamelle Holieway uncorked for 150 passing yards in the fourth quarter. The sophomore quarterback hit Keith Jackson with a 17-yard TD pass to tie the game, and the defense fought off the ensuing Nebraska drive. When the OU offense came back on the field, Holieway hit Jackson again for a 41-yard gain. Tim Lasher then nailed the field goal that sent OU to Miami. Sooner Magic had struck again.

NORMAN, 1971

Of course, any list of great OU-Nebraska games will end with "The Game of the Century."

Although OU lost, 35–31, the game was so epic that Sooner fans still remember it with some fondness. Nebraska quarterback Jerry Tagge recalled years later that a Husker fan told him more than two decades later that he still had the jersey he'd torn off Tagge's back in the mayhem that followed the game.

A standing-room only crowd of 62,884 jammed into Memorial Stadium to see undefeated Nebraska (10–0) take on the unbeaten Sooners (9–0). ABC broadcast the game to an audience of 55 million; Chris Schenkel was joined in the broadcast booth by none other than Bud Wilkinson.

Everyone remembers Johnny Rodgers's 72-yard punt return for a TD just minutes into the game. What we don't remember is the detail: Joe Wylie's high, deep punt put the Sooner defenders in good position to bring down Rogers deep in Nebraska territory. Greg Pruitt (a Heisman Trophy candidate on the kickoff team!) hit Rodgers, but the elusive Cornhusker shook it off and took off running. OU fans to this day insist there should have been a clipping penalty on the play, but the officials called it a touchdown, putting Nebraska up, 7–0.

The Sooners clawed their way back into the game. Down 14–3 with eleven minutes left in the first half, Pruitt was stuffed on first down from his own 20, but fullback Leon Crosswhite popped one for twenty-four yards up the middle. Mildren carried six times for forty-three yards on the drive and scored from the 3.

With less than two minutes to go before the half and the ball on their own 22, everyone assumed OU would run out the clock. Mildren had other ideas, however, and the crafty senior began running option plays. This sucked Nebraska in.

Nebraska had put a wrinkle in its defense to take away Pruitt's deadly runs on the corner. It largely worked, but left the Huskers vulnerable to split end Jon Harrison, an old high school teammate of Mildren's. Harrison told Mildren in the huddle that he could beat Cornhusker safety Bill Kosch, so Mildren launched one, which Harrison pulled in for a 43-yard gain to the Nebraska 24. Fifteen seconds were left.

The Abilene Boys did it again, scoring with five seconds left. John Carroll's kick gave a huge boost to the Sooners, who went into the locker room with a 17–14 lead.

OU had outgained Nebraska at that point, 312 yards to 91. Realizing that his team needed to get more physical, Nebraska coach Bob Devaney in the second half ordered handoff-after-handoff to tailback Jeff Kinney, who would finish with 174 yards.

It worked.

On Nebraska's second drive, after an OU fumble, Tagge weaved his way for thirty-two yards, before Kinney scored from the three.

Kinney later scored on another short run, giving Nebraska a 28–17 lead.

OU resorted to some trickery to try to narrow the gap. On a third down play, Harrison pulled up on a reverse and threw a 51-yard pass to tight end Albert Chandler, who burned the Cornhusker safety again. Shortly afterward,

Photo courtesy of *Lincoln Journal Star*

SURE LOOKS LIKE CLIPPING: With a little "help" from his teammates, Johnny Rodgers returns a punt seventy-two yards for a touchdown in the Game of the Century

Mildren scored on an option keeper, bringing the Sooners to within four heading into the final quarter.

After a Nebraska fumble, OU marched downfield. On fourth down from the 16, Mildren hit Harrison, who yet again outran the lead-footed Kosch into the endzone. Sooner fans were delirious, with just over seven minutes remaining.

Facing third down from OU's 46, Nebraska pulled off a play for the ages, one that surely indicated that fate had sadly decreed that the visitors would win. Tagge rolled out to throw and was pressured by Raymond "Sugar Bear" Hamilton. Sugar Bear had a sprained toe and couldn't quite get enough push to bring Tagge down. The cool Nebraska senior wobbled a pass to Rodgers, who made a diving catch for a first down. From there, Devaney ordered a ground march, and Kinney scored from the two with 1:38 left.

OU fans who saw it will always remember Mildren throwing desperation passes as the last two minutes ticked off the clock. But Nebraska held on to

THE TYLER ROSE

EARL CAMPBELL

If you thought our pronouncement in Chapter Seven of Joe Golding as the greatest forgotten player in Sooner history was arbitrary, then just wait till you read this one: The Greatest Player Against Whom OU has Ever Played. After consulting himself for the past thirty years, the Die-Hard Fan can announce that OU's greatest opponent ever was...

Earl Campbell.

Earl. The Tyler Rose. The One That Got Away.

Coming out of high school, Earl was torn between playing for Texas or Oklahoma, so he prayed intensely about it. Waking up on Signing Day in 1974, the blue-chip fullback decided to stay close to home, and went on to become a legend in Austin. With a sick combination of power and speed, Campbell scared opponents stiff. The Sooners managed pretty well in games against Earl, who went 1–2–1 against OU in his career, but they sure did respect him. At five-foot-eleven and 240, with halfback speed and a punishing running style, Campbell was the real deal.

Although he didn't have huge games against OU save his senior year, when he registered 124 yards after Fred Akers compelled him to lose twenty pounds and move to tailback, containing Campbell was still a major priority for Sooner coaches and players.

During that senior year, in 1977, Campbell terrorized the Southwest Conference, finishing the season with a fantastic 1,744 yards. Only a Notre Dame team led by Joe Montana kept Texas from winning the national title. Campbell was taken in the NFL draft by the Houston Oilers. His punishing runs and freakish speed (the 81-yard TD run against Miami is still shown on highlight reels often) made him one of the game's truly great runners.

This Year The REAL No. 20 Will Stand Up

Big Earl Campbell is down to 220 pounds and fit as a (bass) fiddle, all of which ells trouble for SWC foes

THE TYLER ROSE should be bloom for his final season, afte out much of last year with injur if Earl Campbell is 100 percent, yo be sure there will be a lot of Heis Trophy talk this season around Austi

The jersey number was the same nd the brawny silhouette unmistaka- e, but whoever was wearing No. 20 the University of Texas last fall was

on his brooding face.

Early in the year, the one time he did look like Campbell, breaking loose on an 83-yard run against North Texas State, he suddenly pulled up, dragging one leg behind him, like a cavalry with an arrow in his

Whoever masqueraded as the Longhorn fullback never ran freely or very convincingly until the merciful end to an humbling season. Finally, in the Texas-Arkansas watching on television as he out 131 yards on 32 carries, ourself almost believing his was the real Earl

THE TYLER ROSE, Earl Campbell.

Photo courtesy of *Dave Campbell's Texas Football Magazine*

win the game. Tagge was named ABC's most valuable offensive player, while noseguard Rich Glover, with an insane twenty-two tackles against one of the best centers OU ever had, won top honors on defense.

The headline in the *Daily Oklahoman* the next day said it all: "Sad Day in Soonerland." OU went on to clobber Auburn in the Sugar Bowl, while Nebraska flattened Alabama in the Orange Bowl to win a second-consecutive national championship. Incredibly, Colorado finished No. 3 in the country, even though both OU and Nebraska crushed the Buffs during the season.

Bud Wilkinson knew a few things about football, and his analysis was dead-on:

"Oklahoma runs a high risk offense," he noted. "They handle the ball a lot close to the line of scrimmage. That can lead to fumbles and if they lose more than three fumbles, the Sooners can't beat a team as tough as Nebraska."

We'll wrap up our discussion of this titanic clash with a classic account penned by one of the world's greatest sports writers, *Tulsa World*'s Bill Connors, who vividly captured the excitement of this historic showdown:*

Nebraska-OU Finest of Super Shootouts

In his consoling remarks to Chuck Fairbanks, President Nixon said he thought the only college football game that compared with Nebraska's 35–31 victory over Oklahoma was Notre Dame-Michigan in 1966.

"And that one (10–10) did not quite come up to expectations," the President said.

There have been two other No. 1 vs. No. 2 games with climactic ballyhoo in modern times. Notre Dame-Army in 1946, when Mr. Nixon was first getting himself elected to Congress, may have had the all-time buildup. But the 0–0 stalemate lacked suspense, because the super offenses were negated by conservative strategy.

---

*Reprinted with permission, *Tulsa World*

Texas-Arkansas in 1969 wound up as an epic cliffhanger, but it was mostly three quarters of Arkansas and two plays of Texas. There was a widespread feeling the No. 1 team stumbled into its 15–14 victory.

But what they played at Norman Thursday was an epic confrontation, that followed an epic script, full of superstars, spectaculars and comebacks plus so much drama and emotion it seemed the whole stadium might buckle any minute from one massive heart attack.

At the finish, the record crowd at Owen Field was limp. Spectators and participants alike sensed they had witnessed an unforgettable game; the incomparable game as Mr. Nixon indicated.

For Oklahoma, the defeat was disappointing but not shattering because the Sooners had no cause to be ashamed. They spent themselves emotionally; but they did not give the game away cheaply; they had their chances, but could not make the one defensive play in the stretch that would save victory. Jack Mildren almost pulled it off.

This was Notre Dame (21–27) of 1952 all over for OU. The Sooners emerged with great respect, and Mildren unraveled a performance that ranks with Billy Vessels' Heisman day at South Bend 19 years ago.

They lost to a class team, one that came into the showdown with an average spread of four points against common opponents and left with the same edge.

It seemed incredible that, under such pressure, both teams could play so efficiently, and so cleanly. Perhaps the most remarkable thing about the game was OU not being penalized and Nebraska drawing only one offside penalty (OU declined) on a clipping penalty and Fairbanks thought the officials missed a clip on Johnny Rodgers' 72-yard punt return.

But except for one late—though not flagrant and not called—hit by monster Dave Mason on Mildren, the combatants displayed impeccable manners.

It was a gold-plated event for college football, showcasing all of the game's best qualities. No one could legitimately feel the game was lost (as most are), but rather that the No. 1 team won strictly on its own merit. For sure, it was all that it was advertised to be, with Nebraska doing the one thing it had to do—keep Greg Pruitt from getting outside.

The game seemed to last for about 20 days, and about every other snap something noticeable happened. But the most vivid impression was of Nebraska's offensive unit on the sideline preparing to take over following Mildren's final heroics.

For only the second time all year they were behind (28–31). Only seven minutes remained and the ball was 74 yards from OU's goal. But the Cornhuskers were absolutely unshakeable. They oozed with what seemed like illegal poise and confidence, knowing somehow that Jerry Tagge, Jeff Kinney and Rodgers would make the plays needed to win.

And, against an OU defense which by then was hurt and tired and perhaps drained of its confidence, the Cornhuskers made the plays.

"Bring it; I like pain."

—Defensive tackle Darren Kilpatrick, after hearing Nebraska players commenting that they would make their game painful for OU in 1987. The Sooners won, 17-7.

Tagge was a schoolboy at Green Bay, Wis., when the Packers were at their Super Bowl peak and Bart Starr was, despite a lack of artistic talents, a peerless leader who was never ruffled.

Tagge makes you wonder if there really is a sore-armed, disabled Bart Starr in Green Bay, or if he has come back under another name at Lincoln. Tagge, at 6–3 and 215, looks like an NFL fullback. His passes will never make you think of Arkansas' Joe Ferguson, and his speed is only so-so.

But what a wonderful quarterback he is, and what poise! Statistically, Tagge did not have a typical day. He almost surely lost the Big Eight Conference total offense championship to Mildren. OU's surprising ability to cover Nebraska's receivers sharply reduced Tagge's passing.

Yet, his ability to change plays at the line when he recognized the Sooners' adjustments, and his uncanny ability to come though on third downs keynoted Nebraska's comeback.

Besides his 32-yard run that preceded a go-ahead touchdown in the third quarter, Tagge faced six crucial third down situations when he called on himself, and he delivered on five. The last was an 11-yard pass to Rodgers on the dreary afternoon's No. 1 'if' play.

OU will never forget it. It was third and nine at OU's 46. Tagge tried to pass but couldn't, and averted a five-yard loss when he escaped Raymond Hamilton, who was slowed by a toe injury. With justification, OU is certain a fit Hamilton would have thrown Tagge for a loss.

Of course, there is no assurance Tagge would not have then delivered on fourth and 14. "But I'd sure like to have taken our chances," Fairbanks said, "on fourth and 14 at the 50 instead of what we got."

What they got was first down at the 35, where Rodgers made a super reception, on the ground, of Tagge's low, hurried pass.

Once the Cornhuskers reach the 35, only a turnover will stop them. And, they average one fumble a game and Tagge's interception avoidance record is the best in the country. When they get in the four-down territory they let the 210-pound Kinney take over.

He was devastating in the second half. After being held to 14 yards on eight carries in the first half, Kinney battered the Sooners for 160 yards on 23 carries in the second half.

He got most of this by taking the handoff as though he intended to run up the middle, then cutting outside the tackles. Poor play by

GAMEDAY HAUNTS

JR's Family Bar-B-Q, at 353 Interstate Drive in Norman, is a great new location for hungry families after games. JR is the WWE announcer and a die-hard OU fan.

OU's ends and outside linebackers resulted. Kinney repeatedly ran over and through defenders. So did Tagge.

> **"[The 1971 OU-Nebraska game had] so much drama and emotion it seemed the whole stadium might buckle any minute from one massive heart attack."**

But, as OU defensive coordinator Larry Lacewell noted, "both of them are bigger than anybody on our defensive unit except the tackles."

Their effectiveness is enhanced by the breathtaking Rodgers, who looks as though he may score every time he touches the ball. His punt return was the one thing OU knew it could not afford. The importance of that score cannot be minimized, despite the closing developments. It was all the Conrhuskers lived on for much of the first half.

Because of it Nebraska led, 7–3, after one quarter despite having no first downs. Because of it, Nebraska trailed only 14–17 at halftime, despite being out-yarded, 311–91. You had to feel then that with those kind of statistics the Sooners should be farther ahead.

By then, too, the handwriting was on the wall for OU's defense. Hamilton was hurt. So was Derland Moore. John Shelley was in such shape that had there been an available replacement he would have been used. And Steve Aycock later was knocked out and had to leave a game for the first time in his career. No patched up defense will hold Nebraska.

So, it was all up to OU's offense, and it came close without being able to fire its hottest guns. This was, of course, a tribute to Mildren. Had OU won, Mildren's two-touchdowns-by-running-two-by-passing-267-yard total offense performance would surely have made Auburn's Pat Sullivan grateful the Heisman votes had already been counted.

Here was Nebraska, with the best defensive record in the country, with the quickness and talent to deny OU the pitchout and eventually shut off the middle—and yet almost shattered by Mildren.

Ten Nebraska victims averaged 171 yards per game. Before he was thrown for 20 yards in losses trying to pass, Mildren had 287 yards and OU had 467–96 under its average, but 296 over Nebraska's defensive average. So, the offense could not be faulted.

The Sooners had to drive 68 yards for their field goal and their touchdown drives were 80, 78, 72, and 68 yards. And, 31 points should be enough to win. But they might have scored more. They lost three fumbles, once at Nebraska's 27 and twice at midfield when they were moving, and which Nebraska converted into touchdowns.

"I thought our fumbles hurt our offensive production more than it hurt us defensively," Fairbanks said. "We were moving well each time. And, even though Nebraska scored after two fumbles you have to have a defense that can stop them at the 50 if you're going to win."

"I don't think I've ever seen a big team that plays it straight as quick as Nebraska."

OU was held to 158 yards in the second half and the following figures offer tell-tale proof that Nebraska forced the Sooners to drop their Wishbone basics: Pruitt carried but four times; Leon Crosswhite gained only five yards and Tim Welch 10 and neither Joe Wylie or Roy Bell carried the ball. Bell did not carry in the first half, either.

Nebraska was able to execute a plan that others tried but failed. The Cornhuskers closed to corners, made Mildren keep and used their great speed to keep him from breaking a long run.

OU, the explosive team, had only four running plays to gain 13 yards or more; Nebraska, the methodical team, had seven such plays in the second half.

"I knew that if we couldn't run inside on them we were in trouble," OU offensive coordinator Barry Switzer said. The Sooners had some success inside in the first half, when they took advantage of middle guard Rich Glover's eagerness. But in the second half the sensationally quick, 237-pound Glover shut off everything except Mildren's draws.

"Glover is a super player," Switzer said. "We've never been whipped inside like that. He gets off the blocks and is super quick."

OU may have under estimated Glover, because his best games had been against passing teams (Kansas and Colorado, especially). But the Sooners' offensive line could not cope with the speed Nebraska had throughout its defensive front.

Switzer said, "It is hard to compare Nebraska's quickness to a real quick little team that stunts a lot—like Alabama's great teams of a few years ago. Little teams always look quicker when they stunt. But I don't think I've ever seen a big team that plays it straight as quick as Nebraska."

It was ironic that such a defense, which has been murderous against passing, would almost be undone by a passer with a bad reputation. But Mildren twice brought the Sooners from 11-point deficits into leads with his passing.

DID YOU KNOW?

Perhaps the greatest name of an OU opponent was Wonderful Monds, Jr., an All-American defensive back at Nebraska in 1975. While at NU, he became a father; his son's name is Wonderful Monds III.

Curiously, Mildren passed poorly in the first quarter with the win, then passed stunningly against the wind in the second and fourth quarters. (Six of the eight touchdown drives were made against the wind.)

Meanwhile, Fairbanks dismissed the players until Monday, when they begin preparations for the Oklahoma State finale. OU will not scout Sugar Bowl opponent Auburn against Alabama Saturday. Auburn did not scout OU Thursday. There was no need, with both games on television. They will exchange five films.

OU's defensive players and coaches took the defeat awfully hard. "I honestly think I cost us the national championship," defensive coordinator Larry Lacewell said in the gloomy aftermath.

But before the night was over the gloom was beginning to fade. Switzer, the staff optimist, told Fairbanks he had "figured out a way we can still be No. 1."

He explained, "If Auburn beats Alabama, we beat Auburn, Texas beats Penn State and Stanford beats Michigan...."

HALF-A-HUNDRED QUIZ

Scoring:

» If you can correctly answer ten questions from this list, you might qualify as a walk-on—but probably not.

» If you can answer twenty questions, you will be considered a freshman on the junior varsity.

» If you can answer thirty questions, you've made the Sooner team.

» Thirty to forty-five correct answers garner all-conference honors – maybe even All-American.

» And if you can answer more than forty-five correctly, you earn the right to be...Barry Switzer's personal assistant. Study hard!

1. How many quarterbacks have made All-American at OU?
2. When was OU's first televised football game?
3. What is the all-time average score in OU games?
4. What was the "team hotel" for many years in downtown Oklahoma City?
5. Forrest "Spot" Geyer is considered the first great passer at Oklahoma. Who actually played quarterback during his senior year?
6. Who were the three fullbacks who blocked for Heisman Trophy winners Billy Vessels, Steve Owens, and Billy Sims?
7. Who scored the winning touchdown in OU's first overtime game, against Texas, in 1996?
8. Who was Bob Stoops's first offensive coordinator?
9. Name the center who competed with Tommy McDonald for the Heisman Trophy in 1956.
10. Which game started OU's 47-game winning streak? (Hint: it was 1953)
11. In his autobiography, *Bootlegger's Boy*, Barry Switzer revealed that one of his assistants went by the nickname "Deadset." Who was the assistant?
12. How many conference championships has OU won under Bob Stoops?
13. In which city did the Sooners make their first appearance in a bowl game?
14. What OU quarterback has the lowest interception percentage for a season?
15. Who holds the career interception mark at OU?
16. Who quarterbacked OU to its second-consecutive Sugar Bowl championship in 1972?
17. In what year did Sooner players win both the Heisman Trophy and the Lombardi Trophy, and who were the players?
18. Four players have won the Walter Camp Trophy; who were they? (Hint: not all were Heisman winners!)
19. What was the name given to the offense refined by Barry Switzer when he was an assistant and later head coach at OU?
20. What Oklahoma town are the Selmon brothers from?
21. Who are OU's only three-time All-Americans?
22. Name Bud Wilkinson's long-time assistant who succeeded him in 1964.
23. How many bowl games has OU appeared in?
24. Who was the starting fullback in Adrian Peterson's record-breaking freshman year?
25. How many years did Bud Wilkinson coach before he lost a conference game?

26. What former player succeeded Barry Switzer as head coach?

27. What term was coined to describe OU's dramatic victories over Nebraska at Lincoln?

28. What two prestigious bowls did Bob Stoops-coached teams win for the first time for OU?

29. What is the longest pass play in Sooner history?

30. How many national championships has the school claimed?

31. OU has beaten teams 77–0 twice since 1986. Name the victims.

32. What OU cornerback had the same name as a famous television detective?

33. What father-son combination won national championships at OU?

34. In what years did OU win back-to-back national championships?

35. Who was the university president who brought Bud Wilkinson to Oklahoma?

36. Since World War II, which three former players have become head coaches at OU?

37. In 1974, the Sooners had three defensive linemen make first-team All-America. Who were they?

38. Before Josh Heupel, who was the last Sooner quarterback to make first-team All-America?

39. Name the birth states of Bud Wilkinson, Barry Switzer, and Bob Stoops.

40. Name the eastern Oklahoma town that is known as a "football factory" for the Sooners.

41. What neighboring state has OU consistently raided for top high school talent?

42. Who was OU's opponent in the 1971 "Game of the Century"?

43. Who did Oklahoma defeat in the Orange Bowl to win its sixth national championship?

44. What was the name of the conference in which OU competed under Barry Switzer?

45. In what year did the Sooners play their first game?

46. How many consecutive games did the Sooners win under Bud Wilkinson to establish an NCAA record that still stands?

47. What two teams are considered OU's top traditional rivals?

48. Who returned an interception for a touchdown to defeat Texas A&M in 2000?

49. Who quarterbacked OU to its only Orange Bowl win of the 1960s?

50. How many native Oklahomans started for the 2000 national champions?

Answers

1. Six
2. November 8, 1952 at Notre Dame
3. Oklahoma wins the average game 26–12
4. Skirvin; now the Skirvin Hilton
5. Hap Johnson
6. Buck McPhail, Mike Harper, and Kenny King
7. James Allen
8. Mike Leach
9. Jerry Tubbs
10. Texas (19–14)
11. Wendell Mosley
12. Five
13. Miami (1939 Orange Bowl)
14. Monte Deere, 1962 (no picks in 71 attempts)
15. Darrell Royal (18)
16. Dave Robertson
17. 2003; Jason White won the Heisman and Tommie Harris won the Lombardi
18. Jerry Tubbs (1956), Steve Owens (1969), Billy Sims (1978), and Josh Heupel (2000)
19. Wishbone
20. Eufaula
21. Buddy Burris (1946–48) and Rod Shoate (1972–74)
22. Gomer Jones
23. Forty-one
24. J.D. Runnels
25. Twelve
26. Gary Gibbs (class of 1974)
27. "Sooner Magic"
28. Cotton (2002) and Rose (2003)
29. 95 yards, Ronnie Fletcher to Ben Hart, in the 1964 Gator Bowl
30. Seven
31. Missouri and Texas A&M
32. Jim Rockford (class of 1984)
33. Jim and Seth Littrell (1974, 1975, and 2000)
34. 1955–56, and 1974–75
35. Dr. George Cross
36. Dewey "Snorter" Luster, Gary Gibbs, and John Blake
37. Jimbo Elrod (DE), LeRoy Selmon (DT), and Dewey Selmon (NG)
38. Jack Mildren (1971)
39. Minnesota, Arkansas, and Ohio, respectively
40. Muskogee
41. Texas!
42. Nebraska
43. Penn State
44. Big 8
45. 1895
46. Forty-seven
47. Texas and Nebraska
48. Torrance Marshall
49. Bobby Warmack
50. Fourteen

Acknowledgments

When R.E.M. was inducted into the Rock and Roll Hall of Fame, Michael Stipe revealed that his grandmother had once asked him a lovely question: "Do you know what R.E.M. means? Remember Every Moment." A wonderful sentiment, and one that perfectly describes my experience writing this book.

I would like to thank my wife, Dianna, because she has given me the greatest gift of all for the past twenty years—her companionship. By profession, she is a registered nurse, but she would make a pretty good editor; her eye for detail and dislike of sycophantic feedback has provided me with the kind of critique I most needed: blunt. A writer is dead without it. She also has taught me if we only have courage, our dreams are like the old British empire: the sun never sets on them.

I also need to convey my gratitude to Brian Bishop, the publisher of OUInsider.com. I first spoke with Brian while I was on my way to a Who concert in Little Rock. He was unnecessarily kind to me, and I always remember acts of needless kindness. Brian opened my path to contact and interview former OU greats. And to a man, they have been generous with their time and memories.

Jakie Sandefer is the perfect ambassador for OU football, and I thank him for his accessibility.

Joe Washington was patient with my obsession with minutiae, a hallmark of Sooner fans. ("What was your exact height and weight when you played at OU?") Bob Stoops and Brent Venables were also kind enough to give me some of their time, which is in short supply.

Barry Switzer... words can't describe him, really, but as they say among fans, "It's good to be the King." Coach was kind enough to sit for an interview in his office. Amidst the fun of talking to him, it really hit home that at his core, he is still a country boy from Crossett.

Frank Broyles and Darrell Royal are gentlemen and college football royalty in every way. Sometimes we fans go overboard in our smack-talking about our Texas rivals (usually from the safe confines of our living rooms), but speaking to Royal made me realize, above all else, that the man was—and is—a Sooner.

I'd also like to pay tribute to Jack Mildren, a great man and a great Sooner who passed away shortly after he granted me an interview for this book.

A huge thank you to OU Sports Information Director Kenny Mossman for helping me set up interviews. Many thanks also go to the staff at the Oklahoma Historical Society for their professionalism and assistance.

For another book, I once interviewed former Israeli prime minister Ariel Sharon. But even that could not compare with the pure thrill of accompanying Claude Arnold to Norman one afternoon for a meeting with Josh Heupel. Listening to these two legends reminisce, bound forever by their national titles, is an experience I will always treasure. Like the other players I interviewed, Claude is too humble for his own good, but it should be remembered that it was his passing ability that enabled Bud Wilkinson to modify his Split-T enough to exploit the throwing and beat teams like Texas A&M. Even more impressive, though, is the hospitality of Claude and Nancy, who hosted me in their home. They exemplify the quality that binds all Sooners together, from the greatest players to the common fans: a good heart. There are too many helpful players and coaches to thank each one by name here, but my gratitude goes out to every Sooner who took the time to contribute to this book.

My publisher, Marji Ross of Regnery, shares a quality with Oklahoma players like Jimbo Elrod who, when I asked him to describe what it was like to play against big rivals, leaned in and said "PURE FUN!" I've spent fifteen years in the publishing business as an editor and now as a writer, and I can say with certainty that Regnery's success with *New York Times* bestsellers starts with Marji's calculated, instinctive gambles. She isn't afraid to take chances other publishers would pass up, and that's why they always seem to be playing catch-up with her. Her staff at Regnery is the best; editor Jack Langer has been amazing to work with. It has truly been my privilege.

I'd like to thank my cousin, Julian Rotramel, and our buddy, Dale Rains, for all the times they gave me a place to crash after games in Norman. To this day, we still celebrate each sweet win via email and phone. The same goes for my friend, David Lindsey, who has watched a few demolitions of Texas with me.

Much love to Mamie Hasty in Bristow, for being my third grandmother. You're right; we sure did have some good times.

A huge thanks to Randy Horn for allowing me to use some great pictures taken by his dad, Bill, who was the unofficial "sideline photographer" for years at Owen Field.

To Curtis, Matt, Sarah, and Jonathan—four exceptional children who've never given us a day of grief—thanks for putting up with my insane screaming, hair-pulling, and pathetic, middle-aged-man strutting when I celebrate the wins achieved by the players themselves. And to my grandson, Garret, thanks for being the latest member of the family to join the Sooner Nation.

And to that Sooner Nation—we share memories no one else can. There are more to come!

Finally, the Bible says in the great book of Isaiah that one day, God will restore all things, and that "the former things will not be remembered." Still,

I say with sincerity and trepidation that I can't imagine forgetting having breakfast with Jimmy Harris at the Legends Hotel in Norman—or a hundred other such meetings with the fellows who, unknown to them, have played such a big role in my life.

I will indeed remember every moment.

Index

0 20 30 40 50 40 30 20 10

D

E

F

G

H

I

J

K

L

M

N

O

P

R

S

T

U

V

W